Iron Dome

Iron Dome

A History of Israel's Military Strategy

Jean-Loup Samaan

BLOOMSBURY ACADEMIC
LONDON • NEW YORK • OXFORD • NEW DELHI • SYDNEY

BLOOMSBURY ACADEMIC
Bloomsbury Publishing Plc, 50 Bedford Square, London, WC1B 3DP, UK
Bloomsbury Publishing Inc, 1359 Broadway, New York, NY 10018, USA
Bloomsbury Publishing Ireland, 29 Earlsfort Terrace, Dublin 2, D02 AY28, Ireland

BLOOMSBURY, BLOOMSBURY ACADEMIC and the Diana logo are trademarks of
Bloomsbury Publishing Plc

First published in Great Britain 2026

Cover design by Paul Smith
Cover image: © Getty Images

A catalogue record for this book is available from the British Library.

Library of Congress Cataloguing-in-Publication Data available

ISBN: HB: 978-1-3504-9961-4
PB: 978-1-3504-9960-7
ePDF: 978-1-3504-9963-8
eBook: 978-1-3504-9962-1

Typeset by Amnet
Printed and bound in Great Britain

For product safety related questions contact productsafety@bloomsbury.com.

To find out more about our authors and books visit www.bloomsbury.com
and sign up for our newsletters.

Contents

List of Illustrations   vi
List of Abbreviations   vii
Acknowledgments   viii
Note on Conventions   x

Introduction   1
1   The Rise of Rocket Warfare   13
2   Iron Dome Enters   45
3   An Unlikely Military Hero   73
4   A New Pillar of US–Israel Defense Cooperation   103
5   October 7 and the End of the Iron Dome Decade   135
6   Beyond Iron Dome: The Future of Missile Defense in the Middle East   163
Conclusion   193

Select Bibliography   201
Index   219

Illustrations

Map

I.1.   Israel and the Gaza Strip   3

Charts

2.1.   Number of rockets launched from the Gaza Strip (2000–2012)   61
3.1.   Number of rockets launched from the Gaza Strip (2012–22)   96

Figure

3.1.   Iron Dome portrayed as a superhero   76

Table

4.1.   Defense Budget Appropriations for US–Israeli Missile Defense
       (Fiscal Years 2006–24)   107

Abbreviations

AI	Artificial intelligence
AIPAC	American Israel Public Affairs Committee
BMD	Ballistic Missile Defense
CENTCOM	Central Command
C4I	Command, Control, Communications, Computers, and Intelligence
C2	Command and control
DARPA	Defense Advanced Research Projects Agency
FMF	Foreign Military Financing
HCOC	Hague Code of Conduct against Ballistic Missile Proliferation
IAI	Israel Aerospace Industries
IAMDC	Integrated Air and Missile Defense Center
IDF	Israel Defense Forces
IRGC	Islamic Revolutionary Guard Corps
JCPOA	Joint Comprehensive Plan of Action
MAFAT	Directorate of Defense Research & Development
MoD	Ministry of Defense
MoU	Memorandum of understanding
MTCR	Missile Technology Control Regime
NSC	National Security Council
PA	Palestinian Authority
PIJ	Palestinian Islamic Jihad
PSI	Proliferation Security Initiative
SAM	Surface-to-Air Missiles
SDI	Strategic Defense Initiative
THAAD	Terminal High Altitude Area Defense
THEL	Tactical High-Energy Laser
UAE	United Arab Emirates
UAV	Unmanned aerial vehicle
UNIFIL	United Nations Interim Force in Lebanon
WMD	Weapons of mass destruction

Acknowledgments

Though this book was written after the events of October 7, 2023, and the subsequent wars in Gaza and Lebanon, it originated in a series of short papers written over a decade ago about the introduction of Iron Dome in Israel. At that time, I served as an adviser on Middle Eastern affairs at the NATO Defense College and was visiting Israel for the first time. Missile defense was then a major, though contentious, pillar of the transatlantic organization's strategic planning. However, whereas NATO discussions on missile defense seemed to me conceptual and futuristic (with endless disputes among French, German, and American officials over the implications for NATO's deterrence), Israel's experience was immediate and concrete. In the following years, I kept a close eye on the topic, especially as Iron Dome moved from obscurity to international fame and now holds a special place as an element of pop culture in Israel and beyond.

It was my wife, Emilie, an art historian by training, who convinced me that a book entirely dedicated to a missile defense system, a biography of Iron Dome, would find an audience beyond the small crowd of engineers and Middle East wonks.

The book itself was made possible thanks to the trust of my publisher, Bloomsbury, and my editors, Atifa Jiwa, Nadine Staes-Polet, and Raveena Jutley. I am deeply grateful for their support throughout the process of turning a manuscript into this book.

Several institutions also played a crucial role. For the past five years, my home institution, the Middle East Institute (MEI) at the National University of Singapore, has provided me with a fantastic environment in which to conduct research projects. I want to express my sincere gratitude to my bosses and colleagues, including Bilahari Kausikan, Joseph Liow, Michelle Teo, Carl Skadiang, and Clemens Chay. I also thank Damien Tan, who joined MEI while I was finishing the project and meticulously copyedited the final draft of the manuscript.

My fieldwork in Israel was made possible thanks to the generosity of the Moshe Dayan Center at Tel Aviv University, whose team welcomed me as a visiting scholar for two months in the summer of 2024. Brandon Friedman, the center's director of research, deserves special mention. Brandon made it happen and always remained helpful, despite the challenging circumstances of a country at war.

In the United States, the Washington Institute for Near East Policy also hosted me as a visiting fellow in the spring of 2025 and opened its doors to let me test the first rough drafts of the manuscript in front of American and Israeli participants. A special thank-you goes to Robert Satloff, Dana Stroul, and Grant Rumley for offering me this opportunity.

At a personal level, I would like to thank all the people in Israel, the United States, France, and elsewhere who helped me in one way or another, taking time out of their busy schedule to discuss the topic with me, and sharing their contacts to help me improve the fieldwork. Among them, a special thank-you to Yossi Abravanel, Nir Boms, Michael Eisenstadt, Eran Lerman, Ariel Levite, Sarah Perez, Yuval Rotem, and Benjamin Touati.

As with my previous books, I would like to acknowledge my family: my wife, Emilie, and our daughters, Ines and Leila, for enduring my extensive travels more than they should have.

Finally, the book is dedicated to the memory of the late Michael Elleman. Mike was a rocket scientist and an expert in Californian wines, and he was also a mentor to numerous young researchers eager to understand the link between missile technology and military strategy. I owe him an intellectual debt, and I wish he were still around to offer him a copy of this book.

Note on Conventions

The transliteration of Arabic used in the book follows the conventions of the *International Journal of Middle East Studies*. The transliteration of Hebrew is based on the standards introduced by the Academy of Hebrew Language.

However, to avoid confusion, common names (individuals, cities, and organizations) have been kept in their known English spelling.

What if free people could live secure in the knowledge that
. . . we could intercept and destroy strategic ballistic missiles
before they reached our own soil or that of our allies?
. . . Wouldn't it be better to save lives than to avenge them?

—RONALD REAGAN,
Strategic Defense Initiative Address to the Nation,
March 23, 1983, Oval Office, White House, Washington, DC[1]

[1] Ronald Reagan, "Address to the Nation on Defense and National Security," Ronald Reagan Presidential Library, March 23, 1983. https://www.reaganlibrary.gov/archives/speech/address-nation -defense-and-national-security.

Introduction

On the morning of Tuesday, June 18, 2024, I rented a car on Hayarkon Street in downtown Tel Aviv. I drove south toward what the Israelis call the "Gaza envelope" (*Otef Aza* in Hebrew)—the 7-square-kilometer area bordering the Gaza Strip and only 70 kilometers away from Tel Aviv (Map I.1). On a normal day, without traffic, it takes about one hour from Tel Aviv to reach this area, which, for a few days in October 2023, became a battlefield between the Israel Defense Forces (IDF) and Hamas combatants.

That morning, I parked the car at the entrance of one of several kibbutzim built before the establishment of Israel in 1948. Earlier, I had been told to drive there and wait for instructions. Then, out of nowhere, two Israeli soldiers emerged and ordered me to follow their small Peugeot. After a short ride around the kibbutz, I found myself at the entrance of an Iron Dome base.

The term "base" is misleading here. The location looked more like a small, abandoned runway. There, a dozen conscripted soldiers welcomed me. Most of them were extremely young, probably having spent their entire adulthood in uniform. The facility was small and minimalist. Under a tent, one could count four sofas that looked like the main social area. There was one Coca-Cola distributor in the corner. Behind the soldiers, in the distance, was one Iron Dome battery in the open air. The military system stood still at the runway's center, and all these soldiers were here to defend it, not the other way around.

The IDF spokesperson was a middle-aged officer fluent in English and obviously comfortable talking with foreign researchers and journalists. He started our conversation with classic talking points about the success story of Iron Dome. The system was the object of national pride. He reminded me that it had "saved thousands of lives." He went as far as to argue that "Iron Dome saves Palestinian lives": The logic was that by protecting Israeli civilians, the system enabled governments in Jerusalem to refrain from retaliating against all rocket attacks launched from Gaza. I had heard this argument several times before but always found it an odd selling point. Now, I felt that the Hamas attacks on October 7, 2023, and the subsequent IDF operation in Gaza should have forced Israeli officials to stop using that talking point.

The day we met was quiet, almost peaceful, with a cloudless sky typical of a Mediterranean summer. But two weeks before, the same battery I was observing had intercepted rockets fired from Gaza toward Tel Aviv. As explained by the spokesperson, the role of his small unit was only to ensure maintenance and protection of the battery. The biggest decision—to fire the $50,000 interceptor— was taken elsewhere.

The decision to shoot was made by a command-and-control (C2) unit of Israel's air defense. In practice, this C2 unit first receives data on an incoming rocket via the IDF radars and then orders to shoot down the projectile with Iron Dome. The decision is facilitated by a software that calculates the weapon's trajectory fired from Gaza (or elsewhere). But on that morning, the IDF officer in charge insisted, "There is still a human being in the loop: One soldier can always override the system, and he can make sure we don't fire an interceptor unnecessarily—or the other way around, he can order the launching if he deems it necessary."

A surprisingly casual atmosphere could be felt while walking around this facility. The small number of soldiers guarding the battery contrasted with my expectations of entering a forbidden area. The interactions among those troops were also disconcerting. Young soldiers loosely wore their uniforms. They walked around, looking like bored teenagers rather than fighters ready to go to war. They spoke to their commanding officer as if the latter were an older brother, not their superior. This phenomenon has been described by numerous studies before and relates to the unique civil-military relations at the heart of Israel's strategic culture.[1]

The most surprising thing about this Iron Dome site was its relatively easy access. The battery was not concealed. It was in full display, and in the distance, one could see dozens of apartment towers from the biggest town nearby. As one local resident told me, "If we can see them, they can see us . . ." But when I asked about the risk of operational details that could be available to the curious suburbans and onlookers, the IDF spokesperson replied that "local people know that it is in their interest not to disclose sensitive information about the site." When push comes to shove, the functioning of this technologically advanced system relied on trust—trust that villagers will know better than to post on Instagram or TikTok selfies of themselves with a distant Iron Dome battery in the background. They also trusted that day, that a French researcher visiting Israel

---

[1] Edward Luttwak, Eitan Shamir, *The Art of Military Innovation: Lessons from the Israel Defense Forces* (Cambridge, MA: Harvard University Press, 2023).

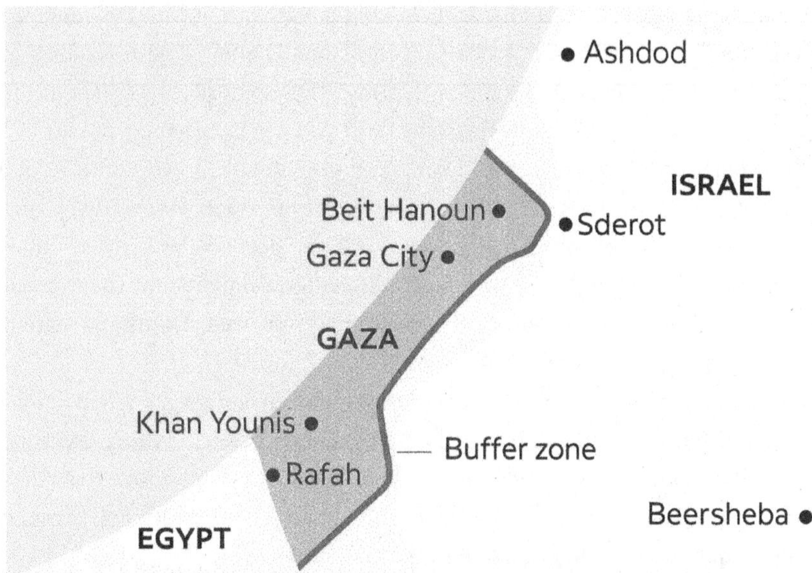

Map I.1 Israel and the Gaza Strip.

would not brag on social networks about his road trip to a southern kibbutz to observe Iron Dome.

As the visit ended, I asked the IDF spokesperson if he had organized visits of foreign visitors like mine in past years. He offered a big smile and said, "All the time." The response was a sobering reality check, if I had been hoping to start this book with an exclusive "behind the scenes" vignette about Iron Dome, but this response was also precisely the reason why I began researching this book in the first place.

The Iron Dome Phenomenon

In the last ten years, Iron Dome became a key component of Israel's military strategy. Government officials, members of parliament, journalists, scientists, and tech entrepreneurs from all around the world traveled to the country to visit an Iron Dome battery. Somehow, this became a necessary item on the agenda for any tour in the country. When Barack Obama conducted his first presidential trip to Israel in 2013, the first thing he did after his plane landed at Ben Gurion

International Airport was to visit an Iron Dome battery that the IDF deployed for the occasion.[2] Former US Ambassador to Israel Daniel Shapiro recalls that he accompanied so many delegations that the "IDF colonel would look at me and say, 'Ambassador, you know this, why don't you do the briefing yourself?'"[3]

Knowledge and interest in Iron Dome also grew thanks to social networks. In the past decade, the system became a sensation when videos displaying interceptions of rockets in real time went viral on Facebook or Twitter. Those videos, often shot at night, felt like Star Wars entertainment, and they served (intentionally or not) as perfect PR campaigns for Iron Dome; its parent company, Rafael; and, more broadly, Israel.

Rarely does a military system enter the common language. When I told friends and family members I visited an Iron Dome battery, almost everyone had an idea about it. Almost none of them knew anything about the other Israeli missile defense systems, like David's Sling and Arrow, which are, in many aspects, much more sophisticated than Iron Dome.

A decade after its introduction, Iron Dome had become part of the pop culture that fed the imagination of people in Israel and abroad. Most of the Israelis I met for this book not only had a strong opinion about Iron Dome but also had a direct experience with it. They shared their own personal "Iron Dome stories": One remembered running on the beach while witnessing a rocket interception in the sky, and someone else told the story of nervously pulling her toddler out of her car after hearing the sirens, only to stare at the Iron Dome exploding light in the distance.

Around the world, Iron Dome has also become a fancy term. At the Republican Party Convention in July 2024, US President Donald Trump went as far as to promise "an Iron Dome missile defense system to ensure that no enemy can strike our homeland."[4] Trump's statement raised eyebrows among military experts, but it highlighted the paradox that Iron Dome had become: A system, initially created to address a technical challenge—that is, to intercept short-range rockets—had become such a success that its aura now exceeded the realm of military strategy and fed the rhetoric of political leaders.

---

[2] Interview with Amir Peretz, Former Minister of Defense (2007–8), IAI Headquarters, Lod, July 29, 2024; Scott Wilson, "Obama and Netanyahu Show Unusual Solidarity," *Washington Post*, March 20, 2013. https://www.washingtonpost.com/world/obama-arrives-in-israel-for-three-day-visit/2013/03/20/a01774aa-914f-11e2-9abd-e4c5c9dc5e90_story.html.

[3] Interview with Daniel Shapiro, Washington, DC, February 20, 2025.

[4] Joe Cirincione, "Can Donald Trump Really Build an Iron Dome over America?," *Defense One*, July 29, 2024. https://www.defenseone.com/ideas/2024/07/can-donald-trump-really-build-iron-dome-over-america/398394/.

A Window on Israel's Strategic Evolution

I started working on this book because I was convinced there was more to Iron Dome than just a military tool. Its biography allows us to reflect on the evolution of Israel and the Middle East in the past two decades. At first glance, it is a perfect illustration of Israel's culture of military innovation and the narrative of a "start-up nation."[5] The story of Iron Dome is the story of how a few individuals, such as Amir Peretz, a defense minister with a limited military background, and Danny Gold, a military engineer from the IDF Directorate of Defense Research & Development, went against the majority of opinions in the government, in the armed forces, and in the media (and even in the US administration) to build a new military system in only three years.

But Iron Dome also reflects an evolution in Israeli military culture from offense toward defense.[6] Traditionally, the IDF focused its training and planning on offensive campaigns, which were deemed the only way to prevent a major war from taking place on its territory.[7] This working hypothesis was ingrained in the IDF ethos since the early years of the state.[8] However, the past decade has seen a gradual rebalancing of this posture, with defense catching up to offense, whether in terms of arms procurement or force structure.

This relates to a third phenomenon at play with Iron Dome: the evolution of civil-military relations. For a long time, IDF commanders assessed rockets and missiles as no more than a nuisance to address by attacking their launchers. Preparing for reprisals was sufficient to deter neighbors. However, by the 2000s, the Israeli population, from either the north or the south, could no longer tolerate living with such a threat, and pressure mounted on the politicians to deal with it in another way.

At the same time, the rise of Iron Dome coincided with the emergence of a new Israeli political approach toward the Palestinians, and in particular

---

[5] Dan Senor, Saul Singer, *Start-Up Nation: The Story of Israel's Economic Miracle* (New York: Twelve, 2009).

[6] Tamir Libel, "Explaining the Security Paradigm Shift: Strategic Culture, Epistemic Communities, and Israel's Changing National Security Policy," *Defence Studies* 16, no. 2 (2016): 137–156. https://doi.org/10.1080/14702436.2016.1165595; Oren Barak, Amit Sheniak, Assaf Shapira, "The Shift to Defence in Israel's Hybrid Military Strategy," *Journal of Strategic Studies* 46, no. 2 (2023): 345–377. https://doi.org/10.1080/01402390.2020.1770090.

[7] Michael Handel, "The Evolution of Israeli Strategy: The Psychology of Insecurity and the Quest for Absolute Security," in: Williamson Murray, MacGregor Knox, Alvin Bernstein (eds.), *The Making of Strategy: Rulers, States, and War* (Cambridge: Cambridge University Press, 1996): 534–578; Yoav Ben-Horin, Barry Posen, *Israel's Strategic Doctrine* (Santa Monica, CA: RAND Corporation, 1981); Ariel Levite, *Offense and Defense in Israeli Military Doctrine* (Boulder, CO: Westview Press, 1989).

[8] Dima Adamsky, "From Israel with Deterrence: Strategic Culture, Intra-war Coercion and Brute Force," *Security Studies* 26, no. 1 (2017): 157–184. https://doi.org/10.1080/09636412.2017.1243923.

toward the Gaza Strip. By 2007, when engineers started designing Iron Dome, the peace process born in Oslo had collapsed, and dreams of coexistence within the framework of a two-state solution seemed long gone. In 2005, Ariel Sharon, then Israel's prime minister, ordered a unilateral disengagement from the Gaza Strip, withdrawing IDF positions and evacuating Israeli settlements. The decision angered the settlers' movement and most of the Israeli right (Sharon's constituency). Later, Hamas took power, first by votes in the legislative elections of January 2006 and then by force, as its militants kicked Fatah's security personnel out of the Gaza Strip the following year. If a military return to Gaza was no longer an option, then containing the threat from Hamas was considered the most realistic approach. In the following years, this led to the implementation of a ground, air, and naval blockade of the Palestinian territory. The new containment approach had its benefits: It enabled most Israelis to feel secure after the bloody years of the Second Intifada. Israel's economy thrived, and it enabled Prime Minister Netanyahu to assert that the Palestinian issue was not, contrary to the traditional beliefs, the mother of all conflicts in the region.

Iron Dome was not designed to serve a political agenda, but its introduction coincided with this new mindset. Eventually, its use on the battlefield and its success in denying the ability of Hamas or the Palestinian Islamic Jihad to inflict major damage to the country became part of this new security concept. During that same period, an influential book, *Catch-67*, written by the philosopher Micah Goodman, argued that instead of trying to resolve what he considered an unsolvable conflict between Israelis and Palestinians, governments should concentrate on reducing its scope and danger.[9] In other words, searching for a political solution with the Gaza Strip was delusional, but ensuring that threats originating from it did not disrupt the lives of Israelis was a realistic endeavor. Maintaining such a "status quo" with Gaza became the central approach of most Israeli governments in the following decade, and to a certain extent, the performance of Iron Dome made it sustainable, at least until the attacks of October 7, 2023.

Iron Dome is also a fascinating window into the evolution of Israel–US relations. The story of Israel's iconic system cannot be told without looking at the role Washington played in supporting the production and deployment of its batteries. Interestingly, the story goes against many assumptions about US military support to Israel. The Bush administration rejected the initial plan for Iron Dome, submitted by the Olmert government to the United States. It was only

---

[9]   Micah Goodman, *Catch-67: The Left, the Right, and the Legacy of the Six-Day War* (New Haven, CT: Yale University Press, 2019).

later, when the system proved reliable on the battlefield, that Bush's successor, Barack Obama, pledged financial support. This American aid to Iron Dome culminated in the signing of a memorandum of understanding in 2016, which specified both an annual allocation for the production of Iron Dome batteries and an unlimited emergency fund to replenish them in the event of a conflict.

During that time, Iron Dome became a cornerstone of the defense for Israeli southern cities such as Ashkelon, Be'er Sheva, and Ashdod. It also became a major topic of Washingtonian politics. Two years before the Gaza War, in 2021, Rashida Tlaib, US representative for Michigan's twelfth congressional district (and the first Palestinian American woman to serve in Congress), called for the suspension of US support for Iron Dome to pressure Israel on its policies in the occupied Palestinian territories. Tlaib's statement was massively dismissed inside the House of Representatives, but it foreshadowed the growing tensions within the Democratic Party on the nature of US military aid to Israel. In other words, the story of Iron Dome also revealed the highs and lows of the US–Israel partnership.

Finally, shedding light on the development of Iron Dome matters not only for those interested in Israel's conflicts with Hamas or Hezbollah. This is a story that also tells us a lot about future trends in warfare in the Middle East and beyond. Iron Dome was born out of the proliferation of missiles and rockets, and particularly the diffusion of such military technologies to nonstate actors. The successes and shortcomings of Iron Dome offer lessons about fundamental themes of strategic studies, such as the equilibrium between offense and defense, the strategic impact of new technologies, the risk of overreliance on them, and the blurred lines between conventional and unconventional wars.

Missiles, Rockets, and Interceptors

Readers taking a glance at a book about Iron Dome may fear that they'll get overwhelmed by technical details and scientific controversies that only rocket scientists would understand. My intention was not to write a technical study on Iron Dome but to demonstrate how the biography of one military system informs us on multiple aspects of Israel's contemporary history. One does not need a scientific or engineering background to grasp the strategic essence of Iron Dome. Given this context, it is helpful to clarify some basic concepts regarding missiles that will be beneficial for the rest of the book.

Missiles and rockets are airborne ranged weapons that deliver explosive warheads to their targets by different means of propulsion. The first use of rockets on the battlefield is ancient, as historians trace it back to China under the Sung dynasty and a battle in 1232 against the Mongols.[10] Four criteria usually distinguish them: their guidance system (which enables accuracy), their range (which allows them to reach distant targets), their payload (which increases the damage inflicted), and their propulsion system (which produces the thrust needed to throw the missile at the target).

Conversely, the logic of missile defense is to design a military system capable of preventing a missile attack. But this field has no "one-size-fits-all" solution. No missile defense system today can intercept all types of projectiles. Defensive systems will vary according to the range or the trajectory of the weapons they want to intercept. In that context, Iron Dome was designed to intercept low-range rockets, which represent the primary and the cheapest weapon system operated by groups like Hamas and Hezbollah. For instance, the Qassam rockets are one of the various systems used by Hamas that can be homemade with material available in the public domain, and their cost is estimated at less than $800. According to Hamas's sources, four models have been developed over the years. The Qassam I has a range of 3 kilometers and can only reach urban areas like Sderot, a city in the western Negev. The Qassam II can reach up to 7 kilometers, which "only" enables it to target Sderot's surrounding areas. However, the Qassam III and IV have ranges of 10 and 15 kilometers, respectively, allowing them to reach Ashkelon. Hamas deployed other systems, such as the J-80 and the R-160, reaching up to 100 and 160 kilometers, respectively.[11]

Like most missile defense systems, Iron Dome is based on three core components: a detection and tracking radar, a missile-firing unit, and a battle management and control system. One Iron Dome battery includes three launchers capable of carrying twenty Tamir interceptors. The Tamir measures three meters in length and uses a proximity-fused explosive warhead, meaning that it automatically explodes when it approaches within a certain distance of its target. Each battery is said to cost approximately $50 million, with one interceptor costing around $50,000.[12] The process of interception can be described as follows:

[10] Jimmy Stamp, "The History of Rocket Science," *Smithsonian Magazine*, February 2013. https://www.smithsonianmag.com/innovation/the-history-of-rocket-science-4078981/.

[11] Yaniv Kubovich, "Mortars, Rockets and Drones: A Look at Hamas' Arsenal," *Haaretz*, May 5, 2019. https://www.haaretz.com/israel-news/2019-05-05/ty-article/.premium/mortars-rockets-and-drones-a-look-at-hamas-arsenal/0000017f-f425-d487-abff-f7ffbe4a0000; Ahmed Qasem Hussein, "The Evolution of the Military Action of the Izz al-Din al-Qassam Brigades: How Hamas Established Its Army in Gaza," *Al Muntaqa: New Perspectives on Arab Studies* 4, no. 1 (September–October 2021): 78–97. https://www.jstor.org/stable/10.31430/almuntaqa.4.1.0078.

[12] Peter Dombrowski, Catherine Kelleher, Eric Auner, "Demystifying Iron Dome," *The National Interest* no. 126 (July–August 2013): 49–59. https://www.jstor.org/stable/42896501.

The moment a rocket is fired at Israel (hypothetically from Gaza, Lebanon, or Syria), a radar will detect and track the projectile. The radar can then provide data to the IDF operators: It calculates the position of the launchers and the impact point of the rocket. Iron Dome's C2 unit can then automatically decide whether to intercept it. For instance, if the radar estimates that the rocket will explode in an unpopulated area, such as the Negev Desert, the system does not order the launch of an interceptor.

Iron Dome may be the most iconic missile defense system today, but it is only one of many others that exist. The IDF currently relies on two other systems: David's Sling, which defends the Israeli territory against long-range rockets and cruise missiles "fired at ranges from 40 km to 300 km," and Arrow, whose third version is currently used to intercept medium-range ballistic missiles.[13] Each of the three systems covers a different threat, defined by its range and trajectory, which often leads Israeli officials to describe their missile defense strategy as one relying on three "layers." As this book went into production, a fourth layer was added : "Iron Beam," a laser-based missile defense system developed by Rafael, the Israeli defense company behind Iron Dome.

Methodology and Sources

This book relies on two different types of sources that allow us to grasp the evolution of Israel's defense policies during the past two decades. First, I use the publicly available data documenting the political, military, and economic evolution of Israel. Through the reports from the International Institute for Strategic Studies (IISS)' Military Balance, the SIPRI Yearbook, official statistics from Israel's government agencies, and other Western states, it is possible to build a comprehensive, if not fully detailed, picture of the environment in which Israel's foreign and defense policies have been conducted. Additionally, for the period of the 1980s and the 1990s, there are numerous declassified official documents and historical monographs that allow us to shed light on Israeli decision-making, especially during the foundational moment that was the Gulf War in 1990–1.

I also used Hebrew and Arabic sources, in particular local military magazines and newspapers. A significant portion of Israeli military literature is available in English (e.g., the publications of the IDF Dado Center), but in some cases, Hebrew

---

[13] US Congressional Research Service, "US Foreign Aid to Israel," December 22, 2016: 16, https://www .everycrsreport.com/files/20161222_RL33222_38d8a59f2caabdc9af8a6cdabfabb963ae8b63ae.pdf.

sources written for a local audience revealed observations and perceptions that were lacking in other sources. Regarding Arabic sources, they were mainly used to illuminate how groups like Hamas and Hezbollah studied the Israeli missile defense strategy and how they gradually learned to adapt.

This leads to the second methodological approach that guided my research: the fieldwork and interviews. The book draws on research trips to Israel (June–July 2024 and February 2025) and the United States (March 2024 and February 2025). I conducted a total of sixty interviews that provided the evidence base for the book. Most interviewees were former officials, from either the US or Israel's government. This included civilian decision-makers at the US Department of Defense, Israel's National Security Council, the US Department of State, and IDF military officers (from the air defense unit, the strategic planning, and the military intelligence). Additionally, I met with representatives of Israel's civil society, local journalists, and social workers involved, for instance, in the treatment of Israelis in the southern communities suffering from traumatic stress disorder due to rocket attacks. I also interviewed current official representatives of the IDF (as detailed in the first paragraphs of the introduction).

Most of the interviews made for this book were recorded, and when possible, I attributed the citations. In specific cases, when information was deemed too sensitive by the interviewee, I kept it anonymous and made every effort to stay as close to the source as possible. For social scientists, interviews are an essential key to accessing the field, and in many ways, this book would not have been possible without them. Former practitioners can help explain the context of past decisions, detailing the motivations of different actors, and reminding us that nothing in public policy follows a natural or evident pattern. Past scholarship has shown that the adoption of a military system is rarely (if ever) the result of a rational process defined by a new technology responding to a need.[14] Personalities, idiosyncrasies, and institutional cultures matter, and the study of Iron Dome reflects all of that.

There are limitations with interviews as well: Individuals can inflate their role in the process, they can use the format to settle scores with old rivals, and they can stick to official statements (especially if they recently left the government and/or if they plan to return soon). However, interviewees can also forget or misremember events. This is why I tried as much as possible to rely on several sources and to cross-reference specific assertions when reliability was uncertain.

---

[14] Ulrich Krotz, *Flying Tiger: International Relations Theory and the Politics of Advanced Weapons* (Oxford: Oxford University Press, 2011); Jean Joana, Andy Smith, "Changing French Military Procurement Policy: The State, Industry and 'Europe' in the Case of the A400M," *West European Politics* 29, no. 1 (2000): 70–89. https://doi.org/10.1080/01402380500389257.

One last caveat is worth acknowledging here. Discussions about the Israel–Palestine conflict usually trigger emotions and passions from all sides involved. Although I hope the book follows a rigorous and objective process, I do not delude myself into believing I am immune to personal biases. I tried as much as possible to keep in check my assumptions and findings.

Structure of the Book

Against that backdrop, the book follows the story of Iron Dome, from its creation against all odds in the late 2000s to its current challenges amid Israel's new security environment. The first chapter starts in the field, specifically in Sderot, a southern Israeli city, to capture the political and social impact of increased rocket attacks from Hamas in the 2000s. It then puts this issue into the broader historical context that led several Arab states (Syria, Iraq), Iran, as well as nonstate actors (Hezbollah, Hamas, the Palestinian Islamic Jihad) to turn to rocket attacks as a key tenet of their strategies against Israel. This culminated with the war of July 2006 between Israel and Hezbollah—the "first missile war," to use the expression of Isaac Ben-Israel.[15]

The second chapter then focuses on the policy process that led to the introduction of Iron Dome. It shows how a small group of civilian decision-makers around former Defense Minister Amir Peretz imposed a program on a reluctant military establishment. It highlights the numerous challenges they faced: financial constraints and technological uncertainties but also a "cult of the offensive" within the IDF that shaped the views of most of its commanders on Iron Dome. Eventually, the successful introduction of the system in 2011 revealed essential lessons, not only on innovation in military technologies but also on civil-military tensions within that context.

The third chapter moves from the development phase to the actual use of Iron Dome on the battlefield, with a close look at its role in the long conflict between Hamas and the IDF that escalated on a full scale in four wars in 2012, 2014, 2021, and eventually 2023. I explain here how Iron Dome improved the safety of civilians against indiscriminate rocket attacks but also how it influenced the Israeli way of war. At the political level, the success of Iron Dome allowed governments to reduce their reliance on ground forces to respond to the

---

[15] Isaac Ben-Israel, *Melkhamat Hatilim Harishona: Israel-Khizballah* ("The First Missile War: Israel Hzbollah") (Tel Aviv University, 2007). https://web.archive.org/web/20110722021710/http://spirit .tau.ac.il/government/Downloads/YitzakBIMissiles.pdf.

rocket challenge, and progressively it fed the security concept that posited the containment of Hamas (and by extension of Gaza) as the prevailing strategy.

Then, the fourth chapter looks at the US–Israel defense cooperation and explains how missile defense in general, and Iron Dome in particular, became an essential pillar of that relationship. US involvement in financing the production of Iron Dome has to be understood in the context of the partnership between the two countries in missile defense programs, which began during the presidency of Ronald Reagan in the 1980s, with Israel's participation in the Strategic Defense Initiative. After initial skepticism on the feasibility of Iron Dome, the US government quickly embraced the system under the Obama administration. If the investigation demonstrates the enduring depth of cooperation between Israel and the United States, it also highlights the rising Israeli reliance, if not overreliance, on US funding and production capacity of Iron Dome.

This leads to the question at the heart of the fifth chapter: How does the Israeli military look at the future of its strategy as the demands for Iron Dome keep increasing? As the research for this book was conducted in the aftermath of Hamas's attack on October 7, 2023, most of the interviewees looked at this dilemma through the lens of that specific military and intelligence failure. In the period preceding October 7, Iron Dome contributed to a rebalancing between offense and defense, but more importantly, it fostered complacency among decision-makers. It allowed them to downplay signs that opposing forces like Hamas and Hezbollah were steadily adapting their tactics vis-à-vis Iron Dome. In retrospect, Iron Dome might be to Israel what the Maginot Line was to France in the 1930s: an impressive military system showcasing technological innovation that blinded its military commanders to the evolving strategy of their enemies.[16]

Finally, the sixth chapter gauges the future challenges surrounding the development of Iron Dome: the trends in the proliferation of rockets, missiles, and uncrewed vehicles in the Middle East; the growing accuracy of those systems; and, conversely, the next technological evolution of missile defense, in particular with the introduction of laser-based systems such as Iron Beam. It considers how Iron Dome progressively overlaps with the other Israeli missile defense systems (David's Sling, Arrow). The chapter also extends beyond the Israeli experience, reflecting on the lessons from the study of Iron Dome concerning the future of warfare, including the impact of new military technologies, and the dilemma between offensive and defensive strategies.

---

[16] Meir Finkel, "Kipat Barzel—Kav Maginot Hachadash?" (Iron Dome—The New Maginot Line?), *Maarachot* no. 461 (June 2015): 11–16. https://www.maarachot.idf.il/media/t13cig4r/כיפת-ברזל-קו-מאזינו-החדש.pdf.

1

The Rise of Rocket Warfare

Susan is an employee of the Sderot Municipality in her late fifties. During her office breaks, she chain-smokes as if she were inhaling her last cigarette ever. She says she moved with her family to Israel from Morocco when she was five years old. At that time, the city was much smaller than the town of thirty-three thousand people it has become today. It wasn't even a city in the true sense of the word. Sderot was founded in 1951 as a "transit camp" for new Jewish migrants (Olim Chadashim in Hebrew) who joined the nascent state of Israel. Approximately ninety thousand Jews from North Africa arrived in the country between 1954 and 1956. Back then, life conditions were difficult for those new citizens who left everything behind and came to a country without speaking the local language or receiving basic welfare services. Until the mid-1990s, the *mizrahim*—Jews of Arab ancestry—made up 85 percent of Sderot's population. It decreased after the massive wave of immigration to Israel from the former Soviet Union and the implementation of various policies to attract Israelis from larger cities. But you can still observe the *mizrahi* character of the town when you engage with the older locals.[1]

When I ask Susan about her view on Gaza, less than 7 kilometers from Sderot, whose buildings can be seen from the hills, she gets uncomfortable. She recalls memories from her youth when she used to stroll through the markets of Gaza City (when the Israel Defense Forces [IDF] still occupied the territory). But as we move closer to the present, she remembers the gradual shift in the 2000s and the first rockets fired at the city during those years. Since then, rocket attacks have been a regular occurrence in Sderot, only stopping periodically in accordance with the latest ceasefire negotiated between Hamas and the Israeli government.

Soberly, Susan describes the psychological impact those attacks have had on her. She talks of how, for months, she was unable to take a shower on the second floor of her house, out of fear that a siren might suddenly scream, and that she

---

[1] Moti Gigi, "Relations Between Development Towns and Kibbutzim: Sderot and Sha'ar Hanegev," *Israel Studies Review* 33, no. 3 (Winter 2018): 121–139. https://doi.org/10.3167/isr.2018.330308; Galit Saada-Ophir, "Mizrahi Subaltern Counterpoints: Sderot's Alternative Bands," *Anthropological Quarterly* 80, no. 3 (Summer 2007): 711–736. https://www.jstor.org/stable/30052721.

would not have enough time to reach her shelter in the basement. Like Susan, many residents of Sderot suffer from what qualifies as post-traumatic stress disorder.[2] Unsurprisingly, the protracted conflict between the IDF and Hamas has had consequences also for the children. "Starting at three years old, children have to be trained to take shelter, to know what to do when the siren blows," says Susan. In Sderot, social life is organized around bomb shelters. Schools and bus stops are all equipped with them, and in 2009, an indoor playground under a 21,000-square-foot bomb shelter was inaugurated.[3]

The IDF assesses that in cities like Sderot bordering Gaza, civilians have approximately 15–30 seconds after the siren rings to take shelter and before an incoming rocket explodes. If you are on the road when that happens, you are told to lie down on the asphalt and cover your head with your hands (assuming you are more likely to recover from a hand injury caused by shrapnel than from one that affects the head).

At first glance, you might think that a city so close to a war zone would inevitably face an exodus. However, when visiting Sderot, I was struck by how wealthy and lively it looked; its infrastructure was modern, and its cultural scene was vibrant. For Israelis, Sderot is famous for its international film festival and its thriving indie rock scene. Residents explain that this is the result of a government strategy aimed at making Sderot appealing. Over the past two decades, many people, weary of the noise and high cost of living in Tel Aviv, have chosen to relocate to Sderot. A train line was established to ease their commute, and tax incentives made the move even more attractive.

Walking on the outskirts of Sderot, you feel an eerie proximity between the Israelis and the Palestinians near the Gaza Strip. In our political imagination, both belong to two worlds far away from each other, but on the ground, the reality is much more complex. People like Susan live in a near-constant fear of assault from Hamas combatants, but when she talks about them, she calls them "our cousins." She says it not to express empathy, but in a matter-of-fact way.

This echoes one of the most famous—and perhaps intriguing—speeches the late Moshe Dayan delivered in 1956, when he was the IDF chief of staff. Addressing the crowd gathered at the funeral of Roi Rothberg, a member from one kibbutz bordering Gaza who was killed by Palestinians who entered

---

[2] Avi Besser, Yuval Neria, Maggie Haynes, "Adult Attachment, Perceived Stress, and PTSD Among Civilians Exposed to Ongoing Terrorist Attacks in Southern Israel," *Personality and Individual Differences* 47, no. 47 (2009): 851–857. https://doi.org/10.1016/j.paid.2009.07.003.

[3] Tal Kra-Oz, "A Look at Israeli Life Just Outside the Gaza Strip," *Tablet*, July 11, 2014. https://www.tabletmag.com/sections/news/articles/a-look-at-israeli-life-just-outside-the-gaza-strip.

the kibbutz, Dayan said, "Let us not cast the blame on the murderers today. Why should we declare their burning hatred for us? For eight years, they have been sitting in the refugee camps in Gaza, and before their eyes, we have been transforming the lands and the villages, where they and their fathers dwelt, into our estate. It is not among the Arabs in Gaza, but in our midst that we must seek Roi's blood."[4]

On October 7, 2023, Sderot was attacked by Hamas gunmen who stormed the police station in the city center while shooting civilians walking in the street or in their homes nearby. At least fifty civilians and twenty police officers were killed during that surprise attack, and it took more than twenty-four hours for the IDF to regain control over the town. The retaking of Sderot Police Station was a violent battle that destroyed most of the building, which was subsequently erased.[5]

When I visited Sderot in July 2024, there was no longer any trace or stigma of the attack, except in the interviews with locals. According to Noam Bedein, a former student of Sderot's Sapir College and the founder of the local media center, the municipality constantly tries to remove traces of rocket attacks as soon as they occur.[6] They even used the shrapnel left over from an attack to build a sculpture on one of the city's roundabouts.

After hearing all the tragic stories shared by locals, I still wondered why the population hadn't deserted cities like Sderot. Some interviewees say they have always lived there and cannot imagine their lives elsewhere. Others also point out their financial dilemma: For middle-class families, Sderot still offers opportunities that are impossible in Tel Aviv or Haifa. Sderot has come to symbolize the predicament of Israeli cities living under the clear and present danger of rockets. Locals lament that their town earned the nickname "the bomb-shelter capital of the world."[7] After Iron Dome entered the battleground, southern cities like Sderot but also Ashkelon, Be'er-Sheva, and Netivot, turned into frontline targets in the protracted conflict between Israel and Hamas.

However, the threat of rocket attacks on Israel's urban areas did not start in the 2000s, nor did it begin in Gaza. A closer look at the history of Middle Eastern wars reveals how it slowly but steadily became a major pillar of the strategies of

---

4 Jewish Virtual Library, "Moshe Dayan's Eulogy for Roi Rutenberg—April 19, 1956." http://www.jewishvirtuallibrary.org/jsource/Quote/dayanq.html.
5 Reuters, "Israel Fights to Regain Control of Sderot from Hamas Gunmen," October 9, 2023. https://www.reuters.com/pictures/pictures-israel-fights-regain-control-sderot-hamas-gunmen-2023-10-08/.
6 Interview with Noam Bedein, founder of Sderot Media Center, Sderot, July 10, 2024.
7 Mitch Ginsburg, "In Sderot, the Bomb-Shelter Capital of the World," *Times of Israel*, July 11, 2014. https://www.timesofisrael.com/in-sderot-the-bomb-shelter-capital-of-the-world/.

Israel's neighbors, starting in the 1970s, as they desperately sought to overcome the IDF's conventional supremacy. Against that backdrop, this first chapter unpacks the key phases that led to the decision to build Iron Dome, starting with the development of missile programs in Egypt, Iraq, Syria, and Iran. It then details the implications of these weapons on the battlefield, first during the Iran–Iraq War and later against Israel during the Gulf War of 1991. But, as the chapter explains, the biggest challenges in the following two decades came from nonstate actors rather than traditional Middle Eastern countries. Namely, Hezbollah and Hamas turned rocket and missile barrages into a central strategy to harass Israeli civilians, forcing in 2006 the government of Ehud Olmert to launch the development of Iron Dome.

Rockets and Missiles Enter the Middle East Battlefield

The proliferation of rockets and missiles in the Middle East started in the early 1970s. By that time, Arab armed forces had been humiliated by the 1967 war and Israel's conquest of Arab lands, including the Egyptian Negev, the Gaza Strip, the Syrian Golan Heights, Jerusalem, and the West Bank (until then controlled by the kingdom of Jordan). Perhaps the most devastating demonstration of the IDF's superiority in 1967 was its bombing campaign in the early hours of June 5 that targeted the bases of the Egyptian Air Force: About 338 planes were destroyed in three hours. Syrian and Jordanian pilots quickly tried to retaliate, but to no avail. By the end of the first day, the Israeli Air Force enjoyed command of the air across the region.[8]

The events of 1967 constituted a major political and military setback for Arab countries, particularly for Egypt. In the following years, Cairo realized that achieving strategic parity with Israel was not a feasible goal, at least through conventional means. Because the Israeli Air Force was superior in terms of the training of its pilots and their capabilities, the Arab armed forces were forced to look for another way to defeat them. Missiles seemed like a convenient option, at least a much cheaper alternative to fighter jets. As a result, Egypt launched a ballistic program in cooperation with the USSR, and by 1973, Frog-7 missiles (70-kilometer range) and Scud-Bs (300 kilometers) went into service. In the following war of October 1973, Egypt fired three Scud-Bs that aimed at

---

[8]   Kenneth M. Pollack, "Air Power in the Six-Day War," in: Ahron Bregman (ed.), *Warfare in the Middle East Since 1945* (London: Routledge, 2017): 53–85.

destroying bridges along the Suez Canal while the Israeli ground forces moved ahead, but none reached their target.[9]

Despite these inconclusive results, Egyptian President Anwar al-Sadat approved the continued development of the arsenal. According to declassified US intelligence estimates, the Frog-7 was later replaced by a similar missile called the Sakr-80, produced by the Egyptians themselves. Meanwhile, international cooperation intensified, and Egypt joined Iraq and Argentina to build a missile with a range of 1,000 kilometers named Badr-2000.[10]

By the early 1980s, there were numerous signs that Arab states were increasingly relying on their new inventory of missiles. However, the IDF had a different reading. In July 2024, I met with David Ivry, the Chief of the Israeli Air Force at the time. Looking back at those developments, Ivry recalls that Arab armed forces "didn't dare to use (missiles) against Israel's territory, only against military targets. So, Israel didn't take it seriously." Ivry adds, "There were a lot of studies that insisted that surface-to-surface missiles are not accurate: the so-called 'circular error of probability' is about two kilometers at those ranges so it's not accurate, it's not a risk from a strategic point of view." Ivry insists on the underlying assumption of the IDF leadership: "They (the Arab states) are not going *to dare* to use it against civilians, because our reaction is going to be overwhelming."[11]

Ivry's recollection highlights one aspect that came back repeatedly during the investigation for this book: For a long time, Israel's military leaders proved reluctant to look at rockets and missiles as a strategic transformation. They often felt that these were the weapons of the poor, that they could not be seriously compared to the advanced systems operated by the IDF, and that they were a mere nuisance. They assumed that Arab forces would not use them against civilians, out of fear of Israeli retaliation. In other words, neighboring states were deterred.

However, events throughout the 1980s and the 1990s seriously questioned these assumptions. One of those events involved a minor clash in 1982 between Israel and Syria inside Lebanon. Several retired IDF generals interviewed for the book recalled the impact of Operation Mole Cricket 19, which pitted the Israeli Air Force against Syrian air defense. Following Lebanon's descent into civil war

---

[9] Joseph Bermudez, "Ballistic Missiles in the Third World: Egypt and the 1973 Arab-Israeli War," *Jane's Intelligence Review* 3, no. 12 (December 1991): 531–537.

[10] Central Intelligence Agency, "Egypt: Aspirations for Missile Production," Intelligence Assessment, April 1, 1988 (Declassified on February 11, 2021). https://www.cia.gov/readingroom/document/05857834.

[11] Interview with David Ivry, former Chief of the Israel Air Force and former Director General of Israel's Ministry of Defense, Ramat HaSharon, July 22, 2024.

in 1975, the Syrian regime of Hafez al-Assad invaded the country, and his armed forces began deploying both mobile and static surface-to-air missiles (SAM) in the Bekaa Valley. The Israeli government feared that these Syrian deployments could easily threaten its troops, as then–Defense Minister Ariel Sharon launched the invasion of Lebanon on June 6 with over sixty thousand soldiers. Three days after the IDF entered the country, the government approved Operation Mole Cricket 19, which tasked the Israeli Air Force with destroying the Syrian missile batteries inside Lebanon. The operation was a significant military success: Nineteen SAM batteries were destroyed in two hours, and when the Syrian Air Force attempted to respond, they lost twenty-six jets in dogfights against the Israelis. Not a single Israeli aircraft was lost.[12]

Later, Operation Mole Cricket 19 became a case study of military innovation, showcasing the IDF's edge over its adversaries. But when David Ivry, then chief of the Israel Air Force, remembers the event four decades later, he does not brag. Instead, he sees the event as an inflection point from the Syrian perspective. Ivry hands me the memoirs of Mustafa Tlass, then Syria's defense minister, that he thoroughly studied. In the book, Tlass ignores the embarrassing defeat of the Syrian Air Force. Instead, he stresses the idea that on the ground, against the Israeli ground forces, the Syrians were much more successful. For Ivry, this proved that the Syrian military establishment was actually learning from its failures. Instead of competing with the IDF in the air with fighter jets and SAM batteries, they would refocus on the ground with surface-to-surface missiles. What was seen as a victory for the Israel Air Force was set to bring about a profound change in the strategic approach of its adversaries.

Iran, Iraq, and the War of the Cities

Syria was not the only Arab state reconsidering its military strategy amid the development of missile inventories. On September 22, 1980, the Iraqi regime of Saddam Hussein launched an invasion of Iran, following months of military escalation around border disputes. The war would last eight long years, making it one of the twentieth century's longest and bloodiest conventional interstate

---

[12] Haim Yogev, Ronen Cohen, Eyal Lewin, "Revolution in Military Affairs—The Operation Mole Cricket 19 as a Case Study for the Technological Race During the Cold War," *International Area Studies Review* 25, no. 2 (2022): 138–156. https://doi.org/10.1177/2233865922107580; Dmitry Adamsky, *The Culture of Military Innovation: The Impact of Cultural Factors on the Revolution in Military Affairs in Russia, the US, and Israel* (Stanford: Stanford University Press, 2010): 93–129.

wars. The conflict saw Iraqi forces using chemical weapons on a massive scale: For the year 1988 only, it was estimated that the Iraqi campaign killed more than fifty thousand Iranians.[13]

Saddam Hussein quickly saw the power of using missiles against urban centers, significantly undermining the morale of the Iranians. According to declassified files, Saddam explained once in 1984 to his air force officers:

> Sometimes what you get out of a weapon is when you keep saying, "I will bomb you" [and] it is better than bombing him. It is possible that when you bomb him the material effect will be 40 percent, but if you stick it up to his face the material and the spiritual effect will be 60 percent, so why hit him? Keep getting 60 percent![14]

In academic terms, the "spiritual effect" Saddam sought is known as compellence: the ability to force his opponent to change behavior through the threat of using or the actual use of force. In his brutal war against the Iranian Islamic Republic, Saddam applied that logic by launching what became known as the "war of the cities," a missile campaign that intentionally targeted urban centers like Tehran, Tabriz, and Esfahan.

According to historians, the "war of the cities" began on February 1, 1984, when the Iraqi regime announced it would target eleven Iranian cities near the front line. Iraqi forces launched a wave of Scud missiles at these cities, resulting in the deaths of forty Iranians and injuring two hundred others. As fighting between frontline soldiers reached a stalemate, Saddam believed that striking Iranian civilians could effectively pressure the leadership in Tehran. His reasoning mirrored that of early airpower advocates, such as the Italian general Giulio Douhet, who argued in the 1920s that air strikes on enemy cities could lead to victory.[15]

Like the Egyptians, the Iraqis received significant Soviet assistance during the seventies and eighties to acquire Scud missiles. Iraqi engineers modified Soviet systems to create the Al Hussein missile, which would be crucial in the war with Iran. In addition to this missile, several projects were launched to develop long-range delivery systems, including one, Project Babylon, focused on developing a system called "Supergun." This massive cannon was designed to have a range

---

[13] Javed Ali, "Chemical Weapons and the Iran-Iraq War: A Case Study in Noncompliance," *Nonproliferation Review* 8, no. 1 (Spring 2001): 43–58, 52. https://doi.org/10.1080/10736700108436837.

[14] Kevin Woods, David Palkki, Mark Stout (eds.), *A Survey of Saddam's Audio Files, 1978–2001: Toward an Understanding of Authoritarian Regimes* (Alexandria: Institute for Defense Analyses, 2010): 259.

[15] Giulio Douhet, *The Command of the Air* (Maxwell AFB, AL: Air University Press, 2019).

of several hundred kilometers. Additionally, Iraq had a diverse array of tactical missiles, including the Laith (derived from the Frog-7), the Ababil-100, and the Ababil-50.[16]

Between February 29 and April 20, 1988, Iraq would launch 190 Al Hussein missiles on Iranian cities. Overall, Iraqi missiles killed more than 2,000 Iranians and injured 6,000. The campaign over Tehran caused the displacement of around 2.5 million Iranians.[17] In total, it is estimated that Iraqis and Iranians fired respectively 523 and 325 ballistic missiles at each other. Almost half of those were launched during the final year of the war.[18]

Still, the Israeli military intelligence considered the surface-to-surface Scud missiles used by the Iraqis a minor challenge. In Tel Aviv, David Ivry, the former chief of the air force, had now been promoted to the position of director general of the Ministry of Defense under then-Minister Yitzhak Rabin. As the "war of the cities" raged between Iraq and Iran, Ivry and his team set up a task force to study its strategic implications. They assessed that after eight years of war, the missile strategy conducted by Saddam Hussein had been a key innovation and the primary reason behind the decision of Ayatollah Khomeini to concede the end of the war.[19]

This suggested two crucial lessons: First, that rudimentary missiles like those employed by the Iraqis could have more than a tactical effect on the battlefield. They could influence the course of the war at the strategic level. Second, the scale of the war of the cities regarding the destruction of infrastructure and the loss of civilian lives challenged the assumption of the Israeli military establishment that Arab forces would not "dare" use those weapons against Israeli cities. Implicit again in that assertion was the belief that the IDF's superiority and its ability to inflict massive casualties in a retaliatory strike deterred such attacks.

The conclusion of Ivry's task force called for a rethinking of Israel's strategy. But the response from the IDF leadership proved underwhelming: According to Ivry, the military intelligence directorate (known as Aman in Hebrew and considered the largest and most influential intelligence unit[20]), then led by Major

---

[16] Michael Eisenstadt, "The Iraqi Artillery Threat," Washington Institute for Near East Policy, February 11, 1991. https://www.washingtoninstitute.org/policy-analysis/iraqi-artillery-threat.

[17] Bernard Rostker, "Information Paper Iraq's Scud Ballistic Missiles," US Department of Defense, July 25, 2000. https://www.gulflink.osd.mil/scud_info/.

[18] Pierre Razoux, *The Iran-Iraq War* (Cambridge: Belknap Press of Harvard University Press, 2015): 541.

[19] Mitch Ginsburg, "Chinks Remain in Israel's Air Defense Armor, Despite Iron Dome," *Times of Israel*, March 14, 2012. https://www.timesofisrael.com/the-chinks-in-our-missile-defense-armor/.

[20] Joshua Krasna, "A Guide for the Perplexed: The Israeli National Security Constellation and Its Effect on Policymaking," Foreign Policy Research Institute, February 2018: 22. https://www.fpri.org /article/2018/02/guide-perplexed-israeli-national-security-constellation-effect-policymaking/.

General Amnon Lipkin-Shahak, downplayed the effects of Saddam's missile strategy. Aman's analysts estimated that damage to Iranian cities remained limited and could not be extrapolated to the Israeli context. In other words, no change in the IDF posture was necessary.

A Reluctant Partner of the US Missile Defense Enterprise

In fact, Israel's involvement in missile defense did not start because of Iraq or Iran but because of one speech delivered in Washington. On March 23, 1983, President Ronald Reagan pronounced his seminal speech on the Strategic Defense Initiative (SDI). For Reagan, missile defense was a means to abandon the logic of mutual assured destruction (MAD). MAD posited that, given the ability of the United States and the USSR to destroy each other, both nations had a vested interest in avoiding nuclear war.

In Reagan's view, ensuring citizens' safety on such a shaky principle as MAD was profoundly immoral. Therefore, he considered the SDI an imperative. In his speech, Reagan asked the question that drove his quest: "What if free people could live secure in the knowledge that . . . we could intercept and destroy strategic ballistic missiles before they reached our own soil or that of our allies?"[21] Later in the speech, Reagan captured the essence of missile defense as opposed to deterrence: "Wouldn't it be better to save lives than to avenge them?" In hindsight, the question echoes the fierce debates among Israeli generals that were to surround the development of Iron Dome two decades later.

While Reagan's speech referenced America's allies, international reactions were lukewarm, to say the least. Only the United Kingdom, West Germany, and Israel accepted the offer to participate in SDI research and development programs. Israel did it with extreme caution. In fact, of the budget allocated to the first US–Israel missile defense project, 80 percent came from the US government and 20 percent from Israel. But more importantly, those 20 percent came from Israel Aerospace Industries (IAI)—not the Israeli government.[22]

On May 5, 1986, US Secretary of Defense Caspar Weinberger and his Israeli counterpart Yitzhak Rabin signed a bilateral memorandum of understanding. The first projects were limited: A $100 million contract was allocated to investigate

---

[21] Ronald Reagan, "Address to the Nation on Defense and National Security," Ronald Reagan Presidential Library, March 23, 1983. https://www.reaganlibrary.gov/archives/speech/address-nation -defense-and-national-security.
[22] Interview with David Ivry, Ramat HaSharon, July 22, 2024.

a combined chemical and electrical propulsion scheme for projectiles fired by a rail gun.[23] Soon, the first director of the SDI Organization, General James Abrahamson, suggested to his Israeli counterparts that they start developing their missile defense system to address the specific threats facing Israel. It would rely on a land-based sensing system and a land-based missile interception system. For Abrahamson, the Israeli project would eventually contribute to the technological development of SDI systems. This Israeli project was to be known as "Arrow," and it began with a contract with IAI, funded by the United States.[24]

IAI's proposal was a bold and innovative one. As Brigadier General Uzi Eilam, then in charge of the research and development for the IDF, remembers, "[T]hey [IAI] offered an eloquent and comprehensive presentation of a new high-powered intercepting missile with dreamlike maneuverability and an interception altitude of dozens of kilometers."[25]

Yet, Israel's involvement in Arrow did not mean a change in its military strategy. The involvement resulted from a decision made by both Defense Minister Rabin and Prime Minister Shamir against the wishes of the military leadership. Both felt it was worth participating in the development of Arrow since the Americans were covering most of its funding. The IDF feared the missile defense program would divert funding allocated to other programs, such as tanks or fighter jets.

The absence of financial commitment from the IDF enabled the government to prevent a fierce bureaucratic battle. It is worth remembering that, by that time, Israel's defense budget was extremely high compared to Western standards: In 1984, its military expenditures accounted for 18.9 percent of its GDP. For economists, this was simply unsustainable. By 1987, the government was forced to cancel the development of Israel's fighter jet, the Lavi, a multirole, highly advanced plane that threatened to bankrupt the country.[26]

The early skepticism of the IDF vis-à-vis Arrow was not only a matter of finances. It was also associated with a deeper aversion to defense as a military strategy. Since the birth of Israel, its armed forces had relied on offensive doctrines. Starting in the late forties, Israel's strategic culture was shaped by constraints such as a lack of strategic depth and limited personnel, which left the country vulnerable to prolonged conflicts. Given these conditions, scenarios of extended wars had to be avoided at all costs. To counteract these challenges, Israeli leaders

---

[23] Harry Waldman, *The Dictionary of Strategic Defense Initiative* (New York: Wilmington, 1988): 80.

[24] Uzi Eilam, *Eilam's Arc: How Israel Became a Military Technology Powerhouse* (Brighton: Sussex Academic Press, 2011): 204–241.

[25] Eilam, *Eilam's Arc*: 242.

[26] Dov Zakheim, *Flight of the Lavi: Inside a US-Israeli Crisis* (Washington, DC: Potomac Books, 1996).

adopted offensive doctrines that enabled the initiation of preemptive campaigns, swiftly shifting the battles onto enemy territory.

Even though the reality of an existential threat coming from Arab conventional armies vanished after the 1967 war, the scenario remained a key driver of the Israeli military planning process in the mid-1980s.[27] Writing in 1989, the Israeli researcher Ariel Levite (who later joined the policy directorate of the Ministry of Defense) described this strong inclination among military planners for an offensive posture as an attitude "characterized by contempt for defensive operations, heavy emphasis on the ephemeral nature of the defensive battle, and a surprising degree of ignorance regarding the doctrinal characteristics or the internal logic of defensive operations."[28]

In 1990, the United States made a $52 billion contribution to the program.[29] Several other bilateral agreements were signed to provide US financial support for the computer facility for the Arrow program and later for its second version. The interceptors were first tested in 1990 and deemed successful. However, this was not the most important development for missile defense that year. In 1990, the unexpected invasion of a small Arab Gulf state triggered a chain of events in the Middle East that were to change Israel's need to defend its territory.

Scuds on Tel Aviv

In 1991, Saddam Hussein put his missile strategy to the test on the Israelis. Following the eight-year war with Iran, Iraq's economy was in terrible shape. The country owed billions of dollars in debt to Saudi Arabia and Kuwait, which financed Saddam's war efforts for most of the conflict. As the war came to an end, Saddam pleaded for the cancellation of his debt to Gulf rulers, to no avail. Tensions escalated between the Iraqi leader and his Gulf neighbors, particularly the small state of Kuwait, which he accused of exceeding its oil production quota to drive down prices. Bilateral relations were also tainted by an old border dispute that Saddam revived to mobilize Iraqi nationalistic sentiments. Eventually, the Iraqi leader launched an invasion of Kuwait on August 2, 1990. In less than

[27] Michael Handel, "The Evolution of Israeli Strategy: The Psychology of Insecurity and the Quest for Absolute Security," in: Williamson Murray, MacGregor Knox, Alvin Bernstein (eds.), *The Making of Strategy: Rulers, States, and War* (Cambridge: Cambridge University Press, 1996): 534–578; Yoav Ben-Horin, Barry Posen, *Israel's Strategic Doctrine* (Santa Monica, CA: RAND Corporation, 1981).

[28] Ariel Levite, *Offense and Defense in Israeli Military Doctrine* (Boulder, CO: Westview Press, 1989): 126.

[29] Jeremy Sharp, "US Foreign Aid to Israel," Congressional Research Service, March 1, 2023. https://www.congress.gov/crs-product/RL33222.

twenty-four hours, the capital was occupied by Saddam's forces, and Kuwait's ruling family, the Al Sabah, escaped to Saudi Arabia.

The invasion of Kuwait was a pivotal moment in the history of the Middle East. For the whole region, the assault from an Arab state on another one was unprecedented. It shattered decades of pan-Arab rhetoric and deeply divided public opinion and leaders in the Middle East. Gulf monarchs condemned the aggression, fearing they could be next. But other prominent figures like King Hussein of Jordan and Yasser Arafat of the Palestinian Liberation Organization supported Saddam's invasion. The divisions within the Arab political establishment would leave scars and grudges for decades.

Eventually, the US administration of George H. Bush assembled a coalition to liberate Kuwait. On November 29, 1990, the UN Security Council passed resolution 678, sanctioning the use of force if Iraq had not withdrawn from Kuwait by January 15, 1991. Iraqi forces stood still. After months of intense diplomatic efforts with European and Middle Eastern partners, Operation Desert Storm started two days later. The first goal of US forces was to establish air supremacy, which involved the destruction of most Iraqi air defenses.

However, on the morning of January 18, 1991, only one day after the start of Operation Desert Storm, Iraq launched eight Scud missiles on Israel, targeting Tel Aviv, Haifa, and Dimona (a city in the Negev near the country's nuclear research center). The Israeli government issued a nationwide alert. Israeli Air Force pilots prepared to take off when radars initially showed Iraqi fighter bombers on their way to Israel—it soon proved to be a false alert.[30] Missiles, *not* airplanes, had been used to attack the Israeli territory.

Through his attack on Israel, Saddam sought to regionalize the conflict. Saddam was aware of the conflicting views on the war within the Arab world. He was then trying to portray himself as a postcolonial leader fighting against a US-led coalition. In other words, targeting Israel was a gamble to turn himself into an Arab commander fighting for the Palestinian cause.

The Bush administration understood Saddam's calculus and feared that an Israeli retaliation against Iraq would jeopardize the Arab support Washington had been able to garner in previous months. The US military presence inside Saudi Arabia was already a delicate move, resented by the local population. If Israel were to retaliate against Saddam, its fighter jets would most certainly cross the airspace of Jordan or Saudi Arabia. The former was supporting Saddam's

---

[30] Michael Gordon, Bernard Trainor, *The Generals' War. The Inside Story of the Conflict in the Gulf* (New York: Little Brown and Company, 1995): 228.

occupation of Kuwait, while the latter hosted US troops. In both scenarios, it fueled the belief of the White House and the Pentagon that an Israeli response would break the unity of the international coalition and possibly trigger a regional war.

As soon as the Scuds reached Tel Aviv, Moshe Arens, Israel's Defense Minister, called his American counterpart, Dick Cheney. The latter expressed the support of the Bush administration and offered to deploy US Patriot batteries to Israel. Arens accepted the American offer. The United States was hoping that the measure would reassure the Israelis against any future threat and that it would buy time for Washington to think of a response to Saddam's attack.

But Arens also formally asked that Washington allow Israel to start preparations for retaliation. Cheney then called Brent Scowcroft, Bush's national security adviser, to brief him on the Israeli demands. According to accounts from former US officials who participated in the consultations, Cheney initially believed Washington could not restrain Israel. The Jewish state could not just stand idly by after an attack on its main cities; this was going against the precepts that were ingrained in Israel's military culture for decades. Furthermore, the damages caused by the attacks were not yet clear, either for the Israelis or for the Americans. Early reports talked of potentially hundreds of deaths; rumors spread that the Iraqis had equipped the Scuds with poison gas (they had repeatedly used chemical weapons against Iran only a few years before). Eventually, by the end of the day, after hours of calls between Washington, Jerusalem, Riyadh, and Cairo, the White House got confirmation from Prime Minister Shamir that the Scud attacks had not caused the number of deaths initially feared. For now, Shamir agreed not to retaliate.[31]

The coalition forces led by the United States tried to detect the Iraqi mobile launchers but failed. Saddam's forces fired other missiles in the following days. The Israelis grew frustrated and demanded to get involved in the air campaign against Iraq's Scud infrastructure. According to David Ivry, then director general of Israel's Ministry of Defense, American officials insisted that there was nothing Israel could do that the United States was not already trying.[32] Still, ten days into the war, tensions were brewing. Moshe Arens and the IDF Chief of Staff Ehud Barak decided to fly to Washington to offer a new plan: An Israeli air campaign on Western Iraq combined with the deployment of special forces on the ground to put an end to the Scud threat.

---

[31] Gordon, Trainor, *Generals' War*: 233.
[32] Interview with David Ivry, Ramat HaSharon, July 22, 2024.

The Bush White House had already dismissed a plan pushed by Defense Secretary Cheney to send troops to Western Iraq to hunt the Scud launchers. But now that Israel was preparing the same operation, the US administration ordered CENTCOM to revisit Cheney's plan to prevent an Israeli intervention. American troops, working jointly with British counterparts, faced numerous difficulties in eliminating the Scuds. As a result, Saddam was able to fire again at Israel.

Overall, between January 18 and February 25, Iraqis fired forty-two missiles at Israeli sites. In the aftermath of the Gulf War, American experts believed the Iraqi use of Scuds on Israel was a turning point. As Keith Payne wrote at the time, "Saddam Hussein surprised the United States by engaging in an invasion that 'should' have been deterred. He again defied the 'logic of deterrence' by launching missile attacks against Israeli cities despite the near certainty that Israel is nuclear-armed and is renowned for its propensity to retaliate."[33]

Patriot Games

The material and human damages inflicted by the Iraqi attacks were relatively low—two Israeli civilians were killed—but it created a climate of angst in the country that caused fifteen heart attacks. More importantly, the Scud attacks crossed a taboo: the presumed inviolability of Israeli cities, particularly Tel Aviv. Yehuda Ben Meir, a former deputy foreign minister, wrote at the time, "The country was virtually under curfew; the last time Tel Aviv had witnessed the sight of empty streets was during the British mandate."[34]

The psychological impact of the missile barrage highlighted an urgent need to reevaluate the Israeli military posture. As a former official from the Israeli Ministry of Defense recalls, "the Iraqi strikes dramatically challenged one of the intellectual foundations of Israel as the homeland of the Jews that would protect them against all persecutions and attacks: the ballistic proliferation jeopardized this belief."[35]

The statement highlights the existential significance of the attack for Israelis. Still, the IDF commanders remained skeptical. According to Joshua Krasna, a former Israeli civilian servant, "In the following days after the attack, the Israeli

---

[33] Keith Payne, *Missile Defense in the 21st Century: Protection Against Limited Threats* (New York: Westview Press, 1991): 144.
[34] Yehuda Ben Meir, "The Israeli Home Front in the Gulf War," in: Jaffee Center for Strategic Studies, *War in the Gulf: Implications for Israel* (Boulder, CO: Westview Press, 1992): 333.
[35] Interview with a former official from the Israeli Ministry of Defense, Tel Aviv, February 2012.

army was still reluctant to distribute masks to the general population because they thought it would fuel panic among the civilians."[36] Later, a report by the state comptroller criticized the skepticism and the slow response of the IDF leadership on the issue of distributing masks.[37]

At the same time, the value of US Patriot batteries in intercepting Iraq's Scud missiles proved dubious. The day after the first attack on Israel, the US armed forces deployed their advanced air defense system to the country. Patriot batteries were regarded as one of the latest examples of US technology primacy. Images of their interceptions of Scuds in the skies over Tel Aviv mesmerized CNN viewers. At first, the US Department of Defense proudly claimed that the Patriot had engaged sixteen out of the forty-two missiles fired at Israel and intercepted 96 percent of them. Then, the official figure was revised to 59 percent in April 1992. That same year, an investigation by the Government Accountability Office highlighted the limited evidence of the actual destruction of Scud missiles resulting from a Patriot interception.[38] Skepticism was also compounded in subsequent publications by the MIT scientist Theodore Postol, who argued that the success rate was much lower. A year after the end of the war, Postol asserted, "Our first wartime experience with tactical ballistic missile defense resulted in what may have been an almost total failure to intercept quite primitive attacking missiles."[39]

Israeli officers shared Postol's skepticism. One former Israeli Air Force general (who preferred to remain anonymous), involved at the time in the air defense campaign against the Scuds, explains,

> The real interception rate was close to zero: the way the Patriot interceptor was designed back then, it would shoot at the Scud missile and it could divert its trajectory so if the Iraqis shoot at Tel Aviv, and your Patriot intercepts the missile which then falls on Ramat Gan (the suburbs of Tel Aviv), you could say it is a success.

Another Israeli officer remembers the sheer cost of the Patriot:

> [F]or each Scud, the Americans told us you shoot two Patriot interceptors, each of them cost $1million, so one day, we saw a Scud coming to Tel Aviv, my guy

---

[36] Interview with Joshua Krasna, June 5, 2024.

[37] Meir, "The Israeli Home Front in the Gulf War": 332.

[38] Jeremiah Sullivan, Dan Fenstermacher, Daniel Fisher, Ruth Howes, O'Dean Juff, Roger Speed, "Technical Debate Over Patriot Performance in the Gulf War," *Science & Global Security* 8, no. 1 (1999): 41–98. https://doi.org/10.1080/08929889908426469.

[39] Theodore Postol, "Lessons of the Gulf War Experience with Patriot," *International Security* 16, no. 3 (winter 1991–2): 119–171, 124. https://doi.org/10.2307/2539090.

pushed the button: he shot one Patriot, two Patriots, but then he didn't stop, he fired three, four Patriot interceptors at it . . . it was nonsense, we laughed, and from then on, we called him "Goldfinger."

In other words, the Israeli experience of Patriot interceptions during the Gulf War convinced the IDF that missile defense could not be an essential mission. Just as the Democratic Party in Washington derided what they considered to be a grandiose enterprise of the Republicans doomed to fail, Israeli generals turned the page on the Scud chapter with the same skepticism they had demonstrated before.

Nevertheless, two major decisions were made as a direct result of the Scud attacks. First, the government of Yitzhak Shamir approved the creation of the Home Front Command in February 1992. The new organization, part of the IDF, would focus on protecting civilian lives. This meant issuing guidance to the general population on civil defense, or training the firefighting and rescue services, and the personnel of Magen David Adom (the Israeli national emergency service). The Home Front Command was initially established due to the threat posed by missiles. It would later play a role in nonmilitary operations such as natural disaster relief. At the time, some questioned the idea of assigning the command to the IDF. They feared it would distract it from its traditional military tasks and recommended instead that it be assigned to a nonmilitary entity such as Israel's police.[40]

The Home Front Command was also responsible for one critical change in Israel's response to the missile threat: its shelter policy. As a result of the Scud missile attacks of 1991, the Knesset passed a law requiring all new buildings in the country to be equipped with shelters. It followed a previous law enacted in 1951 that already called for the construction of "security rooms" made of reinforced concrete in individual apartments and private homes. However, the revised legislation, in the aftermath of the Iraqi attack, had an unprecedented impact, starting with the cost of construction: It is estimated that it drove up the price of residential units by approximately 4 percent.[41]

Shelters would eventually become one of the most visible demonstrations of Israel's adaptation to the missile threat. However, measures such as these are classified as "passive defense." They were mainly intended to minimize the impact of damage caused by the threat. Conversely, "active defense" implies

---

[40] Levite, *Offense and Defense in Israeli Military Doctrine*: 150.
[41] Interview with Ariel Levite, former deputy national security adviser for defense policy, Tel Aviv, June 13, 2024.

preventing that threat, a mission that requires more military capabilities, such as missile defense systems. Nevertheless, the military worried that depending on defensive measures would be a waste of resources. After all, the Scud attacks had not caused massive damage, and the low number of casualties could not reasonably force a change in the overall military strategy of the IDF. In a survey written a year later by the Tel Aviv-based Jaffee Center for Strategic Studies, Ariel Levite acutely described the state of play: "In the course of the war, Israel's rear thus became the front, and vice versa. But given the low likelihood that such a scenario will be repeated in the future, one should not rush to conclude that a fundamental shift in resource allocation toward the defense of the heartland is in order."[42]

For the time being, Israeli decision-makers did not feel the need to revise their defense policy beyond the creation of a Home Front Command and the execution of a new shelter policy. But some voices in Tel Aviv believed the Scud attack was a harbinger of things to come. In 1998, David Ivry articulated his views in a speech delivered at the Begin-Sadat Center: "The looming threat from proliferating ballistic missiles requires us to look at Israel's defense doctrine. Deterrence is no longer a sufficient policy, not when Israel's civilian population becomes exposed to long-range missile attacks."[43]

Ivry's ominous prediction did not prompt a revision of the Israeli military posture. After all, there was no concrete evidence that the country's deterrence strategy had failed. During the next two decades, the IDF's reliance on deterrence against such threats would be tested not by the conventional armed forces of Syria or Iraq but by new nonstate actors who possessed even less sophisticated weapons yet dared to use them against Israel's territory.

Hezbollah and the Katyusha Strategy

The first group that came to epitomize this new strategy was Hezbollah. Born out of the Israeli invasion of Lebanon in 1982, Hezbollah rose both as a resistance movement to the IDF occupation of southern Lebanon and as an offshoot of the young Islamic Republic of Iran and its Islamic Revolutionary Guards Corps (IRGC), which looked at Lebanon as a fertile ground to spread

---

[42] Ariel Levite, "The Gulf War: Tentative Military Lessons for Israel," in: Jaffee Center for Strategic Studies, *War in the Gulf: Implications for Israel* (Boulder, CO: Westview Press, 1992): 149.

[43] David Ivri, "Deterrence Is Not Enough. Israel Needs a Multi-layered Response to the Ballistic Missile Threat," Begin Sadat Center, December 28, 1998. http://www.biu.ac.il/Besa/bulletin/no8art1.htm.

their model of political Islam. For most of the 1980s, the Party of God relied on terrorist tactics such as suicide bombing, kidnappings, and limited insurgency operations (mainly in the southern Lebanese villages and Beirut).[44] Some Hezbollah operatives, particularly Imad Mughniyeh, were known by Western governments for their involvement in major operations such as the April 1983 suicide operation targeting the US Embassy in Beirut and the simultaneous barracks bombing, a few months later, that killed 241 US Marines and 58 French paratroopers. Hezbollah's terrorist footprint was also visible outside of Lebanon, as demonstrated by the December 1983 attack against the French Embassy in Kuwait or the bombing of the Israeli Embassy in Buenos Aires in 1992.[45]

Hezbollah's tactics slowly evolved after the end of Lebanon's civil war in 1989. Although the Taif agreement that marked the end of the conflict called on all militias to disarm, Hezbollah kept its arsenal and justified it, till this day, in the name of its resistance to Israel's military presence in the country.

After Operation Peace for the Galilee and the collapse of Israel's partnership with the Lebanese Phalangists, the IDF retained control of a significant area of the south, named the "security zone," which served as a buffer zone against Hezbollah. About one thousand to two thousand Israeli soldiers stayed there and were backed by a local proxy named "the South Lebanon Army." In 1992, Hezbollah fired a rocket into Israel's territory for the first time. On the morning of February 16 of that year, Abbas Mussawi, the secretary general of Hezbollah, was driving on the road in southern Lebanon, visiting the town of Jibchit. When the IDF confirmed his location, Musawi was with his wife and their six-year-old son. Following consultations between Ehud Barak, then–IDF chief of staff, Defense Minister Moshe Arens, and Prime Minister Yitzhak Shamir, the air force received the green light to fire at the convoy. Musawi and several close operatives were killed, as were his wife and his son.[46]

Musawi had been the leader of the group for less than a year, but he had been part of its military structure since its beginnings in the early 1980s. In haste, a new secretary general was appointed: Hassan Nasrallah, by then a young and relatively unknown member of the organization whose religious or military

---

[44] Nicholas Blanford, *Warriors of God: Inside Hezbollah's Thirty-Year Struggle Against Israel* (New York: Random House, 2011): 40; Joshua Gleis, Benedetta Berti, *Hezbollah and Hamas: A Comparative Study* (Baltimore, MD: Johns Hopkins University Press, 2012): 84.

[45] Benedetta Berti, "Lebanon," in: Assaf Moghadam (ed.), *Militancy and Political Violence in Shiism: Trends and Patterns* (London: Routledge, 2012): 123; Matthew Levitt, *Hezbollah: The Global Footprint of Lebanon's Party of God* (Washington, DC: Georgetown University Press, 2012): 75.

[46] Ronen Bergman, *Rise and Kill First: The Secret History of Israel's Targeted Assassinations* (London: John Murray Publishers, 2019): 394–396.

skills did not stand out.[47] In response to Musawi's killing, Nasrallah ordered the firing of sixty rockets on northern Israel. The government of Yitzhak Shamir was surprised by Hezbollah's reprisal. After initial talks of massive retaliation, the IDF launched a limited operation that merely targeted villages in southern Lebanon from where rockets had been launched.[48]

Hezbollah's use of rockets on that day in February 1992 marked a critical moment. Most of its arsenal comprised Katyusha rockets, unguided rockets initially developed by the USSR in the 1930s and later copied by Iran. While it was not the first nonstate actor to possess and launch them at Israel—the Palestinian Liberation Organization had already fired some at Israel in the previous decade—Hezbollah began systematically targeting Israel's northern cities to pressure the IDF (which was still occupying southern Lebanon). Whenever Israeli soldiers killed Lebanese civilians, Hezbollah retaliated by firing rockets at northern Israel. This represented a level of harassment that the IDF had never faced from a nonstate actor. Although there had been decades of terrorist attacks targeting Israeli civilians, these were isolated incidents. The psychological effect they triggered often distorted their relatively minor impact on the ground. Now, however, Hezbollah, a Lebanese militia, was transforming northern Israel into a potential battlefield.

The tactical shift was explicit in the rhetoric of Hezbollah's leaders. On February 27, 1992, a few days after the party used for the first time its Katyushas against the IDF troops in the south of Lebanon, Hassan Nasrallah gave an interview to the Lebanese newspaper *Al Safir*. Asked about the logic of launching rockets on Israeli forces, Nasrallah replied, "We have to work . . . toward creating a situation in which the enemy is subject to our conditions. We should tell him: 'If you attack us, we will use our Katyushas; if you do not attack us, we will not use our Katyushas.'"[49] In many ways, Hezbollah's secretary general applied the same strategic rationale to the use of rockets that Saddam Hussein employed during the war of the cities against Iran in the previous decade. Rockets were not only a means to overcome the military imbalance with Israel but a tangible instrument to coerce the Jewish state.

The situation escalated in earnest during the summer of 1993, with Operation Accountability conducted by the IDF after Hezbollah's rockets were launched on an Israeli village. A ceasefire was reached after a week of fighting. Israel agreed

---

[47] Aurelie Daher, *Hezbollah: Mobilisation and Power* (London: Hurst, 2019): 158.

[48] Daher, *Hezbollah*: 85.

[49] Quoted in: Nicholas Noe (ed.), *Voice of Hezbollah: The Statements of Sayyed Hassan Nasrallah* (London: Verso, 2007): 62.

to refrain from attacking civilian targets in Lebanon, while Hezbollah pledged to stop firing rockets into northern Israel.[50] This pause was only temporary. In the spring of 1996, a new cycle of escalation erupted when the IDF shelled the Lebanese village of Yatar, and Hezbollah responded by launching rockets on Israeli cities. On April 11, 1996, the Israeli military launched Operation Grapes of Wrath. The campaign lasted for sixteen days, with eleven hundred air raids conducted by the Israeli Air Force. According to Human Rights Watch, Hezbollah fired a total of 639 rockets into Israeli territory, 28 percent of them on the first day of the campaign.[51]

For Hezbollah, the Katyusha arsenal progressively replaced suicide attacks against IDF convoys as the primary tactic. According to local observers, multiple rocket-launching systems were introduced into guerrilla units. Despite the low level of sophistication of Hezbollah's rockets, Israel hitherto did not have any defense system able to counter them. It was only able to detect the launching facilities and subsequently destroy them. Katyusha rockets had become a means of compellence at the military level and a symbol of Hezbollah's resolve at the political level.[52]

The other lesson Israel's military intelligence learned during that period was the shift in regional proliferation trends. In the early 1990s, Iraq was still considered the most significant threat because of its ballistic missiles and its WMD program. However, Iran and Syria were quickly catching up with Saddam's regime. The bloody years of the "war of the cities" had left a major scar on the decision-makers in Tehran. The IRGC embarked on a vast program of investments in rockets and missiles that would turn the country into the fiercest enemy of Israel for the following decades. But in contrast to Saddam's use of missiles, the Iranian regime shared its technologies and military skills with allied nonstate actors like Hezbollah. For Iran and its close Arab ally, the Syrian regime of Hafez al-Assad, empowering Hezbollah was a convenient way to inflict significant damage to Israel without getting its troops on the front line.[53]

The protracted conflict between the IDF and Hezbollah took a toll on the morale of Israeli reservists. In February 1997, two transport helicopters with seventy-three Israeli soldiers on board collided on their way to southern

[50] Augustus Richard Norton, *Hezbollah: A Short History*, 3rd ed. (Princeton, NJ: Princeton University Press, 2018): 83–84.

[51] Human Rights Watch, "Israel/Lebanon: Operation Grapes of Wrath," September 1997. https://www.hrw.org/reports/1997/isrleb/Isrleb.htm.

[52] Jean-Loup Samaan, "Missile Warfare and Violent Non-state Actors: The Case of Hezbollah," *Defence Studies* 17, no. 2 (2017): 156–170. https://doi.org/10.1080/14702436.2017.1295788.

[53] Harald Muller (ed.), *WMD Arms Control in the Middle East: Prospects, Obstacles and Options* (London: Routledge, 2015).

Lebanon. All of them died. The crash shocked public opinion at home, as Israeli families questioned the reason why, fifteen years after the ill-advised invasion of Lebanon, soldiers were still sent there, with no clear end in sight. Soon, protests began, and a movement calling itself the "Four Mothers"—a biblical reference to Sarah, Rebecca, Leah, and Rachel—demanded the withdrawal of Israeli forces from southern Lebanon.[54]

On May 24, 2000, Prime Minister Ehud Barak, who promised a withdrawal during the last election, ordered the complete removal of Israeli troops from the so-called security zone. Barak's decision was driven primarily by domestic politics—to end the protests—but its strategic implications were even more significant. The Israeli withdrawal from Lebanon was a unilateral move in response to discontent at home. But Hezbollah lost no time in declaring it a major victory. Hassan Nasrallah famously described Israel as "weaker than a spider's web" and asserted that thanks to its military resistance, the movement had pushed the IDF out of Lebanon.[55]

Within Lebanon, the episode further consolidated Hezbollah's political influence. The party was no longer advocating for the establishment of an Islamic regime in the country. It adopted Beirut's politics and the distribution of power among the various Lebanese sects. Hezbollah excelled in this arena, establishing itself as a significant player in Lebanese politics—arguably the strongest until the 2024 war—joining blocs and alliances.[56] Even though there were no more Israeli soldiers to fight against, the party did not disarm. The withdrawal may have turned it into a "rebel without a cause," but Nasrallah and his advisers had no intention of letting the Lebanese Armed Forces replace them. The group not only kept its weapons, but it also invested in new ones.[57]

At the regional level, the IDF withdrawal from Lebanon coincided with the unraveling of the Oslo peace process between Israel and the Palestinian Authority. For many in the West Bank and the Gaza Strip, Hezbollah's experience dispelled the belief of the Oslo advocates that the only solution to the conflict was peaceful. After years of negotiations, anger grew among Palestinians, whose hopes for better lives continued to be postponed while Israeli settlements in the occupied territories steadily expanded.

---

[54] Rachel Ben Dor, Daniel Lieberfeld, "Mission Accomplished?: Israel's Four Mothers and the Legacies of Successful Antiwar Movements," *International Journal of Peace Studies* 13, no. 1 (Spring–Summer 2008): 85–97. https://www.jstor.org/stable/41852970.

[55] "Sayyed Nasrallah's 'Spider Web' Speech Has Been Pounding Pillars of 'Israel' Since 2000," *Al Manar*, May 25, 2022. https://english.almanar.com.lb/1611942.

[56] Judith Palmer Harik, *Hezbollah: The Changing Face of Terrorism* (London: I.B. Tauris, 2005).

[57] International Crisis Group, "Hizbollah: Rebel Without a Cause?," Briefing, July 30, 2003. https://www.crisisgroup.org/sites/default/files/hizbollah-rebel-without-a-cause.pdf.

Hamas Adopts Hezbollah's Playbook

After the Israeli withdrawal from Lebanon, Palestinian groups like Hamas looked at Hezbollah as an inspiration. Founded in 1987 as an offshoot of the Muslim Brotherhood in the Palestinian Territories, Hamas—standing for *Harakat al-Muqawama al-Islamiya*, the Movement of the Islamic Resistance in Arabic—initially operated as a terrorist group that employed suicide attacks as its primary tactic.[58] Hamas rejected the Oslo Accords in 1993. Progressively, it outflanked Yasser Arafat's Palestinian Authority by becoming the vanguard of "resistance and revolution" against Israel, particularly during the Second Intifada in the early 2000s.[59]

For most of the Second Intifada, Hamas relied on suicide attacks. But the group also began acquiring a vast amount of so-called Qassam rockets. Like the Katyushas used by Hezbollah, the Qassam is an unguided rocket with a very short range—the first version could reach only up to 5 kilometers. The big difference is that the Qassam was manufactured locally in Gaza starting in 2001. This indicated how much military technology had proliferated in just fifteen years, allowing nonstate actors to build their own artillery.

Qassam rockets were first used in Gaza in July of the same year.[60] In the following seven years, more than six thousand rockets and twenty-five hundred mortar shells were fired at Israel's southern cities.[61] As the topic of Lebanon was pushed to the background of media coverage, the issue of security in the south gained prominence.

While Hamas challenged the power of the Palestinian Authority in the Gaza Strip, Israelis grew disillusioned by the failure of the Camp David summit and the wave of terrorist attacks. In February 2001, they voted to oust Ehud Barak. The leader of the Labor Party was defeated by Ariel Sharon, another former military-commander-turned Likud politician and an ally of the settlers' movement.

Sharon was reluctant to discuss peace talks. He considered that Israel would not treat the Palestinian Authority as a reliable partner as long as terrorist attacks continued. A "roadmap" designed by the US administration of then-President George W. Bush conditioned the resumption of the peace talks on the termination of terrorism, followed by political reform within the Palestinian Authority (PA)

---

[58] Khaled Hroub, *Hamas: Political Thought and Practice* (Washington, DC: Institute for Palestine Studies, 2010).

[59] Khaled Hroub, "Hamas," in: Joel Peters, David Newman (eds.), *Routledge Handbook on the Israeli-Palestinian Conflict* (London: Routledge, 2012): 233–243.

[60] Uzi Rubin, *The Missile Threat from Gaza: From Nuisance to Strategic Threat* (Tel Aviv: Begin-Sadat Center for Strategic Studies, 2011).

[61] Besser, Neria, Haynes, "Adult Attachment, Perceived Stress, and PTSD": 851–857.

that involved free elections. For the Israeli and American governments, Yasser Arafat had become an obstacle to the peace process, and his replacement was deemed a prerequisite for any talks to resume. This led to Mahmud Abbas's rise to the PA presidency in 2005.

Meanwhile, Sharon and his military advisers explored a new idea for the Gaza Strip: a unilateral evacuation of the Israeli settlements and the IDF positions inside the Palestinian territory. In November 2003, Sharon briefed the US administration on his plan for the first time. He called it a "disengagement" from the Gaza Strip.[62] A month later, he made the plan public at the Herzliya Conference. The plan triggered a heated dispute at the Knesset. Members of Sharon's party, the Likud, opposed it. Settlers protested in the streets. Benjamin Netanyahu, then finance minister under Sharon, resigned and denounced a policy that "proceeds blindly toward turning (the Gaza Strip) into a base for Islamic terrorism."[63]

For the past two decades, many observers have speculated on the motivations behind Israel's disengagement from the Gaza Strip. Sharon's approach appeared motivated by a security assessment rather than a belief in peace. There were at the time twenty-one settlements populated by about eight thousand Israelis inside the Gaza Strip. At the military level, protecting those settlements was becoming a major burden for the IDF. There was also a significant demographic factor. The Palestinian population in both the Gaza Strip and the West Bank was growing fast. Sharon may have feared that without a clear political plan for them, their de facto integration into Israel would jeopardize the identity of Israel as both a democracy and a Jewish state.

There has been speculation that Sharon dismantled the Gaza settlements as a strategy to alleviate pressure on the larger ones in the West Bank. The West Bank always played a more significant role in the rhetoric of the settlers' movement. For them, this remains the region of Judea and Samaria, the birthplace of the Jewish people. Sharon did not justify the disengagement in that fashion, though. As far as we can tell from publicly available archives, Sharon considered the disengagement the most realistic option, given the cost of protecting the settlers in Gaza. This was a unilateral move because, as he wrote to US President George W. Bush in April 2004, "there exists no Palestinian partner with whom to advance peacefully toward a settlement."[64]

---

[62] Elliot Abrams, *Tested by Zion: The Bush Administration and the Israeli-Palestinian Conflict* (Cambridge: Cambridge University Press, 2013): 89.

[63] Yossi Verter, "Netanyahu Quits Government Over Disengagement," *Haaretz*, August 7, 2005.

[64] Israel's Ministry of Foreign Affairs, "Exchange of Letters Between PM Sharon and President Bush," April 14, 2004. https://www.gov.il/en/pages/exchange-of-letters-sharon-bush-14-apr-2004.

Sharon and his advisers also thought that the disengagement could then force Palestinians to take responsibility and show good faith.[65] In retrospect, it is easy to affirm that the disengagement from Gaza precipitated the takeover of the territory by Hamas and allowed the latter to fire rockets at Israel. The reality is more complex. The rise of Hamas in Gaza had less to do with the disengagement than with the erosion of support for the PA within the territory. Years of mismanagement and corruption had led Palestinians to grow disillusioned with the rule of the PA. The failure of the peace process also galvanized the leaders of Hamas, who could easily assert that only armed resistance against the Israelis could truly achieve results.

The rivalry came to the forefront on January 25, 2006, when the Palestinians held parliamentary elections. At 77 percent, the turnout was high and displayed the type of democratic process the Bush administration had called for. However, the actual results were much less encouraging: Hamas won 44 percent of the votes against 28 percent for Abbas's organization, Fatah. Even though the possibility of a Hamas victory had been anticipated for weeks, it still caught Israel and Western governments off guard.[66] As a result, a new Palestinian government was formed, with Ismail Haniyeh, a member of the Hamas political bureau, appointed as prime minister.

The electoral victory of Hamas created a major conundrum for the United States. The Bush administration had repeatedly called for Palestinian elections. Now, the White House had to deal with a PA that would include Hamas, still regarded as a terrorist organization. In the following months, both Hamas and Fatah factions failed to reach an agreement on sharing power. Each side looked suspiciously at the other. Rumors of assassination attempts on their leaders spread throughout the Palestinian territories. As a result, Palestinians on both sides took the fight to the streets of Gaza. By the beginning of 2007, thirty-three people had died because of the intra-Palestinian struggle. Saudi Arabia's King Abdallah intervened to force Hamas and Fatah into a ceasefire. Both agreed to sign an agreement in Mecca to pave the way for a national unity government. The truce barely held for more than a few weeks. In June 2007, violence surged again and led to what Palestinians called the "Battle of Gaza." This time, though, Hamas quickly took the upper hand on Fatah, whose security forces in the Strip were either killed or detained in less than five days. In one video emblematic of the new reality on the ground, a combatant from Hamas sits at the desk

---

[65]　Abrams, *Tested by Zion*: 90–91.
[66]　Jean-Pierre Filiu, *Gaza: A History* (London: Hurst, 2014): 289–290.

of Mahmoud Abbas's office in Gaza and makes an imaginary phone call to Washington: "Hello Condoleezza Rice. You have to deal with me now, there is no Abu Mazen anymore."[67]

Many Israelis perceived the collapse of Fatah's rule in Gaza and the Hamas takeover as a consequence of Sharon's gamble with the disengagement two years earlier. In reality, this was less about Sharon's decision than about the failed leadership of Mahmoud Abbas and the growing appeal of Hamas among frustrated Palestinians.

Another common assertion was that rocket attacks on Israel started after the 2005 disengagement. This is not what the residents of the Gaza envelope recall, nor what the historical record tells us. During our meeting, Amir Peretz, the former mayor of Sderot who later served as the defense minister ordering the creation of Iron Dome, was adamant about reminding me, "Many people think the rocket attacks started after the disengagement, but it is a mistake. The rockets started in 2002. The fact is that the IDF could not stop the rocket attacks even before the disengagement."[68]

Peretz's point serves as an important reminder for both military strategy and politics: Two decades after the dismantling of Israeli settlements in the Gaza Strip, many politicians in Jerusalem argue that the root cause of all the ensuing troubles—the successive wars of 2008, 2012, 2014, 2021, and finally the war that started on October 7, 2023—was Ariel Sharon's decision to end Israel's occupation of the Gaza Strip. However, history tells us a different story.

What is true, though, is that the disengagement did not generate the momentum that Ariel Sharon might have hoped for in resolving the Israeli–Palestinian conflict. Quickly after the last settlements were evacuated from Gaza, Hamas and the Palestinian Islamic Jihad fired thirty rockets at Sderot and unpopulated areas in the Negev, injuring five Israelis.

Israelis in the south increasingly felt powerless in front of rockets that kept landing on cities like Sderot. In June 2004, a rocket struck a nursery school in Sderot; one adult and one child were killed. Three months later, another rocket killed two infants.[69] That year, eight people died because of a rocket attack. There were six in 2005.

[67] Conal Urquartm Ian Black, Mark Tran, "Hamas takes control of Gaza," *The Guardian*, June 15, 2007. https://www.theguardian.com/world/2007/jun/15/israel4.

[68] Interview with Amir Peretz, Lod, July 29, 2024.

[69] Molly Moore, "Rocket Attack Kills 2 Children in Israel," *Washington Post*, September 29, 2004. https://www.washingtonpost.com/archive/politics/2004/09/30/rocket-attack-kills-2-children-in -israel/6f0988d1-8d94-42b5-80e9-15eecb432934/.

For military planners in the IDF headquarters of downtown Tel Aviv, those numbers were modest and paled in comparison with the damage caused by suicide attacks in the big cities, a much bigger priority at the time. However, for the residents of Sderot, the rockets hitting schools and houses had become the new, unbearable reality. To alleviate the fears of southern communities, the Home Front Command deployed an early warning system to warn residents in the area of incoming rockets. The system was initially called "Red Dawn" (Shakhar Adom) and activated in 2005. A year later, a family living in one of the kibbutzim nearby complained about the name of the system, "Dawn," which happened to be the name of their seven-year-old daughter. They forced the government to rebrand it as "Code Red" (Tzeva Adom).[70]

The system was simple: The moment a rocket fire was detected by the Home Front Command, a female voice would warn "Code Red" four times. The moment the call was made, people had fifteen to thirty seconds to find a shelter. "Tzeva Adom" was initially designed for the Gaza envelope. Then, in the following years, the Home Front Command deployed it across the whole territory, and the female voice, laconically warning, "Code Red, Code Red," became a familiar sound to all Israelis. This was the first significant measure to address the problem of rockets targeting civilian areas. But it was far from reassuring the residents of Sderot. Susan, the municipality employee I met in the summer of 2024, still recalls (as her other colleagues do) the panic she felt when hearing the siren in the years preceding Iron Dome. Studies have highlighted the negative psychological impact of "Tzeva Adom" on locals, as it often heightened the sense of permanent danger.[71]

In late June 2006, while Palestinian factions were fighting each other, the IDF launched Operation "Summer Rains." This followed the abduction of Israeli soldier Gilad Shalit and aimed to put an end to the rocket attacks from Gaza. Most people have forgotten about this operation, which involved not only air strikes but also a ground offensive by the IDF across the Gaza Strip. The obvious reason why the memory of Operation Summer Rains fell into oblivion was that two weeks after its beginning, another, much bigger, war erupted in the north. This war would oppose, again, Israel and Lebanese Hezbollah. It was later to become a textbook case study in war colleges around the world, and a war that ultimately led the Israeli government to order the development of Iron Dome.

---

[70] Hanan Greenberg, "Sderot: Red Dawn Changed to Color Red," *Yedioth Ahronoth*, September 7, 2006. https://www.ynetnews.com/articles/0,7340,L-3273135,00.html.

[71] Besser, Neria, Haynes, "Adult Attachment, Perceived Stress, and PTSD."

The Rockets of July

The war of July 2006 started in the morning of July 12, when Hezbollah fired rockets at IDF positions near the "moshav" (a cooperative agricultural community) of Zarit, in northern Israel. Quickly, the salvo appeared to be a diversion for another attack. Around 9:00 a.m., a squad of Hezbollah fighters entered Israel's territory to attack an IDF convoy. Three Israeli soldiers died instantly; two others were captured and brought to Lebanon. A tank unit was then sent to retrieve the kidnapped soldiers, but a mine hit it, and five more Israeli soldiers were killed.

In Jerusalem, Prime Minister Olmert called Hezbollah's action an "act of war." He promptly ordered Defense Minister Amir Peretz and the IDF to launch an operation to rescue the two soldiers. Six years after leaving southern Lebanon, the IDF was back. What followed was a massive operation that Hezbollah did not anticipate—later Hassan Nasrallah would publicly confess, "We did not think, even one percent, that the capture would lead to a war at this time and of this magnitude."[72]

In the first days following the abduction of the Israeli soldiers, the IDF responded with air strikes on Hezbollah's positions in the south. The air campaign soon widened, and the Beirut suburb, "Dahya" in Arabic, was added to the target list. The "Dahya" refers to a cluster of small towns between Beirut and the airport. Though its residents are predominantly Shia Muslims, it also houses many Christian and Sunni families. More importantly, the area hosted the Hezbollah headquarters. Overall, the scale of the Israeli air campaign on Lebanon was unprecedented. Planes and helicopters carried out about 12,000 sorties, attacking about 7,000 targets, dropping 19,000 bombs, and some 2,000 missiles.[73] This was more than during the 1973 war against Egypt and Syria.

Despite the intensity of Israel's air campaign, Hezbollah was able to fire hundreds of rockets. On the eve of the war, the Lebanese organization had amassed an inventory of approximately fourteen thousand rockets, with most of a short range (7–40 kilometers) and a small payload (7 kilograms). Rocket systems were often concealed across towns and the countryside of Lebanon's border area.[74]

---

[72] Rory McCarthy, "Hizbullah Leader: We Regret the Two Kidnappings That Led to War with Israel," *The Guardian*, August 28, 2006. https://www.theguardian.com/world/2006/aug/28/syria.israel.

[73] David Johnson, *Hard Fighting: Israel in Lebanon and Gaza* (Santa Monica, CA: RAND Corporation, 2011): 62.

[74] Johnson, *Hard Fighting*: 51–52.

A few days into the war, the IDF launched a ground incursion into Lebanon. By July 23, Israeli troops were fighting against Hezbollah combatants in Bint Jbeil, a town of twenty thousand people. The brutal fighting lasted for twenty days, at the end of which the IDF failed to defeat its enemy. For Nasrallah, Bint Jbeil later became a symbol of the fierce resistance his troops demonstrated against the IDF.

Adding to the calamitous ground operation, the air campaign backfired when, on July 30, an air strike destroyed a building in the town of Qana, killing twenty-eight people, including sixteen children. The IDF admitted responsibility for the targeting of the building but claimed that the strike was intended to destroy Katyusha rockets reportedly stored in the area. The tragedy of Qana eroded much of the support Israel initially enjoyed among its Western partners, particularly the United States. In the following days, calls for a ceasefire grew. By August 5, France and the United States presented a draft resolution to the UN Security Council, which was unanimously approved a week later. The war was over.

A month after the ceasefire, Nasrallah declared, "Today, 22 September 2006, the resistance is stronger than any time since 1982."[75] Although this claim was inaccurate regarding Hezbollah's military capabilities, which had been significantly weakened during the war, the organization still gained unprecedented political support across the Arab world. For thirty-three days, it had succeeded in standing its ground against the IDF, a performance that was embarrassing for Arab states like Egypt or Syria, which Israel repeatedly defeated. The 2006 war quickly became part of the mythology of the party, inspiring urban legends about fighters who bravely stood up to the Israelis in the fights of southern Lebanon villages.[76]

Later, a government-appointed investigation led by Judge Eliyahu Winograd condemned the absence of a clear and coherent political strategy from Prime Minister Ehud Olmert and his Defense Minister Amir Peretz: "The decision to respond with an immediate, intensive military strike was not based on a detailed, comprehensive and authorized military plan (. . .) in deciding to go to war, the government did not consider the whole range of options."[77]

At the operational level, the Israel Air Force did achieve some successes against Hezbollah. According to the American researcher Benjamin Lambeth,

[75] Blanford, *Warriors of God*: 433.
[76] Houda Kassatly, "Des interventions surnaturelles à la victoire divine, le merveilleux dans les récits de la guerre de 33 jours," in: Sabrina Mervin (ed.), *Le Hezbollah état des lieux* (Paris: Actes Sud, 2008).
[77] Wall Street Journal, Official English Summary of the Winograd panel's report, April 30, 2007. https://www.wsj.com/public/resources/documents/winogradreport-04302007.pdf.

"the majority of Hezbollah's long-range Zelzal and medium-range Fajr rockets were destroyed during the campaign's first night."[78] However, as the Winograd Commission wrote, "the Air Force was unable to strike the short-range Katyusha rockets in a way that would limit the attacks on the Israeli home front."[79]

Despite the sustained air campaign launched by the IDF, Hezbollah was still able to fire rockets throughout the whole war. Northern cities like Tiberias and Afula were hit. Residents in Haifa were left hopeless in front of the repeated salvos. Israel's third-largest city was reliving the Scud attacks of 1991. Except that this time, it was not coming from Iraq, which was then considered the biggest Arab military in the Middle East, but from a Lebanese militia. Hezbollah was even able to hit one Israeli corvette, off the coast of Beirut, killing four soldiers.

The 2006 war shaped the views of a generation of IDF commanders, who fought a battle against a nonstate actor using advanced weaponry for the first time. This was a different war from those of 1967 and 1973. And it was not a counterinsurgency campaign either. Hezbollah's way of war had blended conventional and unconventional tactics in a manner no other enemy of the IDF had before.[80] A year later, Isaac Ben-Israel, former director of the research and development agency at Israel's defense ministry, and a professor at Tel Aviv University, wrote in a much-discussed paper, "The very ability to survive, hide and keep rockets so that they can be launched until the last day of the war, constitutes a victory in and of itself for Hezbollah."[81]

While Israel's political and military establishment underwent a bottom-up reassessment of its strategy, the 2006 war marked the first confirmation for Hezbollah that relying on rocket and missile warfare had been its most effective strategic decision to bypass Israeli military power. Hezbollah's rockets soaring over Haifa and other cities shocked the Israeli public opinion regarding the new sense of high vulnerability among the population. For Hezbollah, this provided evidence that its arsenal could pressure Israeli governments effectively.

[78] Benjamin Lambeth, "Israel's Second Lebanon War Reconsidered," *Military and Strategic Affairs* 4, no. 3 (December 2012): 47. https://www.inss.org.il/wp-content/uploads/sites/2/systemfiles/MASA4 -3Engc_Lambeth.pdf.

[79] The Winograd Commission, "The Second Lebanon War, Final Report," Tel Aviv, January 2008: 315. Quoted in: Griff Witte, "Revisiting a War That's Seldom Discussed," *Washington Post*, April 20, 2008. https://www.washingtonpost.com/wp-dyn/content/article/2008/04/19/AR2008041901864. html?hpid=topnews.

[80] Stephen Biddle, *Nonstate Warfare: The Military Methods of Guerillas, Warlords, and Militias* (Princeton, NJ: Princeton University Press, 2021).

[81] Isaac Ben-Israel, *Melkhamat Hatilim Harishona: Israel-Khizballah* ("The First Rocket War: Israel Hezbollah") (Tel Aviv: Tel Aviv University, 2007): 11. https://web.archive.org/web/20110722021710/ http://spirit.tau.ac.il/government/Downloads/YitzakBIMissiles.pdf.

    In the years following the 2006 conflict, Hezbollah shifted its strategic focus to a revised calculus: investing in rockets and missiles with enhanced range and accuracy, while acquiring air defense systems. The logic was to strengthen the party's capacity to strike Israel deep inside its territory while enhancing its ability to mitigate, or at least absorb, the impact of an Israeli bombing campaign.[82]

Conclusion

In Israel, the 2006 war marked the turning point that precipitated the decision of the Olmert government to develop Iron Dome. The waves of rockets fired by Hezbollah at Israeli cities during that summer reached an unprecedented level, leading prominent Israeli scholars like Isaac Ben-Israel to coin it the "first rocket war."[83] But as this first chapter detailed, the rocket barrages on Israel in July 2006 followed two decades that saw a steady evolution in Middle Eastern warfare. In retrospect, Operation Mole Cricket 19 in 1982 was the last hurrah of classic airpower when Israeli planes completely defeated their Syrian counterparts. Two years later, Saddam Hussein turned to his missile arsenal as he saw their strategic potential in the "war of the cities" against Iran. Israel's military establishment initially dismissed the concerns of those who believed Saddam's strategy could be applied against Israel. "They will not dare," as David Ivry recalls the IDF intelligence officers saying. By 1991, they dared. Israel's urban areas were no longer immune to the Middle East wars. Scud missiles were able to question fundamental assumptions of the Israelis about the protection of their territory. Then, in the following decade, the most immediate threat no longer came from a regional power but from Hezbollah and Hamas, two nonstate actors (although supported by Iran and Syria).

The inability of the IDF to decisively defeat Hezbollah in southern Lebanon, or to destroy its rocket launchers, stirred major controversies within the military circles. In its final report on the 2006 war, the Winograd Commission lamented how "a semi-military organization of a few thousand men resisted, for a few weeks, the strongest army in the Middle East . . . the barrage of rockets aimed at Israel's civilian population lasted throughout the war, and the IDF did not provide an effective response to it."[84] After years spent on policing missions in

---

[82] Jean-Loup Samaan, *From War to Deterrence? Israel-Hezbollah Conflict Since 2006* (Carlisle: US Army War College, 2014).

[83] Ben-Israel, *Melkhamat Hatilim Harishona*.

[84] Witte, "Revisiting a War That's Seldom Discussed."

the West Bank and the Gaza Strip, the IDF felt that in the summer of 2006, it had lost its way and underwent a soul-searching moment. Out of this crisis, Defense Minister Amir Peretz asked his staff to come up with a new solution, one that could address the new rocket threat posed by Hezbollah in the north and Hamas in the south. The solution had to be both affordable and deployable within the next three years.

2

Iron Dome Enters

When I meet Amir Peretz in late July 2024 in his quiet and cozy office at Israel Aerospace Industries (IAI), the tensions of national politics feel distant. In 2021, the former leader of the Labor Party was appointed chairman of the IAI board, one of Israel's largest defense companies. Entering his seventies, Peretz was then spending most of his time negotiating arms sales, and he seemed less interested in discussing the endless cloak-and-dagger involved in coalition building within the Knesset.

The trajectory of Amir Peretz reveals a great deal about the evolution of his country. For a long time after the 2006 war with Hezbollah, Peretz bore significant responsibility for his time as defense minister. The Winograd Commission criticized him and Ehud Olmert for serious errors in the preparation and conduct of the war. A former trade union leader, Peretz had minimal experience in military affairs and international security when he was appointed defense minister just two months before the war began. He was not—and still is not—a worldly man. Struggling with English, Peretz needs a translator when he meets foreign officials. His former staff at the ministry still joke that he had to rely on an interpreter to communicate with his American counterpart, then–Defense Secretary Donald Rumsfeld, while most Israel Defense Forces (IDF) generals, often trained in US military schools, expressed themselves fluently in English.

But years have passed, and the criticism surrounding Peretz has faded. His reputation has been slowly restored. Peretz is now also—and perhaps more so— remembered for being the minister who "fought" for the development of Iron Dome. Even former political opponents like Benjamin Netanyahu (not known for handing out free compliments) praise in retrospect how Peretz "wisely overruled" the IDF to launch the system.[1]

It is the same alleged flaws of Peretz, his limited knowledge of the military world, which, in the eyes of many, helped him impose a defense system on the IDF leadership despite all their resistance. "It is no coincidence that the defense minister who forced the IDF to accept Iron Dome was a civilian who had one

[1]   Benjamin Netanyahu, *Bibi: My Story* (New York: Threshold Editions, 2022): 478.

of the smallest experiences in the military world," points out Joshua Krasna, a former Israeli civil servant.[2] During our discussion, Peretz insists, "This was a decision going against all the government agencies, the defense establishment, and the general media."

Peretz had a personal connection to the population of southern Israel. Like many residents of Sderot, he was born in Morocco in 1952 and migrated with his family when he was four. Later in the 1980s, he became the mayor of Sderot before moving into national politics. By the time he had climbed to the top of the Labor Party and Ehud Olmert offered him the position of defense minister in May 2006, the rockets from Hamas had become a significant part of the daily lives of his former constituents. Peretz recalls that in his first meeting with IDF Chief of Staff Dan Halutz and his close military advisers, he told them, "I come from Sderot, and our children there no longer sleep at night: how is it that we have a solution for the most advanced threats, yet we have nothing for simple, primitive threats like rockets?" The IDF leaders explained that the best response was to focus on attacking and destroying the inventories of nonstate groups. This was the kind of military bravado that annoyed Peretz. Therefore, he challenged them: "I asked them, 'Generals, could you tell me if the 'H' in *Tsahal* (the Hebrew acronym for the IDF) stands for *Haganah* (Hebrew for defense) or *Hatkafah* (Hebrew for offense)?' They instantly replied, 'We are an offensive military; our goal is to destroy our enemies.'"

Peretz might embellish the story in retrospect, but it captures the contentious environment in which Iron Dome was to be created. One IDF flag officer present in the room that day allegedly replied to Peretz, "What are we going to do? Put up huge volleyball nets so the Katyusha rockets bounce back to Lebanon and Gaza?" Another one bluntly assessed that "the Qassam and Katyusha rockets are a problem we'll have to live with. It's a tactical issue, not a strategic one. It won't destroy the State of Israel."[3] As Chapter 1 demonstrated, such a defiance toward defensive measures was deeply ingrained in the IDF ethos. But that defiance was eroding.

The Meridor Committee: Going on Defense

In April 2006, a month before Amir Peretz became defense minister, a government-appointed committee released a new report on Israel's national

---

[2] Interview with Joshua Krasna, June 5, 2024.

[3] Dan Raviv, "Inside the Iron Dome," *Moment Magazine*, July–August 2018. https://momentmag.com /inside-the-iron-dome/.

security doctrine. The task force was headed by Dan Meridor, a former minister and a key figure of the Likud Party. It was asked to "examine the validity of the existing paradigm."[4] The paradigm in question consisted of the three "pillars" of Israel's defense policy: deterrence, early warning, and battlefield decisive victory. No written document publicly articulated those pillars. They were based on guiding principles derived from speeches made by the country's founding fathers in the early years of the state.

The Meridor Committee recommended a new, fourth pillar that would acknowledge the role of defense in Israel's modern security environment. For the committee, defense was understood to involve both active and passive defense.[5] Meridor explained that including defense as a fourth pillar meant "to protect the home front which has become the main arena of fighting, and in particular, to defend the population and the strategic infrastructures."[6]

The word "defense" was the object of arguments among the committee members. According to one retired IDF officer involved in the discussions, Gabi Ashkenazi, then director general of the defense ministry, grew uncomfortable with the new emphasis on defense. Ashkenazy reportedly said that "offensive is part of our Israeli defense, it has to be part of the overall solution: we attack the rockets and missiles of the enemy, and by doing that, by degrading his capabilities, we defend the home front."[7]

The Meridor Committee was not the first attempt to include defense as a fundamental mission of the IDF. Still, it was arguably the one that gained the most considerable visibility, thanks to the political influence of Meridor himself. Yet, the concrete impact of the committee is debatable. Ariel Levite, one of the committee's members, explains,

> A lot of the ideas were incorporated, but there was no formal stamp of approval of the conclusion. I mean, nobody in the government formally endorsed it, but in practice, this is what happened. So, we were successful in changing the conception from a three-legged defense doctrine to a four-legged defense doctrine, so from then on, it will be deterrence, early warning, offensive, and defense.[8]

4   Dan Meridor, Ron Eldadi, "Israel's National Security Doctrine: The Report of the Committee on the Formulation of the National Security Doctrine (Meridor Committee), Ten Years Later," Institute for National Security Studies, Memorandum no. 187, February 2019: 7.
5   Interview with Shay Shabtai, Former Head of Strategic Planning, IDF, Tel Aviv, July 4, 2024.
6   Meridor, Eldadi, "Israel's National Security Doctrine": 25.
7   Interview with retired IDF officer, Tel Aviv, July 4, 2024.
8   Interview with Ariel Levite, Tel Aviv, June 13, 2024.

It is against the backdrop of the Meridor report that Amir Peretz engaged the IDF commanders on the need to strengthen the defense of Israelis living in the border areas, both in the south and the north. In the end, the development of a system to defend against rockets did not emerge from thin air; it was built upon various technological innovations that had matured over the past few years. But as often happens in public policy, it needed a significant push from the top to make it possible and turn an idea—to intercept rockets—into an operational military system in under five years.

In this context, the story of how Israel came to build Iron Dome sheds light on the internal power plays between the civilians and the military inside the government. Peretz may have been the highest-ranking political figure in pushing for Iron Dome but in that process, he relied on various entities and individuals who made it possible—people like Daniel "Danny" Gold, an officer at the Directorate of Defense Research & Development (commonly known by its Hebrew acronym as MAFAT) who bypassed bureaucratic procedures to launch the program; or Pinhas Buchris, a retired general who, as director general of the Ministry of Defense, played a crucial role in making sure that the program would not get canceled, especially after Peretz was removed from the Ministry of Defense and replaced by Ehud Barak in June 2007—only a few months after Iron Dome had started.

As the remainder of the chapter explains, the creation of Iron Dome was shaped not only by Israel's politics but also by technical and military challenges that led engineers like Chanoch Levin at Rafael and officers like Doron Gavish in the IDF air defense unit to struggle in finding the most appropriate solution to the rocket threat. Ultimately, examining this process underscores elements that go beyond Iron Dome. It showcases Israel's military innovation, offering insights into the armed forces' ability to adapt to emerging challenges. And, paradoxically, it also reflects the ongoing resistance from some of the same actors involved.

The Nagel Commission and the First Battle for Iron Dome

When Amir Peretz pushed the issue of defending Israel's territory against rockets coming from Gaza or Lebanon, he faced resistance not only from the IDF leadership but from parts of the defense industry as well. At the time, engineers focused on two options to address such a threat: a system that would use laser technology to destroy the rocket or a system that would intercept it kinetically—that is, a missile designed to kill another one.

The kinetic option was expensive, and the technical data was not entirely compelling. The track record of Patriot missiles during the Gulf War had left the IDF deeply perplexed: Not only was its interception rate questionable, but its sheer cost also made it unaffordable for Israel.

For scientists, laser technology was the most attractive option. Laser systems generate power capable of destroying military targets, much like they already burn or cut materials in industrial and medical fields. Theoretically, "a high-energy laser can keep firing as long as it has electrical power."[9] By extension, an interception generated by energy instead of a missile interceptor could be much cheaper.

However, there were limitations to this option as well. Weather conditions significantly affect its ability to operate. Laser-based defense systems work effectively in optimal conditions, such as a sunny and cloudless day, but less so in rainy and cloudy conditions. The laser beam inevitably loses its power upon striking water droplets. Amir Peretz recalls his concerns, "Laser cannot work in the winter, so I didn't want to buy a system we could only use eight months per year (. . .) Moreover, it means that Hamas just has to check the weather to know if it can attack us or not."

In August 2006, Peretz officially ordered the IDF leadership to seek a new solution to the rocket attacks. Before that, Israel had been involved for ten years with the United States in a program initially known as Nautilus, which was to develop a defense system based on a "tactical high-energy laser," THEL. Developed by the American company Northrop Grumman, the system was later renamed Skyguard.[10] By 2000, the program had claimed its first successful field test against a Katyusha rocket. However, in the following years, Israeli officials became increasingly skeptical of Skyguard's viability.

In 2004, as rocket attacks from Gaza intensified, the IDF's deputy chief of staff, Major General Gabi Ashkenazi, ordered MAFAT to review options to address the threat of rockets and surface-to-surface missiles to the air force.[11] MAFAT is the equivalent of the Defense Advanced Research Projects Agency (DARPA) in the US Department of Defense: the agency tasked with designing and experimenting with new concepts and technologies to improve the performance of the IDF on the battlefield.

9   Iain Boyd, "High-energy Laser Weapons: A Defense Expert Explains How They Work and What They Are Used For," *The Conversation*, March 7, 2024. https://theconversation.com/high-energy -laser-weapons-a-defense-expert-explains-how-they-work-and-what-they-are-used-for-225071.

10 Hanan Greenberg, "Peretz to IDF: Develop Anti-Rocket System," *Yedioth Ahronoth*, August 24, 2006. https://www.ynetnews.com/articles/0,7340,L-3295448,00.html.

11 Edward Luttwak, Eitan Shamir, *The Art of Military Innovation: Lessons from the Israel Defense Forces* (Cambridge: Harvard University Press, 2023): 78.

Danny Gold, one of MAFAT's directors, led the interagency team, which studied about a dozen different proposals. They deemed Skyguard's chemical laser solution an immature technology, and they feared that its already high cost could spiral out of control. Gold then suggested the kinetic option, whose technology was more proven and its cost manageable (at least for the system's development). Jacob Nagel, then scientific deputy at MAFAT, recalls, "It was believed that this project (Skyguard) would not lead to an operational weapons system given that there was no foreseeable future for a chemical laser-based system. Clearly, any future laser-based interception system would be based on a solid-state laser. Still, such technology would not be available for at least another decade."[12] As a result, Israel's government suspended Skyguard in 2005.

A year later, the "rocket war" against Hezbollah brought about a new sense of urgency. The development of a defense system was now at the top of the agenda of Defense Minister Amir Peretz. In the aftermath of the Lebanon War, all options were reconsidered. So, when Peretz and his advisers started looking for a response, engineers at Northrop Grumman came back and told them it already existed: Skyguard.

The US administration of then-President George W. Bush continued to support the Skyguard solution. Though the program was jointly designed, most of its $600 million funding came from US taxpayers. Ophir Shoham, the head of the IDF Planning division at the time, remembers, "There were some people back then that said laser is the best solution. They were not necessarily the most professional people to understand the limitations of the laser and the price."[13] Facing a major dilemma between two options, Amir Peretz created a special commission to review them in October 2006. To head it, he chose Jacob Nagel, then the deputy head of MAFAT in charge of weapons development. The commission included a dozen officers and engineers who had spent their careers assessing missile proliferation and defense technologies. They were given three months to decide between Skyguard and Iron Dome. The commission worked under significant political pressure. According to Nagel's recollection, "an unprecedented lobbying campaign for Skyguard kicked off, drafting senior retired military officers, academics, and media personas. This campaign led to significant incitement, with personal attacks lobbed at Director General Pinhas Buchris, DDR&D director Keren, and myself, who were dubbed the 'high priests of Iron Dome' by the campaign. The lobby's efforts included drafting PR

---

[12] Email correspondence with Jacob Nagel, June 8, 2024.
[13] Interview with Ophir Shoham, Former Director MAFAT (2010–16), Tel Aviv, July 17, 2024.

experts, distributing marketing brochures, pushing defamation online and in newspapers."

Eighteen years later, Peretz still remembers the intensity of the attacks: "A lot of people questioned and challenged the decision; they hired PR companies to go against us. At the time, Haaretz's headline was 'Iron Dome a foregone failure'! Every day, the newspapers were killing me."

Despite the frenzy surrounding the process, the Nagel Commission took the time to conduct its review. The commission presented its findings to Peretz in December 2006: Iron Dome was selected. This was a significant victory for Peretz, Gold, Nagel, and everyone who had advocated for the system in the past year. But it was not yet a happy ending. According to Peretz, Prime Minister Ehud Olmert approved the decision, but his support was rather lukewarm. "I cannot oppose your new decision, but I won't give more money to Iron Dome," Peretz recalls him saying.

Circumstances can explain why Olmert made no effort to increase the budget allocated to the new program. The Lebanon War had cost the Israeli government $1.6 billion (about 1 percent of the country's GDP).[14] The economy remained healthy with annual growth in 2006 at 5.1 percent, but Olmert likely sought to keep military expenditures in check after being blamed for the war.[15] According to Jacob Nagel and Shachar Shohat, the prime minister did ask Peretz to "approach the finance ministry to allocate the needed budget."[16] However, the additional funding Peretz hoped for was not secured when he left the ministry.

Therefore, when Danny Gold selected Rafael Advanced Defense Systems LTD to lead the Iron Dome project, he had to find a solution to his financial shortcomings. In an unusual manner for defense contracts, Gold asked Ilan Biran, then Rafael's chairman, to share the cost of the research and development phase: Israel's defense ministry would provide approximately $5–$6 million, and Rafael would do the same.[17] Rafael accepted the idea and started spending money by the fall of 2006, even though the Nagel Commission had not yet released its findings. Officially, the contract only started in January 2008.[18]

14 Julian Borger, "Lebanon War Cost Israel $1.6bn," *The Guardian*, August 15, 2006. https://www .theguardian.com/world/2006/aug/15/israelandthepalestinians.lebanon.

15 Moti Bassok, "2006 GDP Growth: 5.1%," *Haaretz*, March 15, 2007. https://www.haaretz.com/2007 -03-15/ty-article/2006-gdp-growth-5-1/0000017f-df30-df7c-a5ff-df7a300a0000.

16 Email correspondence with Jacob Nagel, June 8, 2024.

17 Charles Levinson, Adam Entous, "Israel's Iron Dome Defense Battled to Get Off Ground," *Wall Street Journal*, November 26, 2012. https://www.wsj.com/articles/SB10001424127887324712504578136931078468210.

18 Luttwak, Shamir, *Art of Military Innovation*: 86.

Finances were not the only obstacle the project faced. It was no secret that military commanders at the IDF headquarters opposed the program. But even after the prime minister approved Iron Dome, the IDF continued to challenge the decision. According to Amir Peretz, the IDF went as far as to create "a committee with seven brigadier generals whose purpose was to reverse the decision!" Throughout the entire process of Iron Dome development, the IDF used multiple ways to demonstrate its resistance to the project. According to one former head of the IDF strategic planning department, this resistance was expressed during the consultations over the threat assessment that drives the need for new air platforms, when the air force dragged its feet in participating in the process. The officer recalls,

> The threat assessment, the strategic thinking was done mostly by the J-5 (a structure in charge of strategic planning and policy within the Joint Staff), with just some guys from the Air Force because the Air Force was not so enthusiastic. Let's say, if you compare, for the F-35, most of the operational analysis is done by the Air Force. J-5 makes a parallel assessment, but the lead is with the Air Force. But here with Iron Dome, the work was done upside down.[19]

Gabi Siboni, a colonel from the reserve and a regular commentator on Israel's military affairs, justifies the attitude: "The main objection of the IDF was a professional one because the IDF has an ethos of offense, not defense, and while you invest in defense, you don't on offense, and we suffer from this decision until now."[20] But Siboni also downplays the idea of obstruction from the top brass: "The IDF did not change its mind, but Iron Dome was forced on it by the Minister of Defense, it was a decision taken by Amir Peretz, and that's it, they had to comply with it." Throughout the process, numerous examples of IDF resistance to Iron Dome emerged, but even at the ministerial level, Peretz's support became uncertain.

A New Believer: Ehud Barak's Conversion to Iron Dome

Soon, another political development added to the tensions surrounding Iron Dome. Weakened by the fallout of the Lebanon War, Peretz started 2007 with much uncertainty about his political future. Voices within the Labor Party called

---

19 Interview with Shay Shabtai, Tel Aviv, July 4, 2024.
20 Interview with Gabi Siboni, Reserve colonel and consultant to the IDF, Tel Aviv, July 18, 2024.

for his resignation. Ehud Barak, one of the most decorated Israeli soldiers and a former prime minister, launched a comeback. In May, primary elections were organized with five candidates: Amir Peretz, Ehud Barak, Ami Ayalon, Ophir Pines Paz, and Danny Yatom. For the defense minister, the final result was a humiliation: Peretz came third, with only 22 percent of the vote, far behind Barak at 36 percent.[21] Two weeks later, Amir Peretz resigned from the government and handed the defense ministry over to Barak.

Barak was no stranger to the threat of rockets. As the former IDF chief of staff in the first half of the 1990s, he closely monitored Hezbollah's evolution from a ragtag militia into a proto-state equipped with advanced weaponry. Then, as prime minister between 1999 and 2001, he ordered the withdrawal of IDF troops from South Lebanon. However, Barak was not a firm believer in missile defense in general, or Iron Dome in particular. Therefore, the day Amir Peretz left the defense ministry, he asked his Director General Pinhas Buchris to ensure that the development of Iron Dome would not suffer from the political transition: "You don't give up, complete the Iron Dome."[22]

Buchris was not among the engineers who designed and developed Iron Dome. He was a former commander of Unit 8200 (an intelligence unit of the IDF), turned bureaucratic warrior, who ensured the IDF accepted the introduction of the system. Buchris was one of the young soldiers involved in the 1976 raid on Entebbe airport to rescue Israeli hostages. Now, he was concluding his career at the Ministry of Defense by ensuring that the new defense system, which many of his military peers and friends considered a misuse of resources, would succeed.

Ehud Barak had made no secret of his skepticism, so there were legitimate concerns that he might suspend the program. Pinhas Buchris says that in his first discussion with Barak, the latter told him, "Listen, we need to leave Iron Dome because we need to promote something else."[23] One former program director at MAFAT also recalls the initial doubts of Barak over missile defense: "The first time I met Barak was in the 1990s when he was still the IDF Chief of Staff; he wanted to get a better understanding of a program, he had a deep knowledge of technology, and wanted to know all the details. But at the time, as a soldier, he

---

[21] Rory McCarthy, "Barak in Run-Off for Israeli Labour Party Leadership," *The Guardian*, May 29, 2007. https://www.theguardian.com/world/2007/may/29/israel1.

[22] Diana Bahur Nir, Meir Orbach, "A Buchris Story: The Rise, Fall, and Comeback of an Israeli Hero," CTECH, December 16, 2022. https://www.calcalistech.com/ctechnews/article/lwigv8m1o#:~:text=Raised%20in%20a%20large%2C%20poor,wound%20up%20in%20a%20coma.

[23] Nir, Orbach, "A Buchris Story."

expressed profound doubts on the value of defensive systems such as Arrow or what would be known as Iron Dome."[24]

Barak also had to deal with the United States refusing to support the development of Iron Dome. In retrospect, given the significant involvement of the United States in the program in later years, it may be puzzling to consider that, in mid-2007, the George W. Bush administration showed no interest in covering the bill for the new program. The motives behind this refusal were not politically driven. "It wasn't an ideological rejection," recalls Dov Zakheim, a former undersecretary of defense during the Bush presidency.[25] According to Jacob Nagel and Shahar Shohat, when Barak met with his counterpart, Robert Gates, the US Defense Secretary revived the idea of supporting Israel via the Skyguard program. Nagel and Shohat add, "This was largely motivated by America's desire to prevent Israel from entering a war with Gaza."[26] In other words, the Bush administration was using Skyguard as a measure of reassurance with the Israelis to avoid a conflict with Hamas, which by 2008 was looming large.

Inside the Pentagon, the assistant secretary of defense for International Security Affairs, Mary Beth Long, and her team managed the bilateral relationship with Israel. After the Israeli defense ministry formally requested financial support for Iron Dome, American engineers traveled there to evaluate the project. They expressed doubts about the feasibility of the Iron Dome project, identifying its "poor performance in initial testing" and deeming the system "doomed to fail."[27] In our correspondence two decades later, Mary Beth Long nuances the analysis. She adds that the technical team considered that

> it was doomed to fail *if* changes were not made. They thought the U.S Phalanx system had more potential if modified to be like the Dome. I don't think that ever happened, and, in the end, they were wrong—within a few short years, the intercept success rate went from single digits to well on its way to a successful program.[28]

Beyond the technical assessment, the American perspective was also shaped by the repercussions of the Skyguard project. After depending on US public funding for two decades, Israel's missile defense program was now seeking an

---

24 Interview with former MAFAT program manager, Tel Aviv, June 5, 2024.
25 Interview with Dov Zakheim, former Under Secretary of Defense (Comptroller) and Chief Financial Officer of the Department of Defense (2001–4), March 12, 2024.
26 Jacob Nagel, Shachar Shohat, "Iron Dome Developers Set the Record Straight on Its Evolution," *Jerusalem Post*, April 8, 2021. https://www.jpost.com/arab-israeli-conflict/iron-dome-developers -set-the-record-straight-on-its-evolution-664542.
27 Levinson, Entous, "Israel's Iron Dome Defense Battled to Get Off Ground."
28 Email correspondence with Mary Beth Long, October 24, 2024.

alternative that did not involve an American system or an American company as the lead contractor. As confirmed by Mary Beth Long, US officials suggested that Israel consider acquiring the land variant of the US-made Vulcan Phalanx system. This system included an automated gun unit and radar, and it had been used by the US Army for several decades.

So, against that backdrop, why did Ehud Barak change his mind on Iron Dome? Two factors played a role: First, Barak was no longer a soldier but a civilian and, more importantly, a politician. "Like Yitzhak Rabin, Ehud Barak changed a lot of his views on strategy and security when he became a civilian and a minister," one former official from the defense ministry says. Barak's shift allowed the program to gain support. Given his intimate knowledge of the IDF and its internal power centers, Barak possessed the skills to secure the development of Iron Dome, which Peretz, a civilian outsider, lacked.

This reminds us of the peculiar nature of civil-military relations in Israel, where most defense ministers first served as military officers, and where the IDF is perceived as a stabilizing force vis-à-vis politicians who come and go. The IDF has traditionally been (and remains) the primary actor in defense policy in Israel. The chief of general staff and his supporting bureaucracy shape the process without significant pressure from other entities. The civilian side of the Ministry of Defense has a role that is mainly limited to defense diplomacy with key allies (the US and European powers) but does not engage in crucial matters such as force structure, doctrine, and procurement.[29]

Another, more mundane factor that influenced Barak's view of Iron Dome was its progress in development. Barak's initial reluctance stemmed not only from a suspicion of defense as a military strategy but also from the negative technical assessments of Iron Dome. The US Defense Department had indicated as much, and many Israeli engineers, including some who worked on the program, shared this sentiment. It was only after the initial tests of the system proved successful that the defense minister fully embraced it.

Navigating the Technical Challenges

The initial instructions provided by the defense minister to MAFAT included the delivery of a prototype in only three years. This created a strong sense of

---

[29] Eva Etzioni-Halevy, "Civil-Military Relations and Democracy: The Case of the Military-Political Elites' Connection in Israel," *Armed Forces & Society* 22, no. 3 (1996): 401–417. https://www.jstor .org/stable/45346755; Yoram Peri, *Generals in the Cabinet Room: How the Military Shapes Israeli Policy* (Washington, DC: US Institute of Peace Press, 2006).

urgency regarding the project. Typically, the development of guided-missile projects lasts between fifteen and twenty years. For instance, it took Raytheon a decade to develop the first Patriot batteries, which the US Army deployed in West Germany in 1981.[30] Another American system, the Terminal High Altitude Area Defense (THAAD), took even longer: The Army began its development in 1992, and after sixteen years marked by several failed tests and the revamping of the program, the first battery was finally activated in 2008.[31] Even the US–Israeli project Skyguard had been consuming the energy of engineers and civil servants for a decade before it got canceled.

This time frame is comparable to that of the most advanced platforms or weapons systems, such as fighter jets or warships. But by the mid-2000s, the experience in the field of missile defense was not encouraging. Skepticism within the IDF was not only cultivated by an institutional preference for the offensive over the defensive. Many decision-makers and military pundits in the United States and Europe also worried that the technical complexity and constant cost overruns made missile defense a perilous enterprise.

If Danny Gold, then head of research at MAFAT, was later to become the face of Iron Dome, another individual played a consequential role on the industrial side: Chanoch Levin. An alumnus of the Technion, Israel Institute of Technology, Levin was no politician. He was an engineer with deep experience in military systems. Yedidia Yaari, Rafael's then CEO, informed him that his next mission was to devise a plan for the new program launched by MAFAT named Iron Dome. Three elements had to be designed: the missile interceptor, the radar, and the command-and-control unit.

Levin's concerns had nothing to do with the political dynamics between the IDF and Amir Peretz or the United States and Israel. His main focus was on how to turn a vague strategic idea into reality. "Imagine a Coke bottle flying several times faster than the speed of sound on an irregular course. Intercepting it seems far-fetched," Levin would joke.[32] In retrospect, Levin explains, "There was not a single person or group who did not oppose it. The entire defense establishment: the chief of staff, the defense minister, and many senior officers all claimed it is a

---

[30] William Delaney, *Perspectives on Defense Systems Analysis: The What, the Why, and the Who, but Mostly the How of Broad Defense System Analysis* (Cambridge: MIT Press, 2015): 64.

[31] Andrew Feickert, "The Terminal High Altitude Area Defense (THAAD) System," Congressional Research Service, July 18, 2024. https://crsreports.congress.gov/product/pdf/IF/IF12645#:~:text=According%20to%20the%20Center%20for,1996%20to%201999—also%20failed.

[32] American Technion Society, "The Technion: Protecting Israel for 100 Years," August 9, 2024. https://ats.org/our-impact/hilla-haddad-chmelnik-a-model-of-public-service/.

fantasy, it cannot be done. It's a waste of money. I'll let you in on a secret. At the beginning, I also thought it was impossible."[33]

The Israeli company Rafael had extensive experience in missile production but less in radar technology. While its engineers designed the interceptor, the company partnered with two firms for the other components. First, Elta, another defense contractor and a subsidiary of Rafael's rival, IAI, was tasked with building the radar. Then, to design the command-and-control unit, Rafael turned to a start-up called mPrest, which had just been founded three years before by Natan Barak, a former commander of the Israeli Navy. Altogether, the teams at MAFAT and the three companies involved about four hundred staff who "worked as near a 24/7 schedule as human physiology would allow."[34]

The first component to be designed was the intercepting missile named the "Tamir." This was a 3-meter-long weapon that weighed 90 kilograms at launch.[35] It was, by all measures, a "small" missile: At the time, the latest variant of the Patriot missile, the MIM-104D/PAC-2, was 5.3 meters long and weighed 900 kilograms. It also operated at a shorter range: A Tamir can engage a target at up to 70 kilometers, whereas the PAC-2 missile was designed to fly up to 160 kilometers. However, the most crucial difference is that while a Patriot interceptor destroys a ballistic missile in a few minutes, the Tamir must catch a rocket that takes approximately 30 seconds to reach its target. Chanoch Levin recalls, "We didn't believe we could do it. We thought that we could intercept 10, 50 percent, that's all. (. . .) No system in the world could intercept 60, 70% back then."[36]

The expected interception rate held equal importance, politically and militarily. It was an obvious indicator of success for the tests and later for the system's first use on the battlefield. However, the exact percentage considered successful was less clear. Doron Gavish, a former air defense commander, recalls the internal debate at the time,

> This was one of the tough decisions we had to take: when is the point when you go out with the system, just like in the private business, when you reach the commercialization point? Should we wait for a 100 percent interception rate, or was 30 percent enough? Some of us (in the air defense) said that before Iron Dome, we had zero percent. Hence, if we are 50%, it's good enough to start and deploy it.[37]

[33] Shlomo Maital, "Iron Dome: The Inside Story," *Jerusalem Report*, July 15, 2021. https://www.jpost.com/jerusalem-report/iron-dome-the-inside-story-673995.

[34] Luttwak, Shamir, *Art of Military Innovation*: 80.

[35] Data available at CSIS Missile Defense Project, https://missilethreat.csis.org/defsys/iron-dome/.

[36] Quote from Podcast "Two Nice Jewish Boys," episode 215, October 12, 2020. https://2njb.com/podcast/episode-215/.

[37] Interview with Doron Gavish, former Air Defense Commander, IDF, Tel Aviv, 10 July 2024.

In the end, Gavish says the IDF was ready to accept an interception rate "around 70%." However, it is difficult to discern behind those numbers an entirely rational calculation, as opposed to a representation of what makes a military system "good enough" to enter service.

In time, the most significant advantage of the Tamir became its production cost. When Iron Dome was declared operational in 2011, one Tamir missile was estimated to cost $100,000. Back then, one unit of the Patriot PAC-2 was valued at approximately $3–$4 million. In the following years, the cost of the Tamir interceptor decreased. It is now estimated to have a $50,000 price tag. The drastic cost reduction made the missile closer in terms of price range to traditional ammunition than other missile defense systems. Its affordability also allowed the military planners to consider its use on the battlefield.

The Tamir may have been cheaper than most other missile defense systems, but it was still fifty times more expensive (at least) than the rockets fired by Hamas at Sderot. Early in the process, engineers and officers considered how not to waste Tamir missiles in useless interceptions. In the memories of IDF officers who witnessed the use of Patriot missiles during the Gulf War, those missiles were excessively fired at Scuds "because the system was in automatic mode." Their astronomical cost had been the object of many jokes, but given the tight budget allocated for Iron Dome, Israelis could not afford a similar burden. A key factor in reducing the expected costs of Iron Dome was to avoid firing an interceptor when deemed unnecessary. They assessed that 75 percent of the rockets fired by Hezbollah and Hamas fell in unpopulated areas, causing no damage.[38] This high number reflected the poor accuracy of the projectiles operated by the Palestinian and Lebanese combatants (though they improved in later years, as discussed later in the book). It meant that only a small portion of them demanded a response. As a result, preventing the Tamir missile from engaging an incoming rocket exploding in open terrain could save money.

As Doron Gavish, former air defense commander, explains, the decision not to engage with all rockets also had a strategic purpose: to "avoid a situation where the enemy simply tries to saturate us with a lot of missiles."[39] A system created to differentiate between rockets fired at populated areas and those detonating in open fields (or wrongly falling inside Gaza, as many did) could save resources. And by extension, it could reduce the ability of the aggressor to exhaust the defenses of the IDF.

---

[38] Luttwak, Shamir, *Art of Military Innovation*: 76.
[39] Interview with Doron Gavish, Tel Aviv, July 10, 2024.

To enable this discrimination, a solution was designed at the level of the command-and-control system built by mPrest. The system would automatically gather data from the Elta radar sensors and calculate the path of the incoming rocket. It would allow soldiers to determine if it threatened infrastructures or a populated area. Theoretically, the software would transmit the order to engage if the trajectory assessment were positive.

Relying on technology and automation was necessary, given the time frame of rocket attacks, which can take just twenty seconds. However, it triggered many questions among military operators regarding accountability and the risk of miscalculation. In practice, the system could not be completely automated: The officer in charge of the command-and-control system had to be able to override it and launch the interception if needed. This philosophy implied that there would always be a soldier "in the loop" to monitor and, if necessary, to abort the mission. As a result, it also meant training soldiers to make such decisions within a time frame ranging from ten seconds to a minute (if a missile aimed at a city in the center of the country like Tel Aviv).

In February 2008, the team assembled by Rafael started the first tests in the desert. Chanoch Levin explains that those tests "were not to intercept a target but rather to evaluate the distance between both objects in the air, between the Iron Dome missile and the rocket."[40] The tests did not go well. There were usual malfunctions with the development of new rocket systems involving combustion in the interceptor engine or radar detection. However, there were also issues regarding the required flight time for the Tamir missile to intercept a rocket. Thirty seconds were necessary for the system to reach its target, so the IDF estimated that projectiles launched from Gaza at a very close distance and within a smaller time window would evade Iron Dome. Given the math, it implied that Iron Dome would catch rockets fired from at least 4 kilometers away. This did not change things for the residents of cities like Ashkelon and Ashdod, but for those in Sderot, 2 kilometers away from the Gaza Strip, it suggested that Iron Dome might not have time to protect them. Those who already opposed Iron Dome immediately politicized the issue. For some, this was an opportunity to repeat that laser technology was a better solution.[41] However, when asked about this particular problem, IDF officers like Doron Gavish insist, "Iron Dome protects Sderot. For the very, very short range, Palestinian groups usually shoot mortar, not rockets. Sure, there is a gap, but it is a small gap."

---

[40] Podcast, "Two Nice Jewish Boys."

[41] Reuven Pedatzur, "Iron Dome System Found to Be Helpless Against Qassams," *Haaretz*, February 22, 2008. https://www.haaretz.com/2008-02-22/ty-article/iron-dome-system-found-to-be-helpless-against-qassams/0000017f-dc43-db5a-a57f-dc6b41ca0000.

Despite the lingering criticism, the Rafael team continued its work. In the summer of 2009, another series of tests was performed, including live fire testing of three Katyusha rockets. This time, the result was a significant success.[42] Then, a few months later, air force officers, MAFAT program managers, and Rafael's engineers met in a battle laboratory named the "Israeli Test-Bed." Designed in the 1990s by Elbit, the battle laboratory was a virtual environment initially meant to test new technologies for the Arrow program. It allowed officers and engineers to run scenarios using real-time data and to examine the performance: What works? What doesn't? What could be the doctrines and procedures for using the military system?

By the end of the simulation, the Iron Dome batteries were assessed to intercept about 80 percent of the rockets launched. This was far more than what Chanoch Levin and his colleagues at Rafael had expected only two years earlier. At the government level, the successful test of Iron Dome was a crucial moment for Ehud Barak and, more broadly, the defense ministry and the IDF. Prototypes were provided to a new battalion of the air defense unit, which was capable of detecting and intercepting rockets launched from the Gaza Strip.

As the national media closely followed the development, public expectations grew. Interviewed by the *Jerusalem Post*, Pinhas Buchris stated that the system would "transform security for residents of southern and northern Israel."[43] Ehud Barak's reaction to the successful test was one of cautious optimism. In March 2011, he told local media, "It's not a 100 percent solution," adding, "It would take us several years to obtain additional batteries."[44]

Cast Lead: War Returns to Gaza

As the engineers of MAFAT and Rafael worked in haste to come up with a prototype of Iron Dome, the Israeli–Palestinian conflict did not stop, and the warring parties did not wait to observe the tests. By the beginning of 2008, Hamas had gotten rid of Fatah in the Gaza Strip and was consolidating its rule inside

---

[42] Reuters, "Anti-rocket Defense System Iron Dome Aces First Live Try," July 15, 2009. https://www.reuters.com/article/us-palestinians-israel-rockets-sb/israel-says-anti-rocket-system-aces-first-live-try-idUSTRE56E61T20090715/.

[43] Yaakov Katz, "In Test, Iron Dome Successfully Intercepts Rockets," *Jerusalem Post*, January 6, 2010. https://www.jpost.com/israel/in-test-iron-dome-successfully-intercepts-rockets.

[44] Tova Dadon, "Barak: Iron Dome Not Perfect," *Yedioth Ahronoth*, March 31, 2011. https://www.ynetnews.com/articles/0,7340,L-4050394,00.html.

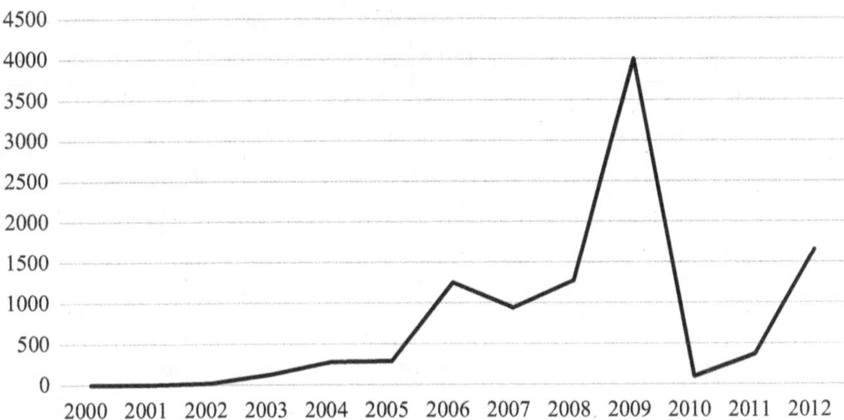

Chart 2.1 Number of rockets launched from the Gaza Strip (2000–2012).

Source: Data compiled by the author. Data based on Byman, *High Price*; Jewish Virtual Library, "Rocket & Mortar Attacks Against Israel by Date." https://www.jewishvirtuallibrary.org/palestinian-rocket-and-mortar-attacks -against-israel.

the enclave. At the same time, Palestinians denounced the blockade imposed on the territory by the Israeli government of Prime Minister Ehud Olmert. The combination of the Hamas takeover and the tight blockade provoked a fall of Gaza's economy from which it never really recovered.

Persisting in its strategy of harassment toward Israel, Hamas faced more difficulties in launching suicide attacks in Tel Aviv, Haifa, or Jerusalem. The Israeli security establishment had adapted its counterterrorism techniques. The Second Intifada was over. But Hamas was looking for ways to attack Israel by other means. The Lebanon War of 2006 provided the ultimate evidence that nonstate organizations like Hezbollah could stand their ground despite the IDF's overwhelming superiority. Missiles and rockets were a cheap solution. It was more reliable than suicide bombers and had the potential to cause even more damage. By the end of the Second Intifada in late 2004, 276 rockets were fired from the Gaza Strip. The data for the following years revealed a steady increase. In 2007, Hamas fired 938 rockets at Israeli cities and kibbutzim in the south. The year after, 1,270 rockets landed in Israel. Then, the number jumped to 4,004 in 2009. All in all, this amounted to a staggering 1,350 percent increase in five years.[45]

---

[45] The data represented in the chart is based on the combination of several sources: the Jewish Virtual Library, Daniel Byman, *A High Price: The Triumphs and Failures of Israeli Counterterrorism* (New York: Oxford University Press, 2011): 183; David Johnson, *Hard Fighting: Israel in Lebanon and Gaza* (Santa Monica, CA: RAND Corporation, 2012): 96.

The rockets of Hamas might not have inflicted severe damage or casualties, but progressively, each salvo triggered a response from the IDF with air strikes on Gaza. Then, Hamas would respond with a more significant wave of rockets. In Jerusalem, the government of Ehud Olmert was slowly getting trapped in a new cycle of escalation. It issued several warnings to Hamas that the continuation of rocket attacks would force Israel to launch an operation on Gaza, but to no avail. On December 21, Hamas fired seventy rockets and released a statement demanding that "Israel stopped its aggression (. . .) and opened up its border crossings."[46]

In retrospect, the leadership of Hamas, around Khaled Meshaal, wrongly assumed the Israeli government would tolerate low-intensity rocket attacks. Ehud Olmert had been the prime minister during the Lebanon War two years earlier, and his government had failed to curb the flow of rockets fired by Hezbollah. The conflict had left painful memories for the residents of northern Israel. Consequently, the government considered that it could not allow Hamas to use the same tactics, and more specifically, use them to pressure Israel to change its policy vis-à-vis Gaza. On December 27, Olmert ordered the response: Operation Cast Lead started. The operation's goal was unclear: "to create conditions for a better security situation in southern Israel," according to official IDF documents.[47] This was, by essence, a limited objective: The IDF was ordered not to destroy Hamas but to "degrade" its military power, to prevent future attacks on Israel's south.

This was motivated more by political factors than by military assessment. Going for the destruction of Hamas, a year after the group had evicted the Fatah security apparatus from the Gaza Strip, would have been a risky enterprise for Olmert. Getting rid of Hamas in Gaza begged the question of the alternative: Olmert had supported Ariel Sharon in 2005 when the former prime minister launched the disengagement from Gaza, so the idea of reoccupying it three years later was out of the question. But there were no other credible options either: The UN Security Council would not deploy peacekeepers like those of UNIFIL in Lebanon, and the Palestinian Authority of Mahmoud Abbas had lost its legitimacy following the bitter conflict with Hamas the previous year.

As a result, Operation Cast Lead was to be the first of several "mini wars" opposing Israel to Hamas. In many aspects, it provided the template for what would become the new Israeli "security concept" toward the Gaza Strip. The military intervention was conceived as a limited response to Hamas's rocket

[46] Johnson, *Hard Fighting*, 96.
[47] Israel Defense Forces, "Operation Cast Lead Against Terror Infrastructure in Gaza Continues," press release, December 27, 2008.

attacks. It was meant as a retaliation to weaken the Palestinian group, but without challenging its grip on Gaza. As one Israeli commentator later described, "We want to break their bones without putting them in the hospital."[48]

Still, the 2008 war triggered an outcry in public opinion in the Arab world and beyond. After three weeks of conflict involving air strikes and a ground invasion in and around Gaza City, some 1,500 Palestinians were killed (including 709 Hamas combatants, according to the IDF), 6,400 public buildings had been destroyed, and 46,000 private residences were hit.[49] Numerous images of civilian victims circulated on Arabic news channels. In January 2009, a few weeks after the end of the war, Recep Erdoğan, then Turkey's prime minister, left a panel at the Davos Summit after a heated exchange about the operation with Shimon Peres, then Israel's president.[50] This marked the erosion of the Turkey–Israel partnership, a cornerstone of the country's regional policy in the past decade. But this was one of many events that saw Israel facing international criticism for its handling of the war. In April 2009, the UN Human Rights Council established a fact-finding mission chaired by the South African jurist Richard Goldstone. What later became known as the Goldstone Report accused both the IDF and Hamas of war crimes. Specifically, the mission accused Israel of deliberately targeting Palestinian civilians as a policy of punishment.[51]

The Israeli government rejected the assertions and denounced what it considered a biased assessment. Two years later, Goldstone himself retracted some of those claims in an opinion piece he wrote for *The Washington Post*, where he wrote that "the investigations published by the Israeli military indicate that civilians were not intentionally targeted as a matter of policy."[52] Beyond the Goldstone Report controversy, Cast Lead was another argument for the missile defense proponents. Reliance on offensive doctrine was relevant when facing conventional armed forces and Arab statesmen who shared the same rationality as the Israelis. But with its new strategy, Hamas was putting the cities of southern Israel under constant threat. Relying solely on retaliatory options would feed

---

48 Quoted in Raphael Cohen, "The Inevitable, Ongoing Failure of Israel's Gaza Strategy," *Los Angeles Times*, October 19, 2023. https://www.rand.org/pubs/commentary/2023/10/the-inevitable-ongoing -failure-of-israels-gaza-strategy.html.

49 Jean-Pierre Filiu, *Gaza: A History* (London: Hurst, 2014): 318.

50 Associated Press, The Guardian, "Recep Erdogan Storms Out of Davos After Clash with Israeli President Over Gaza," January 30, 2009. https://www.theguardian.com/world/2009/jan/30/turkish -prime-minister-gaza-davos.

51 United Nations Human Rights Council, *Report of the United Nations Fact Finding Mission on the Gaza Conflict*, New York, September 15, 2009: 331. https://documents.un.org/doc/undoc/gen/g09 /158/66/pdf/g0915866.pdf.

52 Richard Goldstone, "Reconsidering the Goldstone Report on Israel and War Crimes," *Washington Post*, April 1, 2011.

escalation: The Olmert government was boxed in. After the Lebanon War of 2006, Cast Lead amplified the urgency for decision-makers to find new solutions against the rocket strategy of Hamas. Both the north and the south of the country now needed a response.

In the aftermath of Cast Lead, Ehud Olmert stepped down from the premiership. Olmert had spent most of the previous year fighting against allegations of corruption. By September 2008, he decided not to run for his party's primaries, Kadima, leaving his foreign minister, Tzipi Livni, to position herself as his presumptive successor. Livni proved unable to secure a coalition to form a new government, precipitating new parliamentary elections on February 10, 2009. Although Livni and Kadima came first in the turnout, she again failed to rally a majority at the Knesset.

As a result, President Shimon Peres turned to the leader of the Likud, who came second: Benjamin Netanyahu. A former member of the special forces unit, Sayeret Matkal, Netanyahu had been the prime minister in the 1990s. He had defeated Shimon Peres in the first elections following Yitzhak Rabin's assassination in November 1995. Netanyahu's first term had been marked by tense relations with the US administration under Bill Clinton, especially over the Oslo peace process, which the Israeli prime minister had initially rejected. Later, as finance minister under Ariel Sharon's government, Netanyahu played a significant role in reforms that changed Israel's economy. He imposed an austerity plan to reduce government expenditures while pushing for the liberalization of the economy. However, in 2005, Netanyahu left the Sharon government to express his opposition to the Gaza disengagement plan.

Now, he was back in the prime minister's office. And he would stay there without interruption for the next twelve years. At the Ministry of Defense, the election results again led to many uncertainties. A new minister could potentially suspend the development of Iron Dome and resume the contentious debate over Skyguard. Ehud Barak had no intention of leaving. Although Labor did not share much with the platform of the Likud, Barak signed an agreement to join the new governing coalition and retain his position as defense minister. Barak's rivals within his party castigated his decision, viewing it as a self-serving move that revealed a lack of principles. But with Barak still in charge, programs like Iron Dome would not be at the mercy of political turbulence. In fact, for the next four years, until Barak's last day as defense minister on March 18, 2013, the duo of Barak and Netanyahu was behind most national security decisions, from the deployment of Iron Dome batteries to their use during Operation Pillar of Defense in November 2012.

A few months after Barak decided to stay in Netanyahu's government, the IDF revamped its internal structure, creating the 947th Battalion, entirely dedicated to the future deployment of Iron Dome. This was a strong signal: Iron Dome was here to stay, and from now on, military personnel were to be trained to operate batteries.

The Israeli military was slowly accepting the reality of Iron Dome. But there was still resistance within the administration. The haste with which Danny Gold at the Ministry of Defense had launched the program, the fact that Rafael even started working on Iron Dome before the contract had been signed, caught the attention of Israeli authorities, in particular, the state comptroller's office—a public entity mandated to evaluate public policies and their use of public funding. In 2010, the office published a scathing report stating, "Brigadier General Dr. Danny Gold started the development of the Iron Dome in August 2005 in an unruly manner, violating regulations to order the overlapping of the pre-development stage with the full-scale development stage, thereby overriding the exclusive jurisdiction of the IDF Chief of Staff, the Minister of Defense, and the Israeli government as a whole."[53]

Gold rejected the conclusion of the state comptroller, telling *The Wall Street Journal* at the time, "I just canceled all the unnecessary bureaucracy; I left only the most crucial bureaucracy needed for success."[54] According to IDF sources, "the State Comptroller said Gold had to be kicked out (. . .) in Europe or the US, he would be out of the system after that." In retrospect, Ophir Shoham, who became the head of MAFAT in 2010, around the same time the report from the state comptroller came out, says, "I think they were wrong, they may have had some points where I could agree, about the regulation, the formal processes, but this was a case where a high ranking officer (Danny Gold) took the risk to invest MAFAT funds, he took the responsibility and in the end the system saved lives."[55] Ultimately, the report did not have any repercussions.

"Mazal Tov, You Have Your First Interception"

By the end of 2010, Iron Dome was approaching the point of being declared operational. Pinhas Buchris, the director general of the defense ministry for the

---

[53] The State Comptroller & Ombudsman of Israel, Readiness for Emergency, Annual Report no. 51A 2009: 85. Translation from Luttwak, Shamir, *Art of Military Innovation*: 88.
[54] Levinson, Entous, "Israel's Iron Dome Defense Battled to Get Off Ground."
[55] Interview with Ophir Shoham, Tel Aviv, July 17, 2024.

past four years, stepped down in December of that year. In his words, completing the Iron Dome project was "the best farewell gift I could have received upon completing my term."[56] As Pinhas Buchris left his position at the defense ministry with the sentiment that the fight for Iron Dome was over, the IDF top brass got into new heated arguments.

Now that Iron Dome was turning into an operational reality, and that the system could be considered a reliable option, new questions emerged: Who would be the first beneficiaries of the system? What should be its priorities? The discussion was partly based on technical parameters: Both the radar coverage and the interceptor range had limits. That meant not all cities and kibbutzim across the country could be defended. Other strategic considerations were also raised: For some commanders, the priority should be Israel's critical infrastructures (e.g., its nuclear plant in the Negev or its military bases around the border areas). Around that time, Gadi Eisenkot, then Northern Commander, delivered a speech at Haifa University, during which he bluntly asserted, "The residents of Israel shouldn't be under the illusion that someone will open an umbrella over their heads (. . .) the systems are designed to protect military bases, even if this means that citizens suffer discomfort during the first days of battle."[57]

Eisenkot's statement was meant to manage expectations from the Israeli public, who had closely followed the saga surrounding Iron Dome, and from those who hoped that this could end their fears of rocket attacks. However, it also reflected the enduring skepticism of Israel's military leaders. Eisenkot was affirming that systems like Iron Dome were not going to change the lives of Israeli citizens; at best, they would act as fortifications for the IDF bases.

Such a military argument did not please the members of parliament or government ministers. Israeli politicians were facing constant pressure from residents (and voters) in the south who accused the state of leaving them at the mercy of Hamas's rockets. One IDF officer recalls, "We were working on testing Iron Dome, and at the same time, we were hearing that during municipal elections, local candidates were promising to voters, 'I will bring Iron Dome to our city.'"[58] According to one former head of the IDF's strategic planning department, it was Ehud Barak who put an end to this debate: "Barak said, 'I don't want to have this discussion, I want Iron Dome to protect all of Israel.'"[59]

[56] "Outgoing Defense Ministry Director: Iron Dome Best Farewell Gift," *Yedioth Ahronoth*, December 1, 2010. https://www.ynetnews.com/articles/0,7340,L-3833456,00.html#:~:text=Outgoing%20Director%2DGeneral%20of%20the,received%20upon%20completing%20my%20term.%22.

[57] Ahiya Raved, "Eisenkot: Missile Defense—for IDF Bases," *Yedioth Ahronoth*, January 12, 2010. https://www.ynetnews.com/articles/0,7340,L-3992238,00.html.

[58] Interview with retired IDF officer, Tel Aviv, July 4, 2024.

[59] Interview with Shay Shabtai, former Head of Strategic Planning, IDF, Tel Aviv, July 4, 2024.

Barak's decision was remarkable, given his own evolution on Iron Dome. But more than his military thinking, it reflected his political instinct: With the growing rocket threat facing Israeli cities, the IDF's logic of downplaying the menace and relying on retaliatory strikes was not sustainable. The public needed a strong message of reassurance.

Still, in 2010, Iron Dome was a long way from becoming a system with comprehensive coverage of Israel's territory. Its first batteries were to defend the southern population against Hamas. For Doron Gavish, former air defense commander, "the first deployment on the first day was in the south. The priority was the big cities: Be'er-Sheva and Ashkelon, and then Ashdod. From day one, it was for the civilians." However, Gavish minimizes the influence local politics may have had on the selection of cities: "I don't remember that they interfered in the process. The main criterion was the threat assessment; at the time, it was undoubtedly the towns in the south. We also calculated the density of the area: the denser areas needed to be defended. Hence, the big cities and the small towns around it."[60] IDF officers talked then of creating a "polygon" between Ashdod, Ashkelon, and Be'er-Sheva that would provide Iron Dome coverage. One IDF major said, "[A]s deputy commander of the battery, I recall working with a compass to figure out the optimal location for the radar as we set up."[61]

In late 2010, multiple new tests were conducted on a military site in southern Israel. The air force went through five different scenarios of engagement with rockets coming from Gaza that proved successful. The success of those tests was a relief for the team behind the program. It also allowed Ehud Barak to return to the US administration and ask them to update their assessment of Iron Dome.

Washington's environment had changed since the first time the US Defense Department negatively assessed the feasibility of Iron Dome. After winning the 2008 election, Barack Obama retained Robert Gates as the head of the Pentagon. Gates and his policy team (which had completely changed when the Israelis resumed the conversation on Iron Dome) were observing the new, positive findings of the tests performed by the Israeli Air Force. This time, Washington agreed to provide financial aid: In early January 2011, Congress passed the appropriations law for the new fiscal year, authorizing the secretary of defense to "provide up to $205,000,000 to the government of Israel for the Iron Dome short-range rocket defense system."[62] Not only did the Israeli government

---

[60] Interview with Doron Gavish, former Air Defense Commander, IDF, Tel Aviv, July 10, 2024.

[61] Israel Air Force, "A Decade Since the First Iron Dome Interception." https://www.iaf.org.il/9327 -52853-en/IAF.aspx.

[62] "Ike Skelton National Defense Authorization Act for Fiscal Year 2011," Public Law 111–383, 111th Congress, January 7, 2011. https://www.congress.gov/111/plaws/publ383/PLAW-111publ383.pdf.

succeed in getting US funding, but it was also able to protect its license rights to the Iron Dome system. Jacob Nagel, who took part in the bilateral talks, wrote, "An important element of the committee's proposal insisted that assistance be limited to equipping the Iron Dome system to prevent any future potential export restrictions on the system."[63]

In March 2011, the first three batteries were deployed to protect Ashkelon and Be'er-Sheva. On Thursday, April 7, Hamas fired an anti-tank missile at an Israeli school bus. One child and the bus driver were critically injured. Then, three rockets were fired at Israeli towns. One of them, targeting Ashkelon, was intercepted by the Iron Dome battery deployed to the area a few weeks before. In an official report from the IDF, Lieutenant Colonel Maor shares his recollections of the day: "We sat in the interception management room and saw a real operational target on our screens for the first time—the moment we had anticipated for months."[64]

For the first time, Iron Dome was used on the battlefield. For the engineers at MAFAT or Rafael, as well as the officers of Israel's air defense, this was a day of celebration. Lieutenant Colonel Maor, present in the command-and-control center, recalls, "We were excited," but he adds immediately, "After a few seconds, we began to prepare for the next interceptions since the event was not over."[65] On that day, the prime minister, Benjamin Netanyahu, was in France for a diplomatic visit. His national security adviser at the time, Jacob Amidror, remembers, "We were in Paris, and the military secretary of the prime minister got a phone call, and he said, 'Mister Prime Minister, mazal tov, you have your first interception!' We were all very glad."[66]

Outside of this small circle, the reaction was lukewarm. On that day, news agencies around the world had other top stories. NATO was intensifying its air operations in Libya against the regime of Muammar Gaddafi, while in Syria, protests against the Assad regime were getting more violent by the day. Against that backdrop, the news in Ashkelon appeared secondary. In its first coverage of the new defense system, the BBC emphasized, "It is a very expensive system," concluding with a tad of sarcasm, "Compared with the technology used by the Palestinians, it is like tossing an expensive BMW car into the air to knock down a basic Ford."[67] The international reputation of Iron Dome was yet to come.

[63] Email correspondence with Jacob Nagel, June 8, 2024.
[64] Israel Air Force, "A Decade Since the First Iron Dome Interception."
[65] Israel Air Force, "A Decade Since the First Iron Dome Interception."
[66] Interview with Jacob Amidror, former National Security Advisor (2011–13), Raananah, June 17, 2024.
[67] Jonathan Marcus, "Israeli New Missile Defence in Action," BBC, April 8, 2011. https://www.bbc.com/news/world-middle-east-13013322.

A Tale of the Start-Up Nation?

In several aspects, the study of Iron Dome's development reveals common traits with the broader history of the IDF, whether for its capacity to foster innovation or for its enduring resistance to defense as a strategy. Interestingly, Isaac Ben-Israel, a professor at Tel Aviv University and a former head of MAFAT, sees this evolution as part of a larger pattern of Israel's military innovations:

> When MAFAT thinks it has a good idea, MAFAT is allowed to develop it. The user/customer like the Air Force or the Army, may object. Many times, you come to them with an idea, and they dismiss it as science fiction. Still, if you can prove them wrong with a demonstrator, or a working prototype that you build with your own budget, usually they will change their mind.[68]

This may sound like a romanticized view of Israel's culture of military innovation. But it is one that surfaced many times during our interviews.

This can be captured at the individual level, examining how Danny Gold and his team openly disregarded administrative procedures to expedite the development of Iron Dome. Gold's management style, unusual in a military context, was often described by interviewees as reflecting the "culture of improvisation" prevailing in Israeli society. As scholar Dima Adamsky writes, "the Israeli military tradition glorified the ability of its officers to orient quickly, rely on personal judgment, think on their feet when confronting uncertainty, seize the initiative, and give on-the-spot solutions."[69] Additionally, Gold's persistence with the development of Iron Dome reminds us of the mythology surrounding stories of Ariel Sharon disregarding his commanders to lead his troops across the Suez Canal in October 1973.

It also reveals the process of developing new technology within the IDF, akin to creating a new app in a small tech company in Silicon Valley, and the motto of its entrepreneurs, "Fake it till you make it." In that perspective, the story of Iron Dome belongs to the bigger story of Israel as a "start-up nation," as popularized by Dan Senor and Saul Singer.[70]

Many interviewees also underlined how Iron Dome reflects the culture of risk-taking within the IDF and the broader Israeli society. In 2017, the Israeli

---

[68] Interview with Professor Isaac Ben-Israel, Tel Aviv University, July 2, 2024.

[69] Dima Adamsky, *The Culture of Military Innovation: The Impact of Cultural Factors on the Revolution in Military Affairs in Russia, the US, and Israel* (Stanford: Stanford University Press, 2010): 117.

[70] Dan Senor, Saul Singer, *Start-up Nation: The Story of Israel's Economic Miracle* (New York: Twelve, 2009).

Ministry of Science, Technology, and Space released a poll asking citizens to name the greatest Israeli invention ever. Thirty-one percent of the interviewees named Iron Dome, far ahead of technologies such as the navigation app Waze and the USB flash drive developed by the local start-up M-Systems.[71]

There was an element of risk and uncertainty behind the decision to launch the project. But it would be an overstatement to describe Iron Dome as a project that suddenly, in less than three years, was built merely out of the skills and the *chutzpah* of a small group of engineers. Ophir Shoham, the former head of MAFAT between 2010 and 2016 and now an investor in technology start-ups, nuances this view:

> It's not as if we started completely from scratch for every component of Iron Dome, MAFAT had invested for years in rocket motors, sensor technologies, aerodynamics, computation capabilities, all things that are needed in order to be matured, to kick off such a program. So this was a very fast program that used available technologies that we developed along the years.[72]

The unusual burden-sharing arrangement between Rafael and the Israeli defense ministry also reflects the nature of the arms market in Israel. When Rafael became involved in the Iron Dome project, the organization had only become a private entity four years earlier. But as Isaac Ben-Israel, a former head of MAFAT, insists, "Rafael became private, but it was a government-owned company: as we reformed Rafael, we wanted the people, its engineers, to continue like it was in the past, to feel that they were still part of the defense system of Israel."[73] The intellectual and institutional proximity between the engineers at MAFAT and those at Rafael enabled them to work faster than in the traditional, demarcated environment of public-private partnerships in the United States or Europe.

There is another aspect to the military–industrial ecosystem that is unique to Israel: the role of reservists. Historically, the IDF relies primarily on reserve units (70 percent of its total personnel as of 2025) composed of civilians regularly called up for military duty. This means that many civilians are well versed in the latest military technologies and understand the operational needs of the armed forces. In the case of Iron Dome, this enabled Rafael and the air force to work hand in hand. As Doron Gavish, former air defense commander, explains,

[71] Haaretz, "TechNation: Iron Dome Antimissile System Named Top Israeli Invention of All Time," March 14, 2017. https://www.haaretz.com/israel-news/business/2017-03-14/ty-article/technation-iron-dome-named-top-israeli-invention-of-all-time/0000017f-db64-d3ff-a7ff-fbe407940000.
[72] Interview with Ophir Shoham, Tel Aviv, July 17, 2024.
[73] Interview with Professor Isaac Ben-Israel, Tel Aviv University, July 2, 2024.

The guys that developed Iron Dome were serving in the reserves, with the air defense, they knew exactly what they wanted. It's not as if something is being developed in the civilian sphere without a close relationship with the military; we officially put our air defense soldiers in, and they were part of the development two years before the system was introduced. Our guys worked with the company; they sat next to the developers and told them exactly what they needed.[74]

Ultimately, the story of Iron Dome's development also highlights the ongoing resistance that emerged against it and never entirely disappeared. One argument against Iron Dome was a strategic or philosophical one, namely, that defense cannot be an effective response to the challenges faced by the country. However, there was another, more technical argument related to the dilemma between a kinetic option, such as Iron Dome, and laser technology, which was represented by the Skyguard program at the time. This dilemma divided engineers, officers, and even those who believed in investing in missile defense. For instance, David Ivry, the former director general of Israel's Ministry of Defense, who had fought against the bureaucracy of the IDF in the 1980s and the early 1990s to change the mindset on the missile threat, had mixed feelings on the debate. When I met him in the summer of 2024, Ivry argued that Israel's missile defense architecture could only be understood through different layers, rendering the debate about either Iron Dome or Skyguard flawed. It wasn't one or the other. In Ivry's view, laser technology was to be the core of Israel's defense, with kinetic solutions like Iron Dome and Arrow playing a "complementary" role.[75]

As we will discuss in the following chapters, the heated debate over the selection of Iron Dome often resurfaced in the following decade. However, as of April 2011, Iron Dome was a victory for the engineers, the officers, and the politicians who had devoted their time and resources to its creation. It would soon take on another dimension when Iron Dome emerged as the new, unlikely hero in Israel's wars against Hamas.

---

[74] Interview with Doron Gavish, Tel Aviv, July 10, 2024.
[75] Interview with David Ivry, Former Chief Israel Air Force, Former Director General MoD, Ramat HaSharon, July 22, 2024.

3

An Unlikely Military Hero

"It is Saturday early in the morning," remembers Yossi. "I'm going out on the beach with my five-year-old daughter, a few joggers are running, and some older people are enjoying a short walk." Suddenly, Yossi sees a bright spark in the sky, chasing after another eluding light. Then, both explode in their collision. Yossi looks at the other bystanders, hoping to find an explanation in their eyes, but everyone seems clueless. When his daughter asks him what they just witnessed, he says, "This was Iron Dome." Later that day, while checking online for information, Yossi learns that on that morning, the early warning system operated by the Home Front Command, *Tzeva Adom*, malfunctioned, and the sirens failed to alert the people on the beach about an incoming rocket. Fortunately, the air defense could still track and intercept it before it fell from the sky.

Yossi's story is one of many stories heard during the preparation of this book. More than a decade after the deployment of the first Iron Dome batteries, almost everyone in Israel had an "Iron Dome story" to share. There is the one in which Eli, a reserve officer, is sent to secure the city center of Sderot on the night of October 7, 2023, only hours after the surprise attack of Hamas. Eli remembers a salvo of rockets fired from Gaza, his unit filled with conscripted teenagers hoping that Iron Dome would protect them. "We are sitting ducks, patrolling the streets as rockets flew one after another. And the only comfort we have is the sound of Iron Dome interceptors, and it's a sound so specific, I could hear it in my brain for months."

An Asian diplomat also shares the story of being relieved to learn that an Iron Dome battery was deployed next to her embassy when she took her position in Israel. Two European diplomats detail their stressful memories of endless nights in Tel Aviv when war broke out in October 2023, and Iron Dome interceptors could be spotted in the sky—though they quickly add, "We can't complain; our colleagues at the Embassy in Beirut can't rely on Iron Dome."

Likewise, Shlomo, a retired Israeli civil servant, remembers how one day, he quickly gets his granddaughter from his car and stops on the highway as sirens scream for an incoming rocket: "This is part of our life now: it's the middle of the night, the siren blows, you need to wake up, you need to realize where you are, to be ready, to rush to a shelter if you have one. You accept it because you hear the Iron Dome interception; you're not defenseless, now we're no longer at the mercy of the rockets."

In the first few years after Iron Dome was introduced, those stories were mainly told by people living in southern Israel. A decade later, they had become part of a collective experience shared by everyone across the country, in peripheral towns like Sderot and Be'er-Sheva and in big cities like Tel Aviv, Jerusalem, and Haifa. They reflected how much Iron Dome, more than any other military system, had entered the lives of all Israelis to become part of popular culture if not national folklore.

At first, the phenomenon was evident in the numerous videos civilians took of Iron Dome interceptions. Usually at night, in the middle of a clash between the Israel Defense Forces (IDF) and Hamas, Israelis would stand and stare at their window, or they would gather on their rooftop to capture on their smartphones the footage of a Tamir missile reaching a rocket. There is an eerily science-fictional quality to those videos that have been shared on social networks for years. The videos have spread across the world. Most international media have used pictures of those interceptions at night in the sky over Tel Aviv. Soon, this unusual coverage for an air defense system (rarely do people share stories involving Patriot missiles or Arrow interceptors) gained Iron Dome its reputation beyond Israel's territory.

Nobody within the team assembled by MAFAT and Rafael had anticipated this phenomenon in 2006. What is also remarkable about those videos is the simplicity of their effectiveness. Watching a video of Iron Dome intercepting a rocket is a different experience from watching a fighter jet maneuvering in the sky. There is no display of human prowess. People in Israel and elsewhere are watching them because, in its rawness, the footage demonstrates the success of Israel's technology. Caught on camera, an Iron Dome interception tells a simple story: that of a technology saving lives by going after the rockets launched by Hamas and other groups. It is an action movie based on a true story that lasts less than a minute and can be accessed and watched for free on YouTube.

The phenomenon went so far that, in May 2021, amid a new war between Israel and Hamas, a cartoon picture of a superhero started circulating on Twitter.[1] At first sight, the superhero's costume resembled a mix of Iron Man and Captain America, except that it displayed the Star of David, and his name was "Iron Dome." Designed by a local artist, Sarai Givaty Luboschits, and shared

---

[1] StandWithUs (@StandWithUs), "Introducing, a New Israeli Superhero: Iron Dome, the Protector/ Defender of Israel. We Love It! #irondome10 ɪʟɪʟɪʟ Credit: Sarai Givaty," X, May 31, 2021. https://x.com /standwithus/status/1399032857713127424?lang=ko.

by a pro-Israel advocacy organization, "StandWithUs," the picture captured a striking phenomenon: In the Israeli popular culture, the new "hero" defending the country was no longer a soldier but a military system.

This perception of Iron Dome is not anecdotal, especially in a country that has long cultivated an intimate relationship between the people and its army. It reflected a profound change in the Israeli social norms and attitudes that predated the system.

By the 2010s, David Ben-Gurion's idea of the IDF as a "people's army" had long faded.[2] As polls revealed, the young generation, more individualistic than their grandparents in 1948, had grown tired of the national service and the reserve. But if the time of the Israeli soldier as a hero was gone, Iron Dome provided a new symbol, a new story of national achievement and pride. It echoed the rise of what Edward Luttwak called "post-heroic warfare," a belief that changes in societies and military innovation led Israelis to become more averse to civilian casualties on the battlefield.[3]

To understand this phenomenon and the role played by Iron Dome as an unlikely military hero, we need to go back to the deployment of the first battery in Ashkelon in April 2011 and the implications of its success. As this chapter explains, the following decade saw the political elite and the general public embrace the new defense offered by Iron Dome. There were some critical voices within the IDF and the scientific community. Still, overall, the impressive (and unexpected) performance of the system lent credence to a belief or security concept—the *conceptzia* in Israeli parlance—that Hamas would no longer go to war because Israel's military power deterred it and because its grip on Gaza had led the organization to become more interested in governance than militancy.[4] This *conceptzia* would be tragically proven wrong after October 7, 2023. But for more than a decade, Iron Dome denied the rockets of Hamas and became a convenient means for the successive governments in Jerusalem that tried to avoid at all costs dealing with the reality of Gaza. As Mairav Zonszein, a senior analyst for the NGO Crisis Group, argued, "Iron Dome, in many ways, was a tactical response to a strategic issue that's never been dealt with."[5]

---

[2] Stuart Cohen, *Israel and its Amy: From Cohesion to Confusion* (London: Routledge, 2008).

[3] Avi Kober, "From Heroic to Post-Heroic Warfare: Israel's Way of War in Asymmetrical Conflicts," *Armed Forces & Society* 4, no. 1 (2015): 96–122. https://www.jstor.org/stable/48609200; Eitan Shamir, "Israel's Post-Heroic Wars: Exploring the Influence of American Military Concepts on Israel's Adaptation of Post-Heroic Warfare," *Israel Affairs* 24, no. 4 (June 2018): 686–706. https://doi.org/10.1080/13537121.2018.1478788.

[4] David Makovsky, "The Collapse of Israel's Hamas 'Conceptzia,'" *The National Interest*, October 26, 2023. https://nationalinterest.org/feature/collapse-israels-hamas-conceptzia-207058.

[5] Interview with Mairav Zonszein, Senior Analyst, Crisis Group, Tel Aviv, June 19, 2024.

Figure 3.1 Iron Dome portrayed as a superhero.

Source: StandWithUs (@StandWithUs), "Introducing, a New Israeli Superhero: Iron Dome, the Protector/ Defender of Israel. We Love It! #irondome10 ㅣㅣㅣㅣ Credit: Sarai Givaty," X, May 31, 2021. https://x.com /standwithus/status/1399032857713127424?lang=ko.

Iron Dome's Euphoria Takes Off

The previous chapter ended with the first successful use of Iron Dome to protect the population in the south. In the first weeks after Iron Dome batteries were deployed and used against rockets from Gaza in 2011, the IDF air defense unit closely monitored the data to assess the performance of the system. One of their critical metrics was the interception rate. Each interception was reviewed by the air defense commander and his staff to assess what went right or wrong. Given the positive signs that Iron Dome had effectively protected Ashkelon and Be'er-Sheva, the debate quickly shifted to the number of Iron Dome batteries that were needed. The assessment by engineers at MAFAT and Rafael suggested that approximately thirteen to fifteen batteries were necessary to properly defend the south.

This was a very high number that implied a significant increase in procurement. By the summer of 2011, two batteries had already been deployed, and a third was scheduled to enter service by October. Then, in July, the defense ministry ordered Rafael to start working on the production of three additional batteries, using for the first time US funding approved by the Obama administration (the evolution of the US role is discussed in greater detail in Chapter 4). Shortly after, Defense Minister Ehud Barak promised the general public that nine batteries would be deployed before the end of 2011.[6]

Expectations were again surging, as the first use of Iron Dome in April 2011 impressed both the decision-makers and the general public. Then, in August, a new cycle of violence between Hamas and the IDF led to the firing of 300–350 rockets on Israel's southern cities. This time, one Israeli civilian died, provoking a sudden end to the euphoria built in the previous months. Yes, the performance of Iron Dome was impressive, but civilians could still die from rockets. Again, this led IDF officials to issue cautious statements on the purpose of the system. Ophir Shoham, then director of MAFAT, tried to manage expectations in a statement to the press: "We do not presume to shoot down thousands of rockets. Rather, we aim to minimize the damage and let the IDF do other things."

Still, the excitement surrounding Iron Dome was such that in June 2012, Ehud Barak announced that the prestigious Israel Defense Prize had been awarded that year to the developers of Iron Dome, including engineers and managers

---

[6] Yaakov Katz, "3 More Iron Dome Batteries to Arrive by 2012," *Jerusalem Post*, August 21, 2011. https://www.jpost.com/defense/3-more-iron-dome-batteries-to-arrive-by-2012.

from MAFAT, the Air Force, and Rafael.[7] The attribution of such an award was remarkable: At the time, the system had only been used in a few instances against rockets fired from Gaza. However, in the internal politics of the Ministry of Defense, the award ceremony was the culmination of a half-decade-long battle that saw proponents of a military system turned into the heroes of the day. Pictures of the event showed Rafael engineers congratulated by Barak and then–IDF Chief of Staff Benny Gantz. Among the recipients was also Danny Gold, the MAFAT manager whom the state comptroller had blamed for violating public procedures two years before. For the Israeli and international media, Gold was not only a "hero" but a "maverick thinker," a "heretic innovator."[8] In the eyes of many, he was now joining the mythology of Israeli military innovators.

The idea that Iron Dome was denying Hamas the ability to kill Israelis, and by extension, preventing a new war in Gaza, soon became a key talking point of decision-makers in Tel Aviv and Jerusalem. This was a compelling argument, particularly in convincing the US administration to provide support for the system. If the United States were investing more in defending Israel with Iron Dome batteries, it could also expect to avert another conflict between the IDF and Hamas. Israeli officials started to claim that by protecting Israelis, Iron Dome was also saving Palestinian lives.[9]

But in the following years, the assumption that Iron Dome could indeed prevent war was tested on two occasions: during Operation Pillar of Defense in November 2012 and Operation Protective Edge in July 2014. In both cases, Iron Dome played a central role in intercepting rockets launched from Gaza. During those two conflicts, the system secured its raison d'être for the Israeli national security establishment and built its worldwide reputation. In the aftermath of Operation Pillar of Defense, Yiftah Shapir from Israel's Institute for National Security Studies went as far as to name Iron Dome "the queen of battle."[10] But in retrospect, the recurrence of war during that period should have

[7] Yoav Ziton, "Ehud Barak Isher: Price Bitachon Israel Le-Kipat Barzel" (in Hebrew: Ehud Barak Confirmed: Israel Security Price to Iron Dome), *Yedioth Ahronoth*, June 24, 2012. https://www.ynet .co.il/articles/0,7340,L-4246584,00.html.

[8] Gil Ronen, "Israel's New Hero: The Father of Iron Dome," *Israel National News*, July 12, 2014. https:// www.israelnationalnews.com/news/182816; Abigail Klein Leichman, "The Maverick Thinker Behind Iron Dome," Israel21C, August 3, 2014. https://www.israel21c.org/the-maverick-thinker -behind-iron-dome/.

[9] Michael Oren, "Invest in Iron Dome for Peace," *Politico*, March 18, 2012. https://www.politico.com /story/2012/03/investment-in-iron-domeis-investment-in-peace-074149.

[10] Yiftah S. Shapir, "Iron Dome: The Queen of Battle," in: Shlomo Brom (ed.), *In the Aftermath of Operation Pillar of Defense: The Gaza Strip, November 2012* (Tel Aviv: Institute for National Security Studies, 2012): 39–46.

put into question the belief that Iron Dome could indeed deter Hamas and other Palestinian groups.

Eventually, the study of Iron Dome against the backdrop of IDF operations conducted in the past decade reveals a sobering conclusion. The system proved essential in "routine" security operations, *bittahon shotef* in Hebrew—that is, daily interventions to defend against minor aggression—but it had little influence on the planning and execution of operations (in 2012, 2014, and 2021) once they started. To grasp this reality, the chapter examines the political and military logic of those wars.

Pillar of Defense: Iron Dome's Baptism of Fire

As Neri Zilber, a Tel Aviv-based journalist and analyst, explains, "The story starts in 2012: it is the only time Netanyahu actually takes the initiative that starts a war . . . and that is the first time Iron Dome is really deployed in wartime situations." Zilber adds, "It is after 2012 that Iron Dome becomes a tool for the military and political establishment to put off major strategic decisions about Gaza."[11]

Operation Pillar of Defense officially started on November 14, 2012, but it followed months of sporadic clashes between the IDF and Palestinian groups. On March 9, 2012, Israeli forces eliminated Zuhar al-Keisey, commander of the Palestinian Popular Resistance Committee, a militia active in Gaza and opposing both Israel and the Palestinian Authority (PA). Less than three hours later, the Palestinian Islamic Jihad (PIJ) responded by firing rockets at southern Israel. By the evening of that day, Be'er-Sheva and Ashdod had been attacked. About seventy rockets were launched in the first twelve hours of the fighting.[12] In the following days, the Israeli air defense used Iron Dome batteries to counter the launch of over 160 rockets. The success rate of Iron Dome during this short escalation was estimated to reach 86 percent.[13]

Months of escalating violence followed. Hamas and the PIJ declared they were willing to negotiate a ceasefire. Both sides started discussing the conditions of that agreement. But at the same time, they kept firing at each other. Palestinian

---

[11] Interview with Neri Zilber, Correspondent, Financial Times, Tel Aviv, June 11, 2024.
[12] Uzi Rubin, *Iron Dome vs Grad Rockets: A Dress Rehearsal for an All-Out War?*, Begin Sadat Center for Strategic Studies, Perspective Paper no. 173, July 2012. https://besacenter.org/iron-dome-vs -grad-rocketsa-dress-rehearsal-for-an-all-out-war/.
[13] Rubin, *Iron Dome vs Grad Rockets*.

groups launched rockets, and on the Israeli side, Barak and Netanyahu approved the targeted killing of Ahmed Jabari, the second in command of Hamas's Izz ad-Din al-Qassam Brigades. Nicknamed "the general," Jabari was considered the chief commander behind numerous rocket attacks on Israel's south. He was also held responsible for the kidnapping of Gilad Shalit, a young Israeli soldier whom Hamas held for five years between 2006 and 2011. On the morning of Wednesday, November 14, the Israeli Air Force fired a missile at Jabari's car while he was driving. Operation Pillar of Defense had started.

Ehud Barak, who was already the defense minister in the previous Operation Cast Lead, in 2008, recalls in his memoirs that in the 2012 war, "the overall objective hadn't changed since Olmert's premiership: to hit Hamas hard; bring down the number of rocket attacks to as near zero as possible." Barak adds that this time around, "we had Iron Dome, which I was confident would help deal with the inevitable shower of Hamas rockets that would follow our initial attack."[14] In his recollection of the events, the then–Prime Minister Benjamin Netanyahu appears less confident regarding the uncertainties surrounding the use of Iron Dome the moment the war started: "It had been first used seven months earlier, but would this miraculous system work under a heavy barrage of rockets? No one knew for sure."[15]

On the first day of the operation, the government issued a partial call-up of the reserve, preparing for the possibility of a ground invasion of Gaza. The 2012 operation was preventive as there was no imminent threat to Israel. The IDF and the Netanyahu government assessed that Jabari and the military apparatus of Hamas had grown too big and posed a permanent challenge to the safety of Israeli southern residents.

Israel's security establishment also grew concerned about the impact of the Egyptian revolution on Hamas and the Gaza Strip. Following the fall of the Mubarak regime a year earlier, Egypt experienced a transitional period that culminated in the election of Mohamed Morsi in June 2012. As a member of the Muslim Brotherhood, Morsi had a natural affinity for Hamas. In the ensuing months, Cairo established a joint security committee involving Hamas and Egypt. On the Palestinian side, Jabari led the talks. Nevertheless, beyond those consultations, the Morsi government remained cautious not to jeopardize its

---

[14] Ehud Barak, *My Country, My Life: Fighting for Israel, Searching for Peace* (New York: MacMillan, 2018): Kindle Edition, 7946 out of 9267.
[15] Benjamin Netanyahu, *Bibi. My Story* (New York: Threshold Editions, 2022): 492.

ties to the United States or Israel.[16] The day before the killing of Jabari, Egypt was negotiating with him a permanent truce agreement between Hamas and Israel.[17]

At the domestic level, the war also served Netanyahu's political calculations. A month before the operation began, the prime minister announced early general elections for January 22, 2013. In that context, a quick operation degrading Hamas's power could strengthen Netanyahu's credentials as he ran for reelection.[18]

According to IDF statements, the operation led to approximately 1,500 air strikes and the destruction of "140 tunnels, 980 underground rocket launchers, 30 major command headquarters," as well as the killing of "19 leaders of Hamas and the Islamic Jihad terrorist organization."[19] Throughout the war, the IDF showed its ability to target military infrastructure and Hamas combatants while minimizing casualties among the Palestinian population. According to UN estimates, 103 civilians were killed during that week—a significant number, yet still much lower than the 1,400 fatalities during Operation Cast Lead 2008.

Despite the seemingly impressive data of the IDF's performance against Hamas, the latter proved resilient and fired no less than 1,506 rockets on Israel during the campaign (502 were said actually to explode on Israeli territory).[20] In most of the South, schools were closed, and residents were asked to remain near bomb shelters. Tel Aviv came under attack for the first time since the Gulf War. Hamas even reached Jerusalem. Following those attacks, one of its spokesmen told the Associated Press, "We are sending a short and simple message: There is no security for any Zionist on any single inch of Palestine, and we plan more surprises."[21] Iron Dome might have mitigated the cost and the damage inflicted by rockets, but life disruption was still inevitable.

16 Omar Shaaban, "Hamas and Morsi: Not So Easy Between Brothers," Carnegie Endowment for International Peace, October 1, 2012. https://carnegieendowment.org/research/2012/10/hamas -and-morsi-not-so-easy-between-brothers?lang=en¢er=middle-east.

17 Reuven Pedatzur, "Why Did Israel Kill Jabari?," *Haaretz*, December 4, 2012. https://www.haaretz .com/opinion/2012-12-04/ty-article/.premium/reuven-pedatzur-why-kill-jabari/0000017f-ded6 -db5a-a57f-defe58f00000.

18 Tareq Baconi, *Hamas Contained: The Rise and Pacification of Palestinian Resistance* (Stanford, CA: Stanford University Press, 2018): 193.

19 Israel Defense Forces, "Operation Pillar of Defense," October 30, 2017. https://www.idf.il/en/mini -sites/wars-and-operations/operation-pillar-of-defence/operation-pillar-of-defense/.

20 Niccolo Petrelli, *Israel, Strategic Culture and the Conflict with Hamas: Adaptation and Military Effectiveness* (London: Routledge, 2018): 154.

21 Greg Myre, "For the First Time, Rocket Fired from Gaza Hits Jerusalem," NPR, November 16, 2012. https://www.npr.org/sections/thetwo-way/2012/11/16/165271821/for-the-first-time-palestinians -rocket-jerusalem.

Despite those challenges, Operation Pillar of Defense was met with enthusiasm within Israel's military circles. Analysts praised the performance of the IDF. Eran Ortal, former commander of the Dado Center in charge of the IDF military studies, explains with a hint of sarcasm that, "for many, Pillar of Defense seemed like the dream operation from an operational standing point: We bombard Gaza, we severely weaken Hamas, and eight days later, the operation is over, no boots on the ground, all rockets are intercepted by Iron Dome or fall in open spaces."[22] Similarly, Eitan Shamir, a professor at Bar-Ilan University and former researcher for the IDF, called the 2012 operation "a textbook operation: Israel was able to take out a few of the commanders, less than 200 Palestinians were killed, there was no international pressure, no international outcry, no big demonstration and then it's finished, that's it."[23]

In such upbeat assessments, Iron Dome played a significant role. But this success also led to a paradox that undermined Israel's international standing. The images of Israelis protected by sirens, shelters, and Iron Dome batteries contrasted with the video footage of Palestinians in Gaza who had nowhere to go during the air strikes. Many Israelis felt that public opinion abroad turned against them because they were better protected than the Palestinians. Furthermore, Pillar of Defense did not escape scrutiny and criticism from the United Nations. The UN High Commissioner for Human Rights issued a report stating that the IDF "failed in many instances to respect international law" and to "consistently uphold the basic principles of conduct of hostilities, namely, the principles of distinction, proportionality, and precautions."[24]

After Pillar of Defense, Iron Dome changed the way Israeli decision-makers thought about the dynamics of escalation with Hamas. Uzi Rubin, an Israeli expert on missile defense, explained that before Iron Dome, "Israel had no other response option except escalation." From now on, Iron Dome enabled decision-makers to rely on a "non-escalatory strategy"—that is, a way to respond to aggression without amplifying the conflict.[25] Rubin's argument is correct, but it

---

[22] Interview with Eran Ortal, former commander of the Dado Center, Tel Aviv, June 16, 2024.

[23] Interview with Eitan Shamir, director of Begin Sadat Center, Bar-Ilan University, Tel Aviv, June 16, 2024.

[24] United Nations High Commissioner for Human Rights, "Report of the United Nations High Commissioner for Human Rights on the Implementation of Human Rights Council Resolutions S-9/1 and S-12/1," Human Rights Council, March 6, 2013. https://www.ohchr.org/sites/default/files/Documents/HRBodies/HRCouncil/RegularSession/Session22/A.HRC.22.35_AUV.pdf.

[25] Quoted in: US Department of Defense, "Missile Defense Review," 2019: 75. https://www.defense.gov/Portals/1/Interactive/2018/11-2019-Missile-Defense-Review/The%202019%20MDR_Executive%20Summary.pdf.

did not prevent escalation per se. At best, the success of Iron Dome seemed to prevent the launching of a ground invasion of Gaza.

At last, on November 21, Egypt brokered a ceasefire. The agreement called for both sides to cease hostilities and ease the movement of people and goods within the Gaza Strip. Then, domestic politics once again took center stage in Israel. Soon after the war, Defense Minister Ehud Barak announced his resignation. After more than five years in the position, Barak, then seventy years old, said he was leaving politics. His successor, Moshe Ya'alon, from the Likud Party, had also spent his career in the IDF, having held positions as head of the military intelligence (1995–8) and, most recently, chief of staff (2002–5). Like many officers of his era, Ya'alon was initially doubtful about the effectiveness of missile defense. Yet, by 2013, his perspective had shifted, reflecting a similar change among many in the IDF leadership. The reliance on Iron Dome was no longer a subject of debate.

The Road to Protective Edge

For months, the ceasefire between Israel and Hamas held. The year 2013 was relatively calm, with only a few rocket attacks and limited IDF counterstrikes. That same year, the IDF prepared its new five-year defense plan. The plan was called "Oz" (strength in Hebrew) and reflected the lessons drawn by the military leaders from Pillar of Defense. The emphasis was not on scenarios of large-scale conventional wars involving ground forces but rather on short campaigns that rely on airpower, cyber warfare, and defense against ballistic missiles and rockets.[26] In the new security environment, Iron Dome was to be a central component of the IDF Strategy. This was a remarkable shift after years of resistance to the idea of a defensive system.

However, despite the initial hope that the 2012 ceasefire could hold, the status quo eroded. Since 2007, the blockade of Gaza had severely weakened the economy of the territory, and the Israeli government was now accused of not complying with the second provision of the ceasefire regarding the movement of people and goods. The financial collapse of Gaza was exacerbated by the developments inside Egypt: In the summer of 2013, President Morsi was toppled in a coup led by the Egyptian military. Their leader, Field Marshal Abdel Fattah

---

[26] Raphael S. Cohen, David E. Johnson, David E. Thaler, Brenna Allen, Elizabeth M. Bartels, James Cahill, Shira Efron, *From Cast Lead to Protective Edge: Lessons from Israel's Wars in Gaza* (Santa Monica, CA: RAND Corporation, 2017): 63.

Sisi, took power and made the fight against the Muslim Brotherhood and other Islamist groups his priority. Sisi ordered the closing of dozens of tunnels between the Sinai Peninsula and Gaza. This prevented weapon trafficking, but it also reduced the ability of Palestinians to access consumer goods and fuel. For Hamas, the Egyptian decision was another blow, as it cut off a source of revenue and military supplies.[27]

It also coincided with Hamas's troubles with its international supporters, Iran and Syria. Both countries had cultivated close relations with Hamas in the 1990s and the 2000s, but the partnership unraveled amid Syria's civil war that started in 2011. Facing protests against his regime, Bashar al-Assad refused to step down and ordered a crackdown. In 2012, as violence against the Syrian opposition increased, Khaled Meshaal, the then chairman of the Hamas Political Bureau based in Damascus, decided to close the office in the Syrian capital and leave the country.

As Hamas faced economic and diplomatic crises, it intensified its underground activities, expanding its network of tunnels below the Gaza Strip. Suspecting Hamas of using supplies originally imported for civilian buildings, the Israeli government decided to block the transfer of construction materials inside the Palestinian territory. As a result, seventeen thousand Palestinian workers reportedly lost their jobs in 2014.[28] Hamas's clandestine activities and the new Israeli restrictions fueled the climate of mutual suspicion.

The ceasefire negotiated in late 2012 seemed to erode day by day. At first, Hamas looked the other way when other groups like the PIJ resumed their rocket attacks on Israel. For instance, PIJ combatants fired on the Negev area on January 13, 2014, at the end of Ariel Sharon's funeral. Two weeks later, they repeated the attack on Ashkelon.[29] In the following months, rocket attacks steadily increased, and the status quo that prevailed after Operation Pillar of Defense unraveled.

On June 12, three Israeli teenagers were kidnapped while returning from their religious schools in settlements inside the West Bank. Although Hamas leaders denied any responsibility, the kidnappers were later identified as affiliates of the movement. This event triggered further violence between Israelis and Palestinians. The IDF arrested hundreds of Palestinians across the West Bank and launched a failed rescue operation, during which a dozen Palestinian

---

[27] Karin Laub, Ibrahim Barzak, "Hamas Displays Gaza Grip, as Protest Call Fails," Associated Press, November 11, 2014.

[28] Cohen, Johnson, Thaler, Allen, Bartels, Cahill, Efron, *From Cast Lead to Protective Edge*: 77.

[29] Yoav Zitun, "Two rockets fired from Gaza at the end of Ariel Sharon's funeral," *Yedioth Ahronoth*, January 13, 2014. https://www.ynetnews.com/articles/0,7340,L-4476387,00.html.

civilians were killed. Ultimately, the bodies of the Israeli teenagers were found near Hebron. Then, on the morning of July 2, Mohammed Abu Khdeir, a sixteen-year-old Palestinian boy from East Jerusalem, was kidnapped, beaten, and burned alive by Israelis. Soon after, Hamas entered the fray and, on July 7, fired eighty rockets at Israel. That same evening, Netanyahu convened the security cabinet and ordered the beginning of Operation Protective Edge.

In contrast to Pillar of Defense, Protective Edge involved an air campaign and a ground operation. The incursion of the Israeli army into Gaza, more specifically of two battalions of the Golani brigade (about 2,000 men), led to fierce battles not only on the ground, in the Shuja'iyya neighborhood of Gaza City, but also underground, inside the tunnels built by Hamas. The casualties of the operation were much higher than in the 2012 war: 2,133 Palestinians, according to the United Nations (including 1,489 civilians); sixty-six Israeli soldiers and six civilians were also killed.[30]

While Israeli troops fought inside Gaza City, Iron Dome was again pushed to the forefront of the defense of Israeli towns. According to Israeli data, some 4,500 rockets were fired from Gaza during the 2014 war. About 3,400 fell in unpopulated areas, 188 fell inside Gaza, Iron Dome intercepted 730, and 244 landed in urban areas inside Israel. However, Hamas and the PIJ claimed a much higher number (6,780) of rocket attacks.[31]

Overall, Iron Dome appeared successful again, but a close look at the rocket attacks during the 2014 war signaled an evolution in the tactics employed by Hamas. Rather than inflicting severe casualties, rocket attacks were meant to disrupt the Israeli economy, to undermine the morale of the population, and to saturate the Iron Dome batteries. To do so, Hamas relied on the quantity and the improved quality of its inventory. Salvos of dozens of rockets fired at the communities and the cities in the south forced the air defense unit to process multiple interceptions at the same time. Hamas also increased its use of mortar attacks on the closest areas near the Gaza border, knowing that Iron Dome interceptors would not be able to respond. Those cases roughly represented 75 percent of the attacks during the war.

Meanwhile, the improvements in the accuracy and range of the Palestinian inventory allowed Hamas to strike deep inside Israeli territory. Just like in 2012, Tel Aviv and Jerusalem came under attack. But this time, Haifa, located about

[30] Cohen, Johnson, Thaler, Allen, Bartels, Cahill, Efron, *From Cast Lead to Protective Edge*:125.
[31] Uzi Rubin, "Israel's Air and Missile Defense During the 2014 Gaza War," Mideast Security and Policy Studies Paper no. 111, Begin-Sadat Center for Strategic Studies, Ramat Gan, Israel, 2015: 15. https://besacenter.org/wp-content/uploads/2015/02/111eng_web.pdf.

150 kilometers north of Gaza, was also targeted. This forced the IDF to expand the coverage of Iron Dome: Batteries had to be moved around, and new ones had to be deployed. Even though Hamas had only a small number of rockets able to reach so far, it was now assumed that the whole Israeli territory had to be protected. By the time the war started, five batteries were operational. Four others were added through an emergency process. Over time, the IDF addressed critical issues such as improving the mobility of Iron Dome batteries and shortening the waiting time for their replenishment.

For decision-makers in Tel Aviv and Jerusalem, both Pillar of Defense and Protective Edge confirmed that Iron Dome not only functioned but also served the strategic interests of Israel. As rockets kept proliferating in the Middle East, Iron Dome was sending a strong message of reassurance to Israeli civilians. Still, Iron Dome's success in 2014 did not inspire the same enthusiasm as in 2012. If one could argue in 2012 that Iron Dome had prevented a ground operation in Gaza, this was not the case in 2014. Again, this called for a sobering assessment of the system's strategic value.

Questioning Iron Dome's Performance

By 2014, Iron Dome was praised by most of Israel's political establishment, yet there remained significant skepticism regarding its actual effectiveness. One of the strongest arguments against the system came from Theodore Postol, a retired physicist from MIT. Postol had already gained recognition two decades earlier for challenging the initial statement of the US government on the performance of the Patriot batteries during the Gulf War. Now a professor emeritus, Postol focused his attention on the latest missile defense system that was gaining traction. Writing in the middle of Operation Protective Edge, Postol argued in the *MIT Technology Review* that the performance of Iron Dome—reportedly near 90 percent by then—was, in reality, much lower. Similar to the Patriot controversy of the early 1990s, Postol accused the Israeli government of inflating the success rate of its air defense system. The physicist collected photographs and video footage publicly available of Iron Dome intercept attempts and concluded that "the intercept performance of Iron Dome appears to be probably 5 percent or less."[32]

---

[32] Theodore Postol, "An Explanation of the Evidence of Weaknesses in the Iron Dome Defense System," *MIT Technology Review*, July 15, 2014. https://www.technologyreview.com/2014/07/15/172055/an-explanation-of-the-evidence-of-weaknesses-in-the-iron-dome-defense-system/.

According to Postol, the limited number of Israeli casualties from rocket attacks was less a result of Iron Dome's performance and more due to two factors: the small size of the rockets fired by Hamas and the effective early warning system that allowed civilians to find shelter. Due to Postol's reputation, his assessment was widely quoted in the international media. When asked by news reporters, Postol went even further than in his writing, insisting that the intercept rate "might be as low as one percent, it's so low, it's very hard to tell."[33]

It caused a significant controversy among scientists. The first criticism addressed to Postol was the empirical evidence he was using, as his analysis was based on "grainy YouTube downloads of Iron Dome interceptions."[34] Uzi Rubin, one of the former engineers responsible for the Arrow program at MAFAT, overruled Postol's conclusion. Rubin asked, "Of the hundreds of rockets fired at the city of Ashdod to date, for example, only 12 hit residential areas. Are Hamas rockets that inaccurate? Why, after 60 or so heavier rockets have been fired at Tel Aviv, has not one impact been registered to date within city limits, save for the debris of visibly intercepted ones?"[35]

Postol was not the only one to question Iron Dome. Other critics of the system included missile engineer Richard M. Lloyd, who shared some of Postol's doubts but assessed that the interception rate was probably around "40 percent"— still a massive drop from the IDF claim.[36] The late Reuven Pedatzur, a former IDF pilot and journalist, was also a major critic of the system. As a military correspondent for the Israeli newspaper *Haaretz*, Pedatzur wrote numerous pieces that questioned the interception rate, citing Postol as evidence that the Israeli government was inflating the numbers.[37] Pedatzur also challenged the credibility of Iron Dome, in an attempt to revive the old debate between the program and the laser option that Amir Peretz and the Nagel Commission had dismissed in early 2007. In November 2012, a few days before the IDF launched Operation Pillar of Defense, Pedatzur wrote, "The time has come to stop being

[33] Hiawatha Bray, "Israel's Iron Dome System Doesn't Work, Says Missile Defense Critic," *Boston Globe*, October 13, 2023. https://www.bostonglobe.com/2023/10/13/business/israel-iron-dome-does-not-work/.

[34] Rubin, "Israel's Air and Missile Defense During the 2014 Gaza War."

[35] Rubin, "Israel's Air and Missile Defense During the 2014 Gaza War."

[36] William Broad, "Weapons Experts Raise Doubts About Israel's Antimissile System," *New York Times*, March 20, 2013. https://www.nytimes.com/2013/03/21/world/middleeast/israels-iron-dome-system-is-at-center-of-debate.html.

[37] Reuven Pedatzur, "How Many Rockets Has Iron Dom Really Intercepted," *Haaretz*, March 9, 2013. https://www.haaretz.com/opinion/2013-03-09/ty-article/.premium/reuven-pedatzur-does-iron-dome-really-work/0000017f-e3eb-df7c-a5ff-e3fb57020000.

afraid and demand that the Skyguard laser system and the Vulcan Phalanx artillery system be flown to Israel immediately."[38]

Yossi Arazi, a former colonel from the Israeli Air Force, also became a major critic of Iron Dome, explaining that the system was addressing only the issue of short-range rockets and did not even protect the closest cities at the border with Gaza. Arazi openly challenged the conclusions of the Nagel Commission and, just like Pedatzur, recommended that the Israeli government reconsider investing in Skyguard.[39]

Finally, another critic, Mordechai Shefer, often talked to the media to explain all the flaws of Iron Dome. He went further than either Postol or Pedatzur, arguing that Iron Dome was a mere hoax: "Iron Dome is a sound and light show that is intercepting only Israeli public opinion, and itself, of course. Actually, all the explosions you see in the sky are self-explosions. No Iron Dome missile has ever collided with a single rocket." Shefer also went against the assumption that the system was designed for the interceptor not to engage with rockets falling in unpopulated areas: "Open spaces are a myth invented in order to up Iron Dome's interception percentages. The rockets announced as intercepted by Iron Dome either never reach the ground or are virtual rockets invented and destroyed on the Iron Dome control computer."[40] Shefer's assertions were so abrasive that they resonated with conspiracy theories. Still, he was an engineer formerly employed by Rafael, who had won the Israel Defense Prize for his involvement in air-to-air missile technology.

Shefer's argument was also relayed by commentators without any scientific or military expertise, who used it to portray Iron Dome as a propaganda tool of the Israeli government, a tool that inflated the rocket threat in the first place to justify Israel's harsh response in Gaza. The American political scientist Norman Finkelstein disregarded the Israeli assertion regarding Hamas's rockets, describing those as "enhanced fireworks." He concluded that Iron Dome "probably didn't save many and perhaps not any lives."[41] For Rhys Machold, a senior lecturer in politics at the University of Glasgow, "Iron Dome is no superweapon—more like

[38] Reuven Pedatzur, "Iron Dome Is Not Enough," *Haaretz*, November 13, 2012. https://www.haaretz .com/opinion/2012-11-13/ty-article/.premium/reuven-pedatzur-add-iron-to-the-dome/0000017f -e812-dea7-adff-f9fbe5060000.

[39] Yossi Arazi, Gal Perel, "Integrating Technologies to Protect the Home Front Against Ballistic Threats and Cruise Missiles," *Military and Strategic Affairs* 5, no. 3 (December 2013): 89–110. https://www .inss.org.il/publication/integrating-technologies-to-protect-the-home-front-against-ballistic -threats-and-cruise-missiles/.

[40] "Defense Prize Winner Moti Shefer: Iron Dome Is a Bluff," *Globes*, July 13, 2014. https://en.globes .co.il/en/article-defense-prize-winner-shefer-iron-dome-is-a-bluff-1000954085.

[41] Norman Finkelstein, *Gaza: An Inquest Into Its Martyrdom* (Oakland: University of California Press, 2018): 209.

an extravagant monument to Israel's hollow promises of being an exceptional 'innovator' in 'saving life.'"[42]

To be sure, obtaining a reliable and accurate assessment of the interception rate claimed by the IDF is impossible. The data remains, unsurprisingly, classified, and most independent analysis is based on cross-referencing satellite imagery, video footage of bystanders, and official statements from the IDF or Palestinian groups.

The flow of criticism showed at first that the decisions made by Amir Peretz and Ehud Barak were still being contested within policy and media circles. The intensity of some of those attacks further indicated the degree of passion that surrounded the discussions (not something atypical in an Israeli environment). But in time, it faded away. Media outlets progressively stopped running critical stories about Iron Dome as the general public increasingly expressed enthusiasm for the system. Perhaps more importantly, the military establishment stopped worrying about Iron Dome and truly learned to love missile defense.

The Shift in the IDF's Perception of Iron Dome

After Pillars of Defense and Protective Edge, Iron Dome had passed—successfully—the test of the battlefield. Most decision-makers involved in those operations acknowledged the system's added value. Former Defense Minister Amir Peretz argued, "It allows people to make decisions without panic."[43] Similarly, Jacob Amidror, national security adviser during Operation Pillar of Defense, reflects,

> Iron Dome did not change the situation, but it made the life of decision-makers much easier because the pressure which comes together with the destruction inside Israel was not there. The success of the system to prevent 90 percent of the destruction made a difference; you don't feel that you are drifting slowly into a defensive way of thinking ... I don't have to make a decision now to go into Gaza because there is no problem inside Israel.[44]

42 Rhys Machold, "The Iron Dome System Is a Monument to Israel's Hubris," *Jacobin*, May 28, 2021. https://jacobin.com/2021/05/israel-military-iron-dome-system-high-tech-hubris-missile-defense -palestine.

43 Mitch Ginsburg, "Iron Dome—The Newly Beloved Missile Defense System That Nobody Wanted," *Times of Israel*, March 11, 2012. https://www.timesofisrael.com/iron-dome-the-newly-beloved -missile-defense-system-that-nobody-wanted/.

44 Interview with Jacob Amidror, former National Security Advisor (2011–13), Raananah, June 17, 2024.

Amidror's perspective reflected a growing consensus at the political level that Iron Dome had brought about new options. However, at the military level, the assessment was more complex. Avital Leibovich, a reserve lieutenant colonel formerly in charge of media relations within the IDF, argues, "Iron Dome did not change the decision-making process . . . look, I've been in many operational meetings in my life. Never once was the question heard, 'Wait, should we change the target because of Iron Dome?' It doesn't work like that." But Leibovich did recognize a change in the political–military interaction: "Let's say you have an operational plan, and that plan has four different stages. The government can say, 'You know what? You've done stages one and two, but we don't give the permission for three and four.' That's the difference between an all-out war and, you know, just part of it."[45]

In other words, Iron Dome effectively prevented minor skirmishes (i.e., attacks of a few rockets) from escalating into war. But when push comes to shove, it did not change the political logic of confrontation between Hamas and Israel. When either side deemed it necessary to launch a full-scale offensive on the other, Iron Dome could only mitigate the damage to the Israeli communities.

Still, the success of Iron Dome was such that by the second half of the 2010s, Israelis could think that they had found the solution to the rockets that Hamas had been firing at them. For a while, it seemed that the chances of war were diminishing, even though this notion contradicted the trends in rocket proliferation. In the north, Hezbollah was still active, and its armament had grown tremendously since the 2006 war. Not only did the Party of God increase the quantity of its rockets, but their quality also improved. By 2008, Israel's Defense Minister Ehud Barak estimated that Hezbollah had 40,000 rockets.[46]

A new threshold was reached when Hezbollah started acquiring ballistic missiles. It is believed that by 2010, the Syrian regime of Bashar al-Assad supplied Hezbollah with M-600 short-range ballistic missiles, a variant of the Iranian Fateh-110, which could carry a 500-kilo warhead and had a range of 210 kilometers.[47] According to weapon engineers, the inertial guidance system of the M-600 enabled the missile to strike within 460 meters of a target at maximum range. As a result, while Hezbollah was able to reach only northern Israeli urban

---

[45] Interview with Avital Leibovich, American-Jewish Committee, Director, Jerusalem office, July 8, 2024.

[46] Reuters, "Israel's Barak Warns of Growing Hezbollah Arsenal," September 11, 2008. https://www.reuters.com/article/economy/israels-barak-warns-of-growing-hezbollah-arsenal-idUSLA318892/.

[47] Charles Levinson, Jay Solomon, "Syria Gave Scuds to Hezbollah, U.S. Says," *The Wall Street Journal*, April 14, 2010. https://www.wsj.com/articles/SB10001424052702304604204575182290135333282.

centers during the 2006 war, it could now target deep inside Israel. The numbers kept growing. In 2012, the IDF estimated that Hezbollah controlled about 42,000 rockets plus 4,000 short- to midrange missiles.[48] In 2014, Moshe Ya'alon, Barak's successor at the Ministry of Defense, evaluated the arsenal of 100,000 rockets.

Hezbollah may have had greater capabilities to strike Israel, but its priorities were elsewhere. In 2011, Bashar al-Assad, the ruler of Syria, faced an uprising that quickly spiraled into a full-scale civil war. Syria had been a close partner of Hezbollah from the beginning, and the fall of Assad could complicate the movement's access to Iranian supplies. When the regime in Damascus faced a crucial scarcity of manpower due to desertion or defection in its ranks, Hezbollah and Iran's Islamic Revolutionary Guards shored it up by training pro-Assad militias, such as the Shabiha and Jeish al-Chaabi, to replace the conventional forces in several parts of the country. Over the following years, Hezbollah sent around five thousand combatants who fought against the Syrian rebels in protracted battles, such as in al-Qusair in 2013 and Yabrud in 2014.[49]

For the IDF, Hezbollah's deep involvement in Syria was a double-edged sword. It consumed most of the political and military capital of the Lebanese movement, and as a result, it left the Israel–Lebanon border quiet for a long time. In practice, Iron Dome, which had been developed with the memories of the 2006 war in the minds of its engineers, was seldom used against Hezbollah during that period. Based on an assessment prioritizing the Gaza threat, most batteries were deployed in the south.

At the same time, Hezbollah's presence in Syria created a new potential front with the IDF, particularly in the Golan area. Initially, Hezbollah and Iran engaged in a war of attrition against Syrian rebels there. However, they also transformed the Golan region into a new forward base to target Israel. Various reports claimed that tunnels and bunkers were being built to prepare for a future conflict with the Israeli military.[50] As a result, the IDF increased the frequency and the intensity of its air strikes inside Syria, killing Hezbollah commanders and even sometimes Iranian officers: In January 2015, the IDF killed in an air strike one Islamic Revolutionary Guard Corps (IRGC) general, Mohammed Allahdadi, who was scouting the Quneitra area in Syria in a convoy with

---

[48] Interviews conducted by the author with Israeli officers, in Tel Aviv, February 2012.

[49] Massaab Al Aloosy, "Hezbollah in Syria: An Insurgent's Ideology, Interest, and Survival," *Middle East Policy* 29, no. 1 (2022): 125–138. https://doi.org/10.1111/mepo.12608.

[50] Jean-Loup Samaan, "In Golan, a Battle Looms Between Iran and Israel," *The National*, October 26, 2015. https://www.thenationalnews.com/opinion/in-golan-a-battle-looms-between-iran-and-israel-1.32104.

Hezbollah fighters.[51] This shadow conflict between Israel, Hezbollah, and Iran inside Syria remained under the threshold of an all-out war. It did not impact the situation on the front line between Israel and Lebanon. Again, it seemed, for the time being, that everyone wanted to avoid a new Israel–Hezbollah war.

Iron Dome and the New Status Quo

Slowly, in the second half of the 2010s, Iron Dome contributed to the new Israeli approach toward the Gaza Strip and perhaps more broadly toward the Palestinian issue. By then, many Israelis, including on the left, had become disillusioned with the idea of a peace process. In 2013, 46 percent of Jewish Israelis believed in the two-state solution. This fell to 32 percent a decade later (before the October 7 attacks) and dropped to 19 percent after Hamas's attack.[52] The failure of several US-led diplomatic initiatives in the 1990s and 2000s, the Second Intifada, and the takeover of Gaza by Hamas all contributed to the marginalization of the peace process in Israeli politics. The Labor Party, whose leaders Yitzhak Rabin, Shimon Peres, and Ehud Barak were closely associated with the peace process, never recovered and saw its seats in the Knesset decline. In 1992, Rabin's party controlled the Knesset with 44 seats (out of 120). Thirty years later, it clung to four of them.

Benjamin Netanyahu, who had played a significant role in opposing Oslo from the beginning, was now winning elections one after another (2009, 2013, 2015, 2020). Netanyahu succeeded in popularizing two strong beliefs he held: First, the Palestinian issue was not the center of gravity of the Middle East; instead, Iran held that position (in his memoirs published in 2022, Netanyahu repeatedly derides what he calls the "Palestinian Centrality Theory"). Second, even if the international community insisted on solving the Israeli–Palestinian conflict, he had no reliable partner before him, given the fractious intra-Palestinian politics. Under such circumstances, the following years were characterized by the near disappearance of the Palestinian issue from the diplomatic agenda. The US administration of Barack Obama carefully refrained from investing its

[51] Jeremy Sharon, "Report: Six Iranians Killed in Israeli Strike in Syria, Including Revolutionary Guards General," *Jerusalem Post*, January 19, 2015. https://www.jpost.com/Arab-Israeli-Conflict/Report-Six-Iranians-killed-in-Israeli-strike-in-Syria-including-Revolutionary-Guards-general-388210.

[52] Sarah Austin, Jonathan Evan, "Israelis Have Grown More Skeptical of a Two-State Solution," Pew Research Center, September 26, 2023. https://www.pewresearch.org/short-reads/2023/09/26/israelis-have-grown-more-skeptical-of-a-two-state-solution/; Laura Silver, Maria Smerkovich, "Israeli Views of the Israel-Hamas War: Jewish Israelis and Arab Israelis See the War Differently," Pew Research Center, May 30, 2024. https://www.pewresearch.org/global/2024/05/30/israeli-views-of-the-israel-hamas-war/.

political capital as the Clinton presidency had done. Obama might have publicly expressed his support for the two-state solution, but in practice, his national security team did not pursue any significant initiatives.

Netanyahu's political instinct inspired his tactic of prolonging the status quo, but intellectuals in Israel also gave credence to his view. In 2017, the Israeli philosopher Micah Goodman published a best-selling book, *Catch-67: The Left, the Right, and the Legacy of the Six-Day War*. Goodman posited that the Israeli–Palestinian conflict was unsolvable and that neither side should invest time and resources in reaching a definitive solution. Instead, the goal should be to "convert it from a fatal situation into a chronic one." The book ended with the assertion that "the modern world calls on Israelis to lower their expectations of both war and peace, and to move from a politics that attempts to change reality toward a politics that finds a way to live with it instead."[53]

Goodman's idea that Israel should focus solely on conflict management rather than conflict resolution gained traction among politicians from the right and the center, with officials such as Naftali Bennett and Benny Gantz praising his analysis. Goodman's self-proclaimed pragmatism may have been an intellectual justification for preserving the status quo (which meant, de facto, the continuation of the Israeli occupation of Palestinian territories). Still, it captured the mindset of an era.

After the 2014 war, Israel's leadership deemed Gaza a secondary issue. Both the IDF and the political establishment were eager to focus on other priorities, in particular, the threat of Hezbollah in Lebanon and the Iranian nuclear program. The solution, by default, was the prolongation of Gaza's containment. Starting in 2007, it involved a naval blockade. In 2021, this effort was complemented by the building of the so-called Iron Wall, a high-tech 65-kilometer barrier surrounding Gaza and relying on fortifications, sensors, long-range cameras, and remote-control weapons to prevent attacks from Hamas. Engineers took three years to complete this "Iron Wall" at an estimated cost of $1.1 billion.[54]

Within that security architecture, Iron Dome provided a new defensive layer and a convenient political response. The success in the interception rate, either during the military operations of 2012 and 2014 or in the occasional skirmishes in the border area, allowed Israel's southern residents to live an everyday life.

---

[53] Micah Goodman, *Catch-67. The Left, the Right, and the Legacy of the Six-Day War* (New Haven, CT: Yale University Press, 2018): 168.

[54] Judah Ari Gross, "A Wall of Iron, Sensors and Concrete: IDF Completes Tunnel-Busting Gaza Barrier," *Times of Israel*, December 7, 2021. https://www.timesofisrael.com/a-wall-of-iron-sensors-and-concrete-idf-completes-tunnel-busting-gaza-barrier/.

Meanwhile, the IDF still prepared for reprisal raids against Hamas. In the new IDF Strategy, limited campaigns were meant to degrade the military capabilities of the terrorist group and reaffirm Israel's superiority when needed. These operations were designed to "restore deterrence." As Eran Lerman, former deputy national security adviser between 2009 and 2015, explains, "You [the IDF] don't want to conquer Gaza, not because you cannot do it, but because you can do it. You don't fear defeat, you fear victory: if you take Gaza, what do you do with it?"[55]

After a while, combining Iron Dome and other defensive measures became part of Benjamin Netanyahu's strategy vis-à-vis the Gaza issue. "It sits very well with him. His basic instinct, contrary to the image he likes to convey, is to be very cautious. He doesn't like to launch wars; he is not a risk taker," says a former adviser to the prime minister.

In the same vain, Eitan Shamir, a former analyst for the IDF Dado Center and professor of political science at Bar-Ilan University, explains, "Iron Dome allowed the Israeli government to kick the can down the road, to say 'ok, we have a problem in Gaza, but we have Iron Dome, it's fine, we shoot a little bit on the other side, we do a limited operation, we kill some of them and then there are some negotiations, and we can continue our lives.'"[56]

This translated into the emergence of a new term within Israeli military circles: "mowing the grass." Though the expression was never officially endorsed nor articulated in a military publication, it became a common saying among IDF officers to describe the standoff with Hamas in the 2010s. The metaphor of "mowing the grass" implied the idea that the IDF could not achieve total victory against enemies such as Hamas or Hezbollah. From now on, the goal was not to annihilate the opponent but to degrade its military power.[57] However, if war was constrained in its scope under those circumstances, it was also endless. It suggested that Pillar of Defense or Protective Edge may be just one round of a perpetual cycle of violence between both sides.

Hamas and the Politics of the Gaza Status Quo

At the political level, Netanyahu's reluctance to challenge the status quo—either through military intervention or through diplomatic initiative—coincided with

---

[55] Interview with Eran Lerman, former Deputy National Security Advisor, Jerusalem, June 20, 2024.

[56] Interview with Eitan Shamir, Director of the Begin Sadat Center, Bar-Ilan University, Tel Aviv, June 16, 2024.

[57] Efraim Inbar, Eitan Shamir, "Mowing the Grass': Israel's Strategy for Protracted Intractable Conflict," *Journal of Strategic Studies* 37, no. 1 (2014): 65–90. https://doi.org/10.1080/01402390.2013.830972.

a subtle shift in Hamas's politics. In the years after Operation Protective Edge, Hamas also seemed tempted to accept the status quo and shift from a violent organization with a revolutionary agenda to a political actor more focused on governing the Gaza Strip.

On the ground, this was followed by Hamas's greater emphasis on social and economic policies in Gaza, which was read as a shift toward pragmatism. This partly explains successive Israeli governments' acceptance of Qatar's financial aid to Hamas: The assumption was that the group would have more to lose and thus be less likely to resort to violence because it was responsible for governing the territory.

Qatar had cultivated ties with Hamas since the early 2000s. In 2006, after the Palestinian election, the Gulf state had already donated $50 million to the movement. The former Emir Hamad then traveled to Gaza in October 2012 (a month before Operation Pillar of Defense). Following the trip, Qatar established the Gaza Reconstruction Committee, headed by a special envoy, Mohammed al-Emadi, with an initial offer of $400 million in assistance over the next six years.[58] The entity was tasked with channeling investments into the Gaza Strip. The funding was intended to support the infrastructure, housing projects, and administration of the territory.

Publicly, the Israeli government talked suspiciously of the Qatari financial aid to the Gaza Strip, but on the ground, Qataris coordinated their efforts with the Israelis. In 2020, Yossi Cohen, the head of Mossad, wrote in a letter to the Emir of Qatar that was later leaked: "This aid has undoubtedly played a fundamental role in achieving the continued improvement of the humanitarian situation in the Gaza Strip and ensuring stability and security in the region."[59] Once again, the Israeli acceptance of Qatar's finances into the Gaza Strip stemmed from the belief that after 2014, Hamas had been restrained, that Iron Dome and other military technologies rendered its attempts to attack the country ineffective, and that similar to other extremist groups around the world, Hamas leaders would temper their behavior after taking control of Gaza and becoming accustomed to a lavish lifestyle.

The revision of Hamas's charter in 2017 was analyzed through this lens. The document stated, "Hamas advocates the liberation of all of Palestine but

---

[58] Steven Cook, "Hamas' Benefactors: A Network of Terror," Statement before the House Committee on Foreign Affairs, Subcommittees on the Middle East and North Africa and Terrorism, Nonproliferation, and Trade, US House of Representatives, 2nd Session, 113th Congress, September 9, 2014. https://www.govinfo.gov/app/details/CHRG-113hhrg89738.

[59] Jacob Magid, "Documents Show Israel Sought, Valued Qatari Aid for Gaza in Years Leading to Oct. 7," *Times of Israel*, March 22, 2024. https://www.timesofisrael.com/documents-show-israel-sought-valued-qatari-aid-for-gaza-in-years-leading-to-oct-7/.

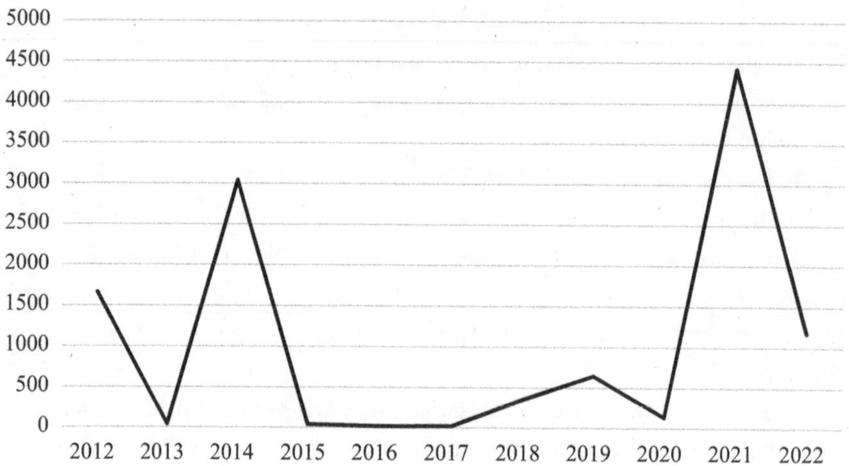

Chart 3.1 Number of rockets launched from the Gaza Strip (2012–22).

Source: Data compiled by the author. Data based on Jewish Virtual Library, "Rocket & Mortar Attacks Against Israel by Date." https://www.jewishvirtuallibrary.org/palestinian-rocket-and-mortar-attacks-against-israel.

is ready to support the state on 1967 borders, without recognizing Israel or ceding any rights."[60] The wording was ambiguous enough to leave room for interpretation of Hamas's motives and the possibility that it was tacitly accepting the status quo with Israel.

It is easy, in retrospect, especially after the tragic events of October 7, 2023, to dismiss this Israeli assessment as delusional. Netanyahu's gamble betrayed a flawed understanding of Palestinian aspirations and an excessive trust in the ability of the IDF to control their trajectory. But as the chart highlights, the period between Operation Protective Edge (2014) and Guardians of the Wall (2021) was marked by a significant decline in rocket attacks, which explains the sentiment of quiet and the belief that the conflict was, after all, manageable.

In reality, many, if not the majority, of the governments in the region accepted the new status quo because it allowed them to push the Palestinian issue to the background. It enabled the government of Benjamin Netanyahu to focus its international efforts on the prevention of an Iranian nuclear weapon and Israel's rapprochement with the Arab Gulf states. This led to the signing of the Abraham Accords with the United Arab Emirates (UAE) and Bahrain in September 2020,

---

[60] Quoted in: Patrick Wintour, "Hamas Presents New Charter Accepting a Palestine Based on 1967 Borders," *The Guardian*, May 1, 2017. https://www.theguardian.com/world/2017/may/01/hamas-new-charter-palestine-israel-1967-borders.

later joined by Morocco and Sudan. The normalization of ties between Israel and those Arab countries occurred without any concession of the sort promised by the Oslo peace process in the 1990s. In the UAE, official statements only referred to the idea that normalization had prevented an Israeli annexation of the West Bank and would "achieve a better future for generations to come."[61] The Emirati assertion was questionable, and it did not prevent, two years later, the same Benjamin Netanyahu from resuming the expansion of Israeli settlements in the West Bank. But what is remarkable is that the Gaza Strip was not part of the conversation even then. It was as if the issue had purely disappeared from diplomatic statements.

Sheikh Jarrah and the Fallacy of the Status Quo

In the spring of 2021, most international media focused on the COVID-19 pandemic and the campaign to vaccinate the world against the virus. But in the Middle East, an old scenario resurfaced. Tensions flared after a dozen Palestinian families were evicted from their properties in the East Jerusalem neighborhood of Sheikh Jarrah.[62] As the protests in Jerusalem escalated, Hamas resumed its fight against the IDF and launched rockets to display its support for the Palestinian population in the West Bank.

This might have been a way for Hamas to send a message to Mahmoud Abbas and the PA entrenched in Ramallah. It was a way to assert Hamas's leadership of the Palestinian cause beyond Gaza. But the consequence was the resumption of war in Gaza after seven years of relative quiet.

On May 11, Hamas and the PIJ fired 137 rockets at Tel Aviv in only five minutes, calling it "the largest ever barrage" at the time.[63] The day after, another 850 rockets landed across the Israeli territory. In total, the new war lasted only eleven days, but during that period, Hamas fired about 4,300 rockets at Israel. This meant that, on average, Hamas fired 390.9 rockets per day. In comparison, the daily frequency of attacks during previous wars was 28.69 in 2008, 188.25 in

[61] "UAE Foreign Minister's Speech at the Abraham Accords Signing Ceremony," *Times of Israel*, September 15, 2020. https://www.timesofisrael.com/full-text-uae-foreign-ministers-remarks-at-abraham-accords-signing-ceremony/.

[62] Rami Ayyub, Zainah El-Haroun, Stephen Farrell, "East Jerusalem's Sheikh Jarrah Becomes Emblem of Palestinian Struggle," Reuters, May 11, 2021. https://www.reuters.com/world/middle-east/east-jerusalems-sheikh-jarrah-becomes-emblem-palestinian-struggle-2021-05-10/.

[63] Joseph Trevithick, "Largest Rocket Barrage from Gaza Ever Hits Central Israel Amid Fears of An Imminent War," *The Drive*, May 11, 2021. https://www.thedrive.com/the-war-zone/40561/largest-rocket-barrage-from-gaza-ever-hits-central-israel-amid-fears-of-an-imminent-war.

2012, and 79.76 in 2014. Before that, in 2006, during the first "missile war" Israel fought against Hezbollah, the latter launched 3,970 rockets in thirty-three days, or a daily average of 120.[64] The accuracy of strikes also improved: It is estimated that 50 percent of rockets fired in 2021 aimed at populated areas, compared to 22 percent in 2012 and 18 percent in 2014.[65]

These salvos did not render Iron Dome irrelevant, but they underlined a pattern. Hamas not only had the resolve but also had the capabilities to use rockets as a means of exhaustion. The purpose was not to inflict one severe attack on Israel but to conduct many of them. For the defender, this meant that the longer the conflict lasted, the more difficult it became to protect its territory against these attacks.

But rockets were no longer the sole weapon used by Hamas. During the 2021 conflict, the latter also launched a few "kamikaze" drones dubbed "Shehab" (similar to the Iranian Ababil-2 drones) that were destroyed either by Iron Dome or, in one case at least, by an air-to-air missile fired from an Israeli F-16 fighter.[66]

The firepower displayed by Hamas—and to a lesser extent by the Palestinian Islamic—showed that despite the drastic blockade of Gaza enforced by the IDF for more than a decade, the Palestinian organizations had found ways to get external support for their inventories. In the later part of the 2010s, Hamas resumed military ties with both Iran and Lebanon's Hezbollah.[67]

This was the result of one individual: Yahya Sinwar. Born in the refugee camp of Khan Yunis in 1962, Sinwar joined Hamas as a teenager. Aged sixteen years old, Sinwar was caught by the IDF after abducting and murdering two Israeli soldiers. He then spent twenty-three years in Israeli prisons, where he learned Hebrew and read history books about Israel and Zionism. Released in 2011 in the context of a prisoner exchange, Sinwar steadily rose through the military ranks of the Palestinian movement.[68]

Soon, Sinwar got close to Qassem Soleimani, the then powerful Iranian commander of the Quds Force of the IRGC. Then, in 2017, when Sinwar replaced

[64] Michael J. Armstrong, "The Effectiveness of Rocket Attacks and Defenses in Israel," *Journal of Global Security Studies* 3, no. 2 (2018): 113–132. https://doi.org/10.1093/jogss/ogx028.

[65] Michael J. Armstrong, "Gaza's Enhanced Rocket Technology Challenges Israel's Defences," *The Conversation*, May 17, 2021. https://theconversation.com/gazas-enhanced-rocket-technology-challenges -israels-defences-160853.

[66] Thomas Harding, "How Iran's Latest Drones Tested Israel's Iron Dome Defence System," *The National*, May 21, 2021. https://www.thenationalnews.com/world/asia/how-iran-s-latest-drones -tested-israel-s-iron-dome-defence-system-1.1227133.

[67] International Institute for Strategic Studies, "Iran's Networks of Influence in the Middle East," IISS Strategic Dossier, 2019: 71.

[68] David Remnick, "Notes from Underground; The Life of Yahya Sinwar, the Leader of Hamas in Gaza," *The New Yorker*, August 3, 2024. https://www.newyorker.com/magazine/2024/08/12/yahya-sinwar -profile-hamas-gaza-war-israel.

Ismail Haniyeh as the leader of Hamas in the Gaza Strip, he decided to deepen cooperation with Tehran. Relations between the Iranian Islamic Republic and the Palestinian organization were at odds at the time. Hamas's political leaders, Ismail Haniyeh and Khaled Meshaal, had distanced themselves from Iran amid the Syrian civil war. Meshaal had led the political office of the movement from Damascus until 2012, when the crackdown on Islamists and Muslim Brotherhood–affiliated groups by the Assad regime forced Hamas to leave the country.

Five years later, the rift had been forgotten. Sinwar prioritized cooperation with Tehran to strengthen Hamas's military arsenal via the provision of Iranian missiles and unmanned aerial vehicles (UAVs). To that end, Sinwar relied on Saleh Arouri, a founding commander of the Izz al-Din al-Qassam Brigades, who handled the operational aspects of the rapprochement.[69] This came along with multiple visits of Arouri to Beirut and Tehran, followed by closer consultations between Hamas and Hezbollah, including the creation of a joint operations cell based in Beirut involving the two nonstate organizations alongside Iran's Islamic Revolutionary Guards.[70]

In retrospect, several trends signaled that the belief in a manageable status quo was shaky. Sinwar's rapprochement with Iran and Hezbollah was no secret. Hezbollah's Secretary General Hassan Nasrallah acknowledged in 2017 that his organization "transferred arms to Gaza."[71] This suggests that the working theory, which posited that Hamas was more interested in the governance of Gaza rather than fighting Israel, was overblown. The data on Hamas's firepower and its use throughout successive wars also shows that Iron Dome may have been successful, but it did not act as a deterrent. Despite those alarming signals, Operation Guardians of the Wall took place, the Israeli government declared victory, and the IDF provided data asserting its military success.

Conclusion

A year after the 2021 war, the IDF launched a brief preemptive operation codenamed Breaking Dawn in Gaza, but this time targeting the PIJ. It started when, five days earlier, Israel arrested Bassem al-Saadi, a senior leader of the PIJ in the West Bank. Following the arrest, tensions quickly rose as Israelis braced

---

[69] International Institute for Strategic Studies, "Iran's Networks of Influence in the Middle East": 74.

[70] Souhayb Jawhar, "Lebanon: New Strategic Base for Hamas," Carnegie Endowment for International Peace, October 17, 2022. https://carnegieendowment.org/sada/2022/10/lebanon-new-strategic -base-for-hamas?lang=en.

[71] Jack Khoury, Reuters, "Nasrallah Admits: Hezbollah Smuggled Advanced Arms Into Gaza," *Haaretz*, November 20, 2017. https://www.haaretz.com/middle-east-news/ nasrallah-admits-hezbollah-smuggled -advanced-arms-into- gaza-1.5467043.

for possible retaliation from the PIJ. Roads in southern Israel were closed, and soldiers were deployed to the border with Gaza. The government of Prime Minister Yair Lapid decided to launch air strikes before the threat from the PIJ materialized.

This small war in 2022 lasted only three days and ended in an overwhelming military victory for the IDF. In the first twenty-four hours of the conflict, the Israelis killed two of the most important military commanders of the PIJ (Tayseer Jabari and Khaled Mansour). Considering those killings as a "declaration of war," the PIJ retaliated by firing about eleven hundred rockets and mortars at Israel. These attacks failed as they landed in unpopulated areas or were intercepted by Iron Dome. The system again demonstrated impressive performance with a reported 97 percent interception rate.[72] The damages caused in Israel were minor, with only 70 people injured. The human toll was much more significant for the Palestinians: 46 were killed (including 17 children), and 360 were injured.[73] After three days, the PIJ's military structure was in such disarray that its dislocation surprised the IDF commanders, who had initially prepared for a one-week campaign. Overall, the PIJ suffered a significant blow in only three days, taking them "back decades," according to Israeli officials.[74]

For the Israelis, this short and almost forgotten operation fed the belief of a prevailing status quo with Hamas. The episode showed an apparent absence of solidarity between the PIJ and Hamas, which was again interpreted as evidence that the latter was not interested in a new war. This was the essential gamble behind the campaign: that the IDF could launch an offensive that singled out one Palestinian movement while betting that the other one would stay quiet. Hezbollah in Lebanon also stood by. Its Secretary General Hassan Nasrallah condemned the operation and praised the operations of the PIJ, but the Lebanese group refrained from joining the fray.[75]

At the time, Operation Breaking Dawn garnered many upbeat comments from military analysts in Israel, even though, just like previous wars, it did not fundamentally alter the equation of the Israeli–Palestinian conflict. At best, it weakened the PIJ. This was a tactical win, nothing more. Israeli governments

[72] Reuters, "Israel Says Iron Dome Shoots Down 97% of Gaza Rockets," August 7, 2022. https://www.reuters.com/world/middle-east/israel-says-iron-dome-shoots-down-97-gaza-rockets-2022-08-07/.

[73] "Fresh Israel-Palestinian Islamic Jihad Truce Prevents 'Full-Scale War,'" UN News, August 8, 2022. https://news.un.org/en/story/2022/08/1124212.

[74] Neri Zilber, "Israel and Gaza Keep Up Their Precarious Dance," *New Lines Magazine*, August 9, 2022. https://newlinesmag.com/reportage/israel-and-gaza-keep-up-their-precarious-dance/.

[75] *Al Mayadeen*, "Sayyed Nasrallah: The Resistance in Palestine Can Protect Its People and Focus on the Deterrence Equation" (in Arabic), August 7, 2022. https://www.almayadeen.net/news/politics المقاومة-في-فلسطين-تستطيع-حماية-شعبها-وتكر يس السيد-نصر-الل:-.

had stuck to the status quo with Gaza for so long that lingering issues, such as the dire humanitarian conditions for the two million Gazan population or the enduring rocket threat on southern Israel, did not call for a change.

In other words, the Israeli rationale for staying the course was not the result of a thorough assessment of its security environment. It originated from a political compromise: Without a diplomatic resolution, the immediate solution was to manage the conflict rather than resolve it. In this regard, Iron Dome served as an ideal tool for managing the conflict. Admittedly, the fact that Palestinian politics were frozen by the Fatah-Hamas standoff for over a decade further fueled the belief that the conflict was intractable.

Even at the military level, the logic of "mowing the grass" was starting to reach its limits. The firepower of organizations like Hamas and the PIJ was growing after each round. The proliferation of military technologies, such as UAVs and precision-guided kits, in the hands of nonstate actors added new concerns about Israel's ability to protect its territory. For all its impressive performance, Iron Dome had to be constantly upgraded—and by extension, it implied that Israel would increasingly rely on the United States for the replenishment of its capabilities. It was an Israeli success story, yet one that was increasingly cowritten in Jerusalem and Washington.

4

A New Pillar of US–Israel Defense Cooperation

On Wednesday, July 23, 2008, a forty-six-year-old US senator, who had just become the Democratic presidential nominee, walked through the streets of Sderot, a southern city in Israel near the Gaza Strip. Locals gathered behind the cortege, intrigued by this young and relatively unknown American politician who came to town. Braving the heat of the Mediterranean summer, Barack Obama visited the home of Pinhas and Aliza Amar, which had been recently hit by a Qassam rocket. He then moved to the police station in the city center. There, accompanied by Sderot's mayor Eli Moyal, Defense Minister Ehud Barak, and Foreign Minister Tzipi Livni, Obama addressed the public. Israelis gathered to listen to the new star of American politics, who, against all odds, had won the Democratic primaries against Hillary Clinton a month earlier, and who would later that year defeat the Republican candidate John McCain. Standing in front of a pile of shrapnel, the future American president soberly said, "I came to Sderot with a commitment to Israel's security (...) Israelis must not suffer a threat to their lives, to their schools … if missiles were falling where my two daughters sleep, I would do everything to stop that."[1]

More than fifteen years have passed since Barack Obama's short visit to Sderot, but locals still remember it vividly. Noam Bedein, a social activist, recalls, "I remember the day Obama came here, and as much criticism as people had on him, Obama was one of the few world leaders who always mentioned Sderot."[2]

Iron Dome was still in its early development at the time, but the coming of a presidential candidate to a small town hardly known beyond Israel and bordering the Gaza Strip was remarkable. Obama was not the first candidate to visit Sderot in 2008. In March, Senator John McCain also traveled to Sderot and followed the same itinerary, meeting with the Amar family and going to the police station.[3]

---

[1] Fadi Eyadat, "Obama Tours Sderot, and Says All the Right Things," *Haaretz*, July 24, 2008. https://www.haaretz.com/2008-07-24/ty-article/obama-tours-sderot-and-says-all-the-right-things/0000017f-dee5-d856-a37f-ffe5fa210000.

[2] Interview with Noam Bedein, Founder of the Sderot Media Center, Sderot, July 10, 2024.

[3] Michael Cooper, "McCain Visits Israeli Town That Rockets Often Strike," *New York Times*, March 20, 2008. https://www.nytimes.com/2008/03/20/us/politics/20mccain.html.

In the summer of 2008, the Israel–Palestine conflict was not the most significant issue on the agenda of the US presidential campaign. Americans, both in Washington and across the country, looked at the Middle East through the lens of the fight against terrorism and the Iraq War. After a three-week campaign in March 2003 that toppled the regime of Saddam Hussein, the Bush administration faced an unanticipated insurgency that dragged Iraq into a full-scale civil war. US troops were ill-prepared for that scenario, and by 2007, about four thousand American soldiers had been killed in action. That same year, the US military, under the leadership of General David Petraeus, changed course with the so-called surge that increased troops on the ground and mobilized support among local tribal leaders. At home, the United States was caught up in a subprime mortgage crisis that would soon escalate into a global recession when the next president took office. But amid all the other events, the detour of both Obama and McCain to Sderot, a few months before the election, foreshadowed the role missile defense, more specifically Iron Dome, was about to play in the US–Israel relationship.

Barack Obama and Israel

The story of Barack Obama's relations with Israel is often read through the lens of his later troubles with Benjamin Netanyahu. For nearly all of Obama's time in the Oval Office, Netanyahu was Israel's prime minister. From the outset, both leaders clashed over the expansion of Israeli settlements in the West Bank, which Obama publicly opposed during the first year of his presidency.

In June 2009, a few months into his presidency, President Obama addressed a large crowd at Cairo University. The speech was designed to restore ties between the United States and the Muslim world. This was one of a series of foreign policy speeches with lofty objectives that the new president delivered, and which led him to earn the Nobel Peace Prize in October of the same year (less than twelve months after he entered the Oval Office). The Cairo speech addressed the Israel–Palestine conflict, and though Obama carefully called on both sides to reach a compromise, he did not shy away from condemning Israel's occupation of Palestinian territories. "It is time for these settlements to stop," he asserted.[4] The tone of the new American president angered the close advisers of Benjamin

---

[4] White House, Office of the Press Secretary, "Remarks by the President at Cairo University," June 4, 2009. https://obamawhitehouse.archives.gov/the-press-office/remarks-president-cairo-university -6-04-09.

Netanyahu, who "scoffed at what they regarded as Obama's inexperience with the Middle East."[5] Right after the Cairo speech, the US administration demanded a ten-month freeze on the construction of new settlements in the West Bank. From the American standpoint, the freeze was meant to build an environment conducive to new negotiations with the Palestinians. But soon, the Netanyahu government greenlighted the expansion of housing units in East Jerusalem, an area most Israelis consider to be their sovereign territory. This was enough for Mahmoud Abbas, president of the Palestinian Authority, to dismiss the American call for new talks.

Relations between Obama and Netanyahu only grew more tense in the years that followed. In May 2011, during a visit by Benjamin Netanyahu to Washington, the Israeli prime minister sat with the American president for a press conference inside the Oval Office. The meeting came after Obama's announcement that new Israeli–Palestinian peace talks should be based on the 1967 lines in place before the Six-Day War. However, Netanyahu openly disagreed and asserted, "It's not going to happen." In his tone and posture, Netanyahu seemed as if he was "lecturing" the US president about the Israel–Palestine conflict.[6] The video shocked both Democrats and Republicans. On the left, it significantly affected the perspectives on US–Israel relations. For Matt Duss, a former adviser to Senator Bernie Sanders, "[t]hat was seen as deeply insulting by a lot of Democrats, particularly black Democrats (. . .) What they saw was a white man treating a black man, the President of the United States, as his inferior."[7] Meanwhile, on the right, former Bush officials like Dov Zakheim argued, "It was outrageous that Netanyahu could come to the White House and start lecturing my president. He may be a democrat but he's my president."[8]

Then, in the fall of that same year, during a G20 Summit in Cannes, a private conversation between Obama and French President Nicolas Sarkozy leaked to the press. Sarkozy told Obama, "I cannot bear Netanyahu; he's a liar." The American president replied, "You're fed up with him, but I have to deal with him even more often than you."[9]

5   Michael Oren, *Ally: My Journey Across the American-Israeli Divide* (New York: Random House, 2015): 66.

6   YouTube, @obamawhitehouse, "President Obama Meets with Prime Minister Netanyahu," May 20, 2011. https://www.youtube.com/watch?v=ShP8hQ431HU.

7   Interview with Matt Duss, former foreign policy advisor to Senator Bernie Sanders, March 7, 2024.

8   Interview with Dov Zakheim, former Under Secretary of Defense (Comptroller) and Chief Financial Officer of the Department of Defense (2001–4), March 12, 2024.

9   Reuters, "Sarkozy Tells Obama Netanyahu Is a 'Liar,'" November 9, 2011. https://www.reuters.com /article/world/sarkozy-tells-obama-netanyahu-is-a-liar-idUSTRE7A7201/.

Personal animosity peaked in 2015 when Netanyahu openly opposed the White House during the Iranian nuclear negotiations, delivering a speech at the US Congress convened by the Republican Speaker of the House of Representatives John Boehner. Netanyahu's address to American lawmakers was coordinated by the prime minister's advisers and the Republican Party without notifying the White House. Moreover, the unhidden objective of the speech was to prevent congressional support for the deal that the Democratic White House was then negotiating with Tehran. As a result, the Obama administration defined the Joint Comprehensive Plan of Action (otherwise known as the Iran nuclear deal) as a "nonbinding agreement" rather than a treaty requiring the Senate's approval.

However, notwithstanding the tensions that characterized the relationship between President Obama and Prime Minister Netanyahu, the former oversaw a considerable expansion of US–Israel defense cooperation. Indeed, it was the Obama administration that decided to finance Iron Dome (and later coproduce it). It was also the Obama administration that, in its final year in office, signed a memorandum of understanding (MoU) that not only secured US funding for Israel's missile defense programs but also pledged a total of $38 billion in military assistance over the next decade.[10] In that perspective, Iron Dome also reflects the evolution of the US–Israel partnership. It shows not only how Israel's missile defense enterprise has been closely dependent on American support but also how this cooperation transcended the occasional tensions between both governments and their respective domestic politics, at least until the Israel–Hamas war of May 2021 (Table 4.1).

An American Passion for Missile Defense

As discussed in the first chapter, the United States and Israel started cooperating in missile defense after President Reagan launched the Strategic Defense Initiative (SDI) in 1983. Israel's contribution to SDI was not particularly significant in and of itself. Moreover, American military planners hardly saw the added value of that cooperation in the context of the US–USSR competition, which remained the main driver of SDI.

On the Israeli side, as mentioned earlier, the Israel Defense Forces (IDF) leadership considered missile defense, and by extension, defense strategies, as

---

[10] Matt Spetalnick, "U.S., Israel Sign $38 Billion Military Aid Package," Reuters, September 15, 2016. https://www.reuters.com/article/world/us-israel-sign-38-billion-military-aid-package-idUSKCN11K2CI/.

Table 4.1 Defense Budget Appropriations for US–Israeli Missile Defense (Fiscal Years 2006–24)

Fiscal Year	Iron Dome	Arrow 2	Arrow 3	David's Sling	Total
2006		122.866		10.0	132.866
2007		117.494		20.4	137.894
2008		98.572	20.0	37.0	155.572
2009		74.342	30.0	72.895	177.237
2010		72.306	50.036	80.092	202.434
2011	205.000	66.427	58.966	84.722	415.115
2012	70.000	58.955	66.220	110.525	305.700
2013	194.000	40.800	74.700	137.500	447.000
2014	460.309	44.363	74.707	149.712	729.091
2015	350.972	56.201	74.707	137.934	619.814
2016	55.000	56.519	89.550	286.526	487.595
2017	62.000	67.331	204.893	266.511	600.735
2018	92.000	82.300	310.000	221.500	705.800
2019	70.000	163.000	80.000	187.000	500.000
2020	95.000	159.000	55.000	191.000	500.000
2021	73.000	173.000	77.000	177.000	500.000
2022	1108.000	173.000	62.000	157.000	1500.000
2023	80.000	173.000	80.000	167.000	500.000
2024	80.000	173.000	80.000	167.000	500.000
Total	2995.281	1972.476	1487.779	2661.317	9116.853

Source: Congressional Research Service & US Congress.
Note: Current US dollars in millions.

a perilous posture that could not, and should not, replace offense as the best way to deter Israel's neighbors. Yitzhak Rabin, then prime minister, shared many of those reservations on SDI. Still, he also considered that the program would enable the Israeli defense industry to participate in new R&D projects that could be beneficial. As a result, even though Israel was officially invited in April 1985 to join SDI, it took one year for the government in Jerusalem to accept it.[11] Most strikingly, the US government provided approximately 80 percent of the funding for the US–Israeli projects, while the remainder was covered by the Israeli defense industry, primarily Israel Aerospace Industries. The IDF may have been involved in the projects, but they made sure that they did not incur any financial commitments.[12]

Initially, Israeli companies were expected to contribute only to a few research and development projects, focusing on space and laser missile defense applications. However, by 1986, the Reagan administration offered to develop a system to counter long-range ballistic missiles named "Arrow." Historical scholarship underscores that, contrary to initial assumptions, this cooperation did not stem from Israeli aspirations. It worked the other way around. When the White House first announced SDI in 1983, both Democrats and Republicans in Congress were skeptical of its strategic logic and its technical feasibility. In that context, cooperation with Israel was seen as a way to build support in Washington: "The idea was that if Israel got involved, the Jewish groups would support the program," explained Dov Zakheim, who acted as Deputy Undersecretary of Defense for Planning and Resources at the time.[13]

The link between SDI and Israel enabled Reagan and his national security team to build a justification for the programs that was much more appealing to Congress than before. The decision to invite Israel into SDI was also shaped by tensions between both governments regarding another military procurement program: the Lavi fighter jet. Developed in the early 1980s, the Lavi was meant to be Israel's indigenous fourth-generation fighter jet. However, as its cost continued to soar, it faced mounting opposition. The Reagan administration, which financed about 90 percent of the program, pressured the Israelis to suspend the Lavi. Ultimately, the program was canceled in August 1987, leading some five thousand Israeli engineers to lose their jobs. According to one former US official, the United States "needed to help Israel build something."[14] That same year, the Reagan administration declared Israel a "major non-NATO ally," a status that provided Israel with greater access to the US defense industry.

[11] Or Rabinowitz, "'Arrow' Mythology Revisited: The Curious Case of the Reagan Administration, Israel and SDI Cooperation," *The International History Review* 43, no. 6 (2021): 1312–1329, 1312. https://doi.org/10.1080/07075332.2021.1883094.

[12] Interview with David Ivry, Former Chief Israel Air Force, Former Director General MoD, Ramat HaSharon, July 22, 2024.

[13] Quoted in: Rabinowitz, "'Arrow' Mythology Revisited": 1315.

[14] Duncan L. Clarke, "The Arrow Missile: The United States, Israel and Strategic Cooperation," *Middle East Journal* 48, no. 3 (Summer 1994): 475–491, 477. https://www.jstor.org/stable/4328717.

US funding enabled Israel to produce the first versions of the Arrow system in the 1990s. The fact that Arrow was primarily funded by the United States allowed the Israeli government to participate in the project. Still, it did not alter the military's mindset. Benny Peled, a retired major general from the IDF, claimed at the time, "The Arrow is simply not worth the cost."[15]

Israel was also provided with Patriot batteries amid Saddam Hussein's Scud attacks on the country during the Gulf War. Subsequently, the United States and Israel explored airborne laser technology through the Skyguard program, which was eventually superseded by Iron Dome (see Chapter 2). In addition to these investments, the US and Israeli militaries also conducted joint training exercises. In 2001, the Bush administration launched the Juniper Cobra exercise, bringing together air defense units from the IDF and the US Army to simulate a coordinated operation against incoming missiles. Over the following twenty-five years, Americans and Israelis organized additional joint drills, often with intriguing codenames such as "Austere Challenge," "Juniper Oak," and "Juniper Falcon." They allowed both militaries to share experiences and learn to work together—a process that arguably would prove precious when the United States supported Israel in defending itself against Iran's missile and drone attacks in 2024.

For successive US administrations, cooperation with Israel in the sector of missile defense served two primary purposes. It addressed the immediate needs of an ally facing a close and immediate threat from ballistic missiles. Therefore, it fulfilled a cornerstone of US Middle East policy—that is, to ensure Israel's security and preserve its "qualitative military edge" as required by US law. Second, in the longer term, bilateral cooperation was also conceived as a process that allowed US engineers and soldiers to test systems that could protect the US homeland.

However, this did not mean that the United States and Israel agreed on all aspects of missile defense. Ironically, when the Israelis, who had long voiced skepticism about missile defense, began developing their own truly indigenous system—namely, Iron Dome—it was the Americans who then expressed doubts.

The Evolution of American Views on Iron Dome

When Iron Dome was first launched, the Bush administration expressed skepticism and declined to provide funding. This was less driven by political motives than technical estimates. Missile defense was a significant pillar of Bush's

---

15 Clarke, "The Arrow Missile": 478.

foreign and defense policy. Bush's first Defense Secretary, Donald Rumsfeld, had chaired a commission established in 1998 by Congress to assess the threat of ballistic missiles. Rumsfeld and other members concluded that the proliferation of these systems to regional powers intensified due to easier access to foreign assistance and greater affordability. As a result, missile defense had to be reconsidered as a necessary means to prevent attacks against the United States.[16]

In June 2002, the US administration left the Anti-Ballistic Missile Treaty, which constrained its ability to invest in national missile defense systems. In the following years, the White House and both the State and Defense Departments made missile defense a key item of the strategic dialogue between Washington and its regional allies. In Europe, plans were made for the deployment of ground-based interceptors in Poland and an X-band radar in the Czech Republic. Meanwhile, in Asia, Japan procured sea-based and ground-based missile defense systems.

At the domestic level, following Ronald Reagan's presidency, missile defense became a topic of increasing polarization in Washington. National security practitioners may have focused on the feasibility of the various technologies developed within the SDI and their military applications. However, this quickly became a topic shrouded in partisan politics. Because of Reagan's passion for missile defense, Republicans kept supporting the programs, politically and then financially. Conversely, Democrats feared that missile defense was akin to a "pie in the sky, destabilizing and as trouble."[17]

Before getting elected president, Obama expressed the same type of skepticism for missile defense as his Democratic peers and promised to downgrade the program decided by the Bush administration. But then, when in office, Obama invested no less than $63.6 billion in maintaining or developing new systems.[18] Obama canceled the deployment of missile defense assets in Poland and the Czech Republic, which the Bush administration had initially planned. But at the same time, he pushed for a broader NATO involvement, known as the "Phased Adaptive Approach," which involved SM-3 and Aegis systems deployed in the Mediterranean and Eastern Europe. The Ballistic Missile Defense Review,

---

[16] Commission to Assess the Ballistic Missile Threat to the United States, "Executive Summary of the Report," 104th Congress, July 15, 1998. https://irp.fas.org/threat/bm-threat.htm; Craig Cerniello, "Rumsfeld Panel Releases Report on Missile Threat to U.S.," *Arms Control Today*, June 1998. https://www.armscontrol.org/act/1998-06/press-releases/rumsfeld-panel-releases-report-missile-threat-us.

[17] Andrew Futter, *Ballistic Missile Defence and US National Security Policy: Normalisation and Acceptance after the Cold War* (London: Routledge, 2013): 16.

[18] Missile Defense Advocacy Alliance, "President Obama's Legacy in Missile Defense," January 19, 2017. https://missiledefenseadvocacy.org/alert/president-obamas-legacy-in-missile-defense/.

released by his administration in 2010, presented a strategy for deploying more systems and strengthening coordination with partners worldwide.[19]

In the end, Obama was a "reluctant convert" to the American passion for missile defense.[20] He did not change his views on the topic due to ideological bias, but rather because of pragmatism and technological progress. In retrospect, Barack Obama may be considered the first US president to separate missile defense from partisan politics and make decisions primarily based on technical assessments.

In the first year of the Obama presidency, the topic of Iron Dome resurfaced. It is difficult to determine how much the US president was influenced by his visit to Sderot a year before. In later speeches, Obama often mentioned his experience there. For instance, speaking in Jerusalem in 2013, he recalled children "whom I met in Sderot, children the same age as my own daughters who went to bed at night fearful that a rocket would land in their bedroom simply because of who they are and where they live." Obama said, "That reality is why we've invested in the Iron Dome system to save countless lives—because those children deserve to sleep better at night."[21]

The idea that Obama played a personal role in changing US views on Iron Dome is confirmed by several practitioners in Washington. Daniel Shapiro, senior director for the Middle East at the National Security Council at the time, explains in our conversation:

> President Obama came back to this repeatedly . . . that the ability to understand the threat that he got by walking in the destroyed house, by meeting the injured boy, by being with the family, by seeing what those rockets looked like in the parking lot of the police station; it really crystallized for him what this threat was and what he saw as our obligations to Israel's defense.[22]

A high-level manager at the American Israel Public Affairs Committee also recalls that "much American interest was generated by then–Senator Obama's visit to an Iron Dome battery when he was running for president."[23]

---

[19] US Department of Defense, "Ballistic Missilie Defense Review Report," February 2010. https://apps .dtic.mil/sti/pdfs/ADA514210.pdf.

[20] Futter, *Ballistic Missile Defence and US National Security Policy*: 134.

[21] White House, Office of the Press Secretary, "Remarks of President Barack Obama to the People of Israel," March 21, 2013. https://obamawhitehouse.archives.gov/the-press-office/2013/03/21 /remarks-president-barack-obama-people-israel.

[22] Interview with Daniel Shapiro, Washington, DC, February 20, 2025.

[23] Email correspondence with an anonymous source at the American Israel Public Affairs Committee, March 26, 2024.

In 2013, Barack Obama made his first presidential trip to Israel. Amir Peretz, the former Israeli defense minister who had played an instrumental role in launching Iron Dome in 2007, remembers that day, "When Obama came to Israel, the IDF made a big show for him, they brought Iron Dome to the airport for him to see. I was there, next to Bibi (Netanyahu), who introduced me to Obama as 'the man who made it possible.' "[24] Immediately following the national anthem, the presentation of an Iron Dome battery constituted the second item on the tight schedule of Obama's visit to Israel.[25]

To understand the evolution of US support for Iron Dome during that period, it is also necessary to consider the actors and processes of US security assistance to foreign countries. While the US president remains the essential player who shapes the priorities for the United States, executing his objectives depends on several executive and legislative entities. The Department of State is the government agency responsible for managing the security assistance budget through its Bureau of Political-Military Affairs. The Department of Defense also gets involved because the funding for missile defense projects comes from its Missile Defense Agency. Additionally, the Office of the Secretary of Defense provides the policy guidance.

The two institutions of Congress—the Senate and the House of Representatives—also play a crucial role in authorizing or amending the funding. According to the Constitution, Congress has the "power of the purse"—that is, the power to control government spending. This means that approval from the legislative branch conditions all foreign policy projects involving federal funding from the executive branch. Military aid to Israel is no exception to this principle. The exercise of Congress's authority in federal financing follows a two-step process: first, an "authorization" that describes policies to be implemented by federal agencies such as the Department of Defense, and the budget estimated to execute them; second, an "appropriation" that allows that federal agency to spend a specific amount for the policy initiated.[26] This two-step process explains the frequent discrepancies between the initial amounts specified in the authorizations and the final numbers in the appropriations. Congress can reject the administration's request and even go so far as to force a federal government shutdown. However, it can also add missions to a federal agency or increase its provision.

---

[24] Interview with Amir Peretz, Lod, July 29, 2024.
[25] White House, "The President's Trip to the Middle East," https://obamawhitehouse.archives.gov /photos-and-video/photogallery/presidents-trip-israel-west-bank-and-jordan.
[26] James Saturno, "Authorizations and the Appropriations Process," Congressional Research Service, May 16, 2023. https://crsreports.congress.gov/product/pdf/R/R46497.

Specialized entities such as the House Foreign Affairs Committee, the Senate Foreign Relations Committee, and the Appropriations Committees oversee the budget of US assistance to Israel. Members of Congress may pursue their objectives, which may be locally oriented—to secure the enduring support of their constituents—or nationally motivated—to align with their party's line. Between the initial request from the executive branch and the final amount authorized, or appropriated, by Congress, the sum of a bill can change. Dana Stroul, a former senior professional staff member on the Senate Foreign Relations Committee (2013–18), explains, "There have been frequent cases, not just specifically to Israel, but often with Israel, where whatever the executive branch negotiates, Congress will come and appropriate or authorize on top of that amount."[27]

In addition to the government actors, US defense cooperation with Israel is also shaped by the activities of various interest groups. The largest, the American Israel Public Affairs Committee (AIPAC), was established in 1954, but its influence and visibility grew significantly in the 1980s. Other smaller groups include J Street and the American Jewish Committee (AJC). One source at AIPAC explains, "When we lobby on an issue, we generally request that Congress allocate a certain level of funding, and we speak about the issue with congressional offices."[28] Specifically, AIPAC, J Street, or AJC can write policy briefs and convene conferences to support their respective agendas. For instance, in June 2021, AIPAC released a two-page "memo" titled "Iron Dome saves Israeli and Palestinian Lives." The document included fourteen bullet points explaining how Iron Dome worked, why it was successful, and how US financial support helped its deployment. Most importantly, it ended with the statement, "Congress should fully support efforts to replenish Israel's Iron Dome missile defense system and continue to support full funding for US-Israel missile defense cooperation under the 2016 MOU."[29]

As political action committees, AIPAC or J Street can raise and spend money for elections. According to AIPAC documents, the organization spent $53 million on congressional elections in 2024 ($31.8 million on Democratic candidates and $21 million on Republican candidates, respectively) and officially endorsed 361 candidates. In comparison, J Street only spent $2 million during the same election

[27] Interview with Dana Stroul, former deputy assistant secretary of defense for the Middle East (2021–3), March 12, 2024.

[28] Email correspondence with anonymous source, March 26, 2024.

[29] American Israel Public Affairs Committee, "Iron Dome Saves Israeli and Palestinian Lives," AIPAC Memo, June 3, 2021. https://aipacorg.app.box.com/s/of63emg1ugo72uy8tlyt1lp31g8hcjt8.

cycle.[30] Significant divergences exist between the different pro-Israel interest groups, but Iron Dome, or more broadly, missile defense, is not one of them. J Street, which is seen as more critical of Israel's policies than AIPAC, includes in its endorsement criteria for candidates "an ironclad commitment to Israel's security . . . including support for the Iron Dome missile defense system."[31]

The topic of pro-Israel lobbies in the United States is beyond the scope of this book. It has been the object of many studies and has often triggered contentious views.[32] However, on the topic of missile defense, and Iron Dome in particular, there is no evidence, either through written documents or interviews, of a specific influence from AIPAC or any other interest group. They undoubtedly contributed to shaping the public debate about Israel's rocket challenge and the value of Iron Dome. It is possible to find some similarities between the talking points that AIPAC prepared and the arguments used during congressional debates. However, many of these ideas also circulated in publications from think tanks and at events that were convened in Washington. As a result, the shift in US policy toward Iron Dome during the 2007–9 period and the subsequent support for the system have less to do with the external intervention from a group like AIPAC than with the evolving assessment of the project's viability within the Defense Department and the US government.

Inside the Pentagon, the topic of US support for Iron Dome was then handled by Colin Kahl, the successor to Mary Beth Long, as deputy assistant secretary of defense for the Middle East. In the spring of 2009, soon after the policy team of Obama's Defense Department was confirmed by Congress, Kahl and his boss, Michelle Flournoy, the undersecretary of defense for policy, raised the issue with then–Secretary of Defense Robert Gates. After his election, Obama had asked Robert Gates, a former cabinet member of the Bush administration, to remain in charge of the Defense Department to ensure that the political transition in Washington did not affect the ongoing wars in Iraq and Afghanistan. Gates' relations with the Israeli government were complicated. According to Israel's then–Ambassador to the United States Michael Oren, Gates was "enormously fond of Ehud Barak," but he looked at Benjamin Netanyahu as "ungrateful for US military aid."[33] Gates expressed solidarity for Israel, but he did not hide

[30] American Israel Public Affairs Committee, "2024 Congressional Report," November 18, 2024. https://aipacorg.app.box.com/s/z2oa78jwjmr2ytmon22xumvxk2d4uphf.

[31] J-Street, "Our Endorsement Criteria and Process: Supporting Pro-Israel, Pro-Peace, Pro-Democracy Leadership." https://jstreetpac.org/jstreetpac-endorsement-criteria-and-process/.

[32] Stephen Walt, John Mearsheimer, *The Israel Lobby and U.S. Foreign Policy* (New York: Farrar, Straus and Giroux, 2007); see also Michael J. Koplow, "Value Judgment: Why Do Americans Support Israel?," *Security Studies* 20, no. 2 (2011): 266–302. https://doi.org/10.1080/09636412.2011.572690.

[33] Michael Oren, *Ally: My Journey Across the American-Israeli Divide* (New York: Random House, 2015): 181.

his disagreements with the country's trajectory: "Israel's strategic situation is worsening, its own actions contributing to its isolation," he wrote in his autobiography *Duty*.[34]

According to several accounts, Gates did not recall the initial rejection of US support for Iron Dome two years earlier.[35] After consultations with Flournoy and Kahl, Gates decided to reinitiate the process and send a technical team to review the program in Israel in the fall of 2009. This time, the assessment was positive: The latest tests of Iron Dome were promising. Kahl and his team then worked on an estimate of what the Defense Department could provide in terms of aid. They then submitted a provisional number of $205 million.[36] The request was first officially mentioned in the National Defense Authorization Act for Fiscal Year 2011.[37]

The Steady Rise of US Support for Iron Dome

Despite the initial package approved by the Obama administration, Israel's need for financial support for Iron Dome resurfaced quickly. As discussed in the previous chapter, Iron Dome became "battle-proven" in 2011 after intercepting rockets fired from Gaza. The technical success demanded more batteries to be deployed. In February 2011, as President Obama steadily prepared for his reelection campaign, Defense Secretary Robert Gates resigned. He was replaced by Leon Panetta, a former head of the CIA and the director of the Office of Management and Budget during the presidency of Bill Clinton. As Obama eyed his reelection, he gave Panetta one primary mission: to reduce the budget of the Defense Department. After a decade of the war on terror involving two major operations in Iraq and Afghanistan, Obama was concerned that American voters could no longer bear the burden that had become the budget of their armed forces. A year before, Obama had announced that all US troops would leave Iraq by the end of 2011. Then, in May of that year, a team of Navy SEALs killed Osama bin Laden in an operation inside Pakistan. The politics within the White House called for financial restraint, and this was now affecting US–Israel relations.

[34] Robert Gates, *Duty: Memoirs of a Secretary at War* (New York: Alfred Knopf, 2014): 398.

[35] Yonah Jeremy Bob, "Getting the US to Fund Iron Dome Against All Odds," *Jerusalem Post*, October 24, 2017. https://www.jpost.com/israel-news/senior-defense-official-tells-jpost-how-he-convinced -white-house-to-fund-iron-dome-508254#google_vignette.

[36] Doron Levin, "Barack Obama and the Legacy of Iron Dome," *The Detroit Jewish News*, June 2, 2021. https://www.thejewishnews.com/opinion/guest-column-barack-obama-and-the-legacy-of-iron -dome/article_85eade1b-6a96-5737-98de-ad06755b5899.html.

[37] US Government Information Office, "Ike Skelton National Defense Authorization Act for Fiscal Year 2011," January 7, 2011: 4173. https://www.congress.gov/111/plaws/publ383/PLAW-111publ383.pdf.

Two months after entering the Pentagon, Leon Panetta met with his Israeli counterpart Ehud Barak, who "calmly asked for $700 million in American defense funding for an expansion" of Iron Dome. Barak argued, in Panetta's recollection, "that might be enough to allow Israel to absorb Hamas's aggression without having to invade to clean out the rocket infrastructure."[38] The Israeli request was extremely high, even by US standards. "We had just announced that we were cutting defense spending by $487 billion in ten years. To turn around and request $700 million more for additional batteries was not going to be easy," wrote Panetta.[39]

Around that time, the Israeli Ambassador to the United States Michael Oren penned an opinion piece for *Politico*, the digital newspaper closely read by the foreign policy community in Washington. The article "Invest in Iron Dome for Peace" made the case for increased funding to aim for "an additional 10 batteries." Oren's talking points were well crafted: According to the ambassador, US–Israel cooperation on Iron Dome "represents a win-win accomplishment" that "can also help defend U.S. facilities and interests around the world." Moreover, Oren argued, "An investment in the Iron Dome system is an investment in diplomacy—helping to create the conditions conducive to peace."[40]

As soon as the Obama administration increased its support for Iron Dome, it raised a classic bureaucratic issue: Where should the money come from? US military aid to Israel is provided through grants under the Foreign Military Financing (FMF) program operated by the Department of State. Each year, Congress reviews and approves the amount. However, support for Iron Dome came on top of that annual package and from a different budgetary line at the Defense Department.

"From a congressional angle, that amount was not capped, so the US and Israel could expand missile defense cooperation because there was a larger amount of money to play around with than there was on the military aid, which was sort of set in stone per actual agreements," explains a congressional staff member who remained anonymous. Daniel Shapiro, NSC director for the Middle East before being appointed US ambassador to Israel by Obama, also recalls that in the first years of the Obama presidency, "the typical pattern was that the Administration would call for a certain ballistic missile defense funding level from Congress

---

38　Leon Panetta, Jim Newton, *Worthy Fights: A Memoir of Leadership in War and Peace* (New York: Penguin Press, 2014): 422.

39　Panetta, Newton, *Worthy Fights*: 423.

40　Michael Oren, "Invest in Iron Dome for Peace," *Politico*, March 18, 2012. https://www.politico.com /story/2012/03/invest-in-iron-dome-for-peace-074149.

that was less than the Israeli request, knowing that Congress would respond by increasing the number, sometimes by a factor of two or three."[41] Still, the money allocated to Israel's missile defense had to come from somewhere. In practice, the Defense Department tapped into the budget of its Missile Defense Agency. But, as Andrew Exum, former deputy assistant secretary of defense for the Middle East (2015–16), adds, "There was no additional money, so that would be like directly taking away from the stuff we wanted to use to counter missile threats elsewhere, in the Persian Gulf or the Korean Peninsula so we wanted to put an end to this."[42] This became an issue to be addressed in the upcoming negotiations of the new US–Israel MoU.

Iron Dome and a New Memorandum of Understanding

In November 2012, Barack Obama won his reelection against the Republican candidate Mitt Romney. Obama's pick for his new secretary of defense was Chuck Hagel. An army veteran and a former senator from Nebraska, Hagel quickly became the center of a controversy for an interview he gave to a researcher in 2006, during which he stated, "The Jewish lobby intimidates a lot of people (. . .) I'm not an Israeli senator. I'm a United States senator."[43] The Republican opposition used the statement to criticize the appointment, and the confirmation process with the Senate proved contentious.

Hagel's foreign policy views were not a significant departure from those of Obama. According to one former close adviser to Hagel, the latter had known Obama well from his time in the Senate. They had traveled together to Israel on congressional trips. Later on, Hagel embraced the Obama approach—that is, to support Israel's defense while urging for a better treatment of Palestinians in the occupied territories. After Robert Gates and Leon Panetta, Hagel became the third secretary of defense to praise the performance of Iron Dome—"it has saved countless Israeli lives," he wrote to Senate Majority Leader Harry Reid in

[41] Daniel Shapiro, "A Review of the Negotiations on the 2016 US-Israel MOU on Military Assistance," in: Sasson Hadad, Tomer Fadlon, Shmuel Even (eds.), *Israel's Defense Industry and US Security Aid* (Tel Aviv: Institute for National Security Studies, 2018): 65.

[42] Interview with Andrew Exum, former deputy assistant secretary of defense for the Middle East (2015–17), March 14, 2024.

[43] Jon Swaine, "Chuck Hagel to Face Questions Over Israel Views Ahead of Defence Secretary Nomination," *The Telegraph*, January 6, 2013. https://www.telegraph.co.uk/news/worldnews /northamerica/usa/9784034/Chuck-Hagel-to-face-questions-over-Israel-views-ahead-of-defence -secretary-nomination.html.

2014—and he asked Congress to increase the amount of US funding.[44] Still, the confirmation of Hagel's nomination proved difficult. Only weeks into the second term of President Obama, it was a reminder that relations with Israel, or more precisely the optics of that relationship in Washington, were now at the center of the power plays between the White House and the Republican opposition.

In the following months, the White House and the Department of Defense announced they had to revise the framework of US military support for Israel and develop a new MoU. This soon became a key milestone in consolidating US support for Iron Dome. Since 1999, MoUs have become official documents defining the level of US support for Israel over the next ten years. They are not legally binding and do not require Senate ratification. The previous MoU had been written by the Bush administration and signed in 2007. Iron Dome did not exist then, and in the following years, the Obama administration used exceptional measures to provide funding for the Israeli system. Before the 2016 MoU, the US government had provided at least $1.3 billion to finance Iron Dome. It was on an ad hoc basis, and the duration of the arrangement was unclear. Additional bills could range from $350 million to over $700 million. By then, it was apparent that support for Israel's missile defense systems had become a permanent element of the US package. Following President Obama's visit to Israel in March 2013, both countries assembled teams to work on the content of the new MoU. The process was led by the White House Middle East Coordinator Phil Gordon and the Israeli Deputy National Security Adviser Jacob Nagel—the same Nagel who had presided over the commission mandated by Amir Peretz and that had selected Iron Dome in 2007.

On the US side, the details of the bilateral agreement were mainly prepared by three officials and their teams: Yael Lempert, senior director for the Middle East at the National Security Council; Daniel Shapiro, then US ambassador to Israel; and Andrew Exum, deputy assistant secretary of defense for the Middle East at the US Department of Defense. The troubled relationship between Obama and Netanyahu and the regional events shaped the MoU negotiations. As the process started, Andrew Exum recalls the political environment:

> The directions we got from the National Security Advisor or the Secretary of Defense were obvious: we're going to have disagreements with the Israelis, but the thing we're not going to compromise on is defense and security cooperation

44 Roxana Tiron, "Israel's Iron Dome Defense in Line for Tripled U.S. Aid," *Bloomberg*, July 23, 2014. https://www.bloomberg.com/news/articles/2014-07-23/israel-s-iron-dome-defense-in-line-for -tripled-u-s-aid.

with Israel, we're not going to allow the Republicans or Netanyahu to say that we're leaving Israel out to dry from a defense and security perspective.[45]

The beginning of the talks coincided with the US involvement in the Iran nuclear deal, which would later be known as the Joint Comprehensive Plan of Action (JCPOA). Only three months after Obama visited Israel in 2013, Hassan Rouhani was elected president of Iran. A former nuclear negotiator, Rouhani was considered a "moderate" in the Iranian political system. The Obama administration quickly saw Rouhani's rise to power as an opportunity to resume the nuclear talks. As the White House focused on the deal with Tehran, discussions on the MoU with Israel were put on hold.[46] The Israelis felt profound frustration regarding the priorities set by the White House. Netanyahu made no secret of his distrust for Hassan Rouhani, whom he had portrayed as a "wolf in sheep's clothing."[47] One former high-level official at the Defense Department recalls Ashton Carter, the then–secretary of defense, during his visit to Israel just before the JCPOA was signed.

When we met Netanyahu, Carter tried to stay on track, he said we are prepared to talk about your security needs, but Netanyahu was having none of this. At one point, he told Carter he didn't even want to talk about the MoU because, according to him, it would almost be an admission on his part that the JCPOA was gonna happen.

Tellingly, in his memoirs, Ashton Carter writes of that trip as a visit "fraught with political peril" and does not mention the MoU at all.[48]

At last, the talks on the MoU resumed. Despite the fierce disagreements between Netanyahu and Obama over the JCPOA, Israel still needed to secure a new MoU. The previous one was set to expire by 2018, which meant that, in the absence of an agreement with the Obama team, the Israelis would have to wait for the outcome of the next election, pitting Hillary Clinton against Donald Trump. The American negotiators felt that this uncertainty forced the Israeli side to be more pragmatic. "They had no idea what was gonna happen in the next administration, so they wanted to do a deal in the last year of the Obama

[45] Interview with Andrew Exum, Washington, DC, March 14, 2024.

[46] Shapiro, "A Review of the Negotiations on the 2016 US-Israel MOU on Military Assistance": 62.

[47] Tom Watkins, "Netanyahu: Iranian President Is 'Wolf in Sheep's Clothing,'" CNN, October 2, 2013. https://edition.cnn.com/2013/10/01/world/meast/israel-netanyahu-iran/index.html.

[48] Ash Carter, *Inside the Five-Sided Box: Lessons from a Lifetime of Leadership in the Pentagon* (New York: Random House, 2019): 298.

administration," said Andrew Exum. The then–US Ambassador to Israel Dan Shapiro wrote, "By not completing the MoU in 2016, the delay would be at least a year, while a new administration appointed its senior officials and negotiations were relaunched from the beginning. That time pressure became an important factor in the Israeli decision."[49]

US support for Iron Dome was only one of several significant items on the agenda that included more broadly funding of other missile defense systems, the question of Israel using US funding to purchase fuel or to procure Israeli-made military items rather than American ones.

The required funding was a delicate subject of the negotiations around the MoU. Andrew Exum, the Pentagon negotiator, remembers, "We demanded a lot of transparency from the Israelis about their own defense requirements; it was important for us to have an understanding of how much they planned on spending because we didn't want to ramp up our spending if Israel's defense spending was going to be flatlining or declining."

The final document stipulated that the total value of US military assistance for the next ten years (up to Fiscal Year 2028) would amount to $38 billion, or $3.8 billion per year. Regarding Iron Dome and missile defense programs, the US team proposed a "flat rate" of $500 million per year. The amount was based on past experiences: "I literally just took an average of the previous years, and 500 million sounded reasonable for what we could guarantee," explains Exum. The fact sheet released by the White House at the time emphasized that "[t]he $500 million in annual missile defense funding under the MOU exceeds the average level of non-emergency support the United States has provided to Israel for missile defense over the last five years."[50]

The decision to put a number on US support for Israel's missile defense was partly made to prevent a fight between the administration and Congress. In the 2014 midterm elections, Republicans retained control of the House of Representatives and won control of the Senate. Increasingly, relations with Israel had become a partisan issue. Republican lawmakers criticized the Obama administration for reluctantly supporting Israel's security, and Prime Minister Netanyahu openly used the tensions when he addressed Congress in 2015 to oppose the nuclear deal prepared by the Obama administration with Iran. Congress could also force the executive branch to increase security assistance if

---

[49] Shapiro, "A Review of the Negotiations on the 2016 US-Israel MOU on Military Assistance": 64.
[50] White House, Office of the Press Secretary, "Fact Sheet: Memorandum of Understanding Reached with Israel," September 14, 2016. https://obamawhitehouse.archives.gov/the-press -office/2016/09/14/fact-sheet-memorandum-understanding-reached-israel.

necessary. Daniel Shapiro remembers, "It created this sort of ping pong" between the executive branch and Congress. It led the negotiators to assess "it was to the benefit of both sides to have a stable, predictable number all the way across the ten years, so that we didn't get into this constant back and forth."[51]

Under these circumstances, guaranteeing a $500 million package for missile defense was meant to prevent new debates about last-minute bills that would need to be reviewed by Congress. Andrew Exum sums it up: "It was a gentleman's agreement: we're going to do something we've never done, we're going to guarantee you missile defense spending as part of this agreement (. . .) and in exchange, you won't go to Congress or tell senators that you're not getting support."[52]

However, this part of the deal excluded "exceptional circumstances such as in the event of a major armed conflict involving Israel."[53] There was no ceiling on the amount of funding that could be submitted in that scenario. As underlined by one congressional staffer involved, "emergency packages aren't delineated by any type of agreement, so it could be, in theory, limitless. But it still has to be approved by Congress."

Overall, the signing of the MoU acted as a means of reassurance. Despite the much-publicized tensions between Obama and Netanyahu, despite the Iran nuclear deal that Israel opposed, the MoU showed that the Democratic president followed the same path as his predecessors. It also confirmed that support for Iron Dome, and more broadly, for Israel's missile defense, had become an essential component of that bilateral cooperation.

The American Defense Industry Gets Involved

Around the time the Obama administration and the Netanyahu government discussed the terms of the new MoU, Congress raised the question of the coproduction of Iron Dome. Given the substantial amount of funding involved in the system, lawmakers began to wonder how it could also benefit American industries. This was first put on the record of the National Defense Authorization Act for the Fiscal Year 2013, in which Congress asked the Defense Department "to obtain appropriate data rights to Iron Dome technology to ensure us the ability

51 Interview with Daniel Shapiro, Washington, DC, February 20, 2025.
52 Interview with Andrew Exum, Washington, DC, March 14, 2024.
53 US Department of State, "Memorandum of Understanding Reached with Israel," September 14, 2016, Archives. https://2009-2017.state.gov/documents/organization/265160.pdf.

to use that data for US defense purposes and to explore potential co-production opportunities."[54] The following year, the National Defense Authorization Act, approved on December 26, 2013, reiterated the call for the "establishment of a capacity for co-production." The document stated, "Congress senses that second-source production of parts and components of the Iron Dome (. . .) based in the United States is in the national security interest of both Israel and the United States."[55]

In Washington, the approval of arms sales typically involves negotiations among lawmakers to ensure that local factories in their districts can benefit from the sales. As one congressional staffer explains, "a member of Congress ultimately cares about jobs in his or her district, that is what they can deliver to their constituents back home. Otherwise, it's just some esoteric foreign policy priority." Jonathan Lord, a former professional staff member for the House Armed Services Committee, also stresses that "members need to be able to go back to their districts and make the case and say, this is in fact providing jobs and economic stimulus for America. This isn't simply charity."[56] Julie Fishman Rayman, managing director of policy at the AJC and a former congressional staffer, nuances the analysis: "It's a bonus, but it's not the main driver. I don't think that there are members of Congress who are saying 'Oh I wouldn't vote for this if this money does not end up coming back to my district.'"[57]

Against that backdrop, in March 2014, the United States and Israel agreed to sign a coproduction agreement. Initially, Congress requested that the Department of Defense explore "coproduction for radar components."[58] A few months later, the late senator from Arizona, John McCain, visited Raytheon's missile plant in Tucson and declared there that he was "very proud that Arizona workers at Raytheon will be helping protect our ally Israel." By 2017, documents from the legislative branch shifted their focus to the coproduction of the Tamir interceptors.[59] Thus, for the fiscal year, the full amount approved by Congress for Iron Dome—$92 million—was provided to Israel for the coproduction of the

54 Jeremy Sharp, "U.S. Foreign Aid to Israel" (Washington, DC: Congressional Research Service, March 1, 2023): 18. https://sgp.fas.org/crs/mideast/RL33222.pdf.

55 113th Congress, "National Defense Authorization Act 2014, Public Law 113–66," December 26, 2013: 713–714. https://www.congress.gov/bill/113th-congress/house-bill/3304.

56 Interview with Jonathan Lord, former political–military analyst in the US Department of Defense, and professional staff member for the House Armed Services Committee, March 12, 2024.

57 Interview with Julie Fishman-Rayman, Managing Director of Policy and Political Affairs, American Jewish Committee, March 11, 2024.

58 114th Congress, "National Defense Authorization Act 2016, Public Law 114–92," November 25, 2015: 1134. https://www.congress.gov/114/plaws/publ92/PLAW-114publ92.pdf.

59 114th Congress, "National Defense Authorization Act 2017, Public Law 114–328," December 23, 2016: 2632. https://www.congress.gov/114/plaws/publ328/PLAW-114publ328.pdf.

interceptors. Then, after a lengthy selection process, Raytheon (now renamed RTX Corporation), one of the oldest American defense companies, was chosen to partner with Israel's Rafael. Raytheon chose its plant in Tucson (Arizona), where it already produced the Tomahawk cruise missile and the AIM-120 advanced medium-range air-to-air missile (AMRAAM), to start manufacturing the Tamir interceptors.[60]

As of this writing, the precise level of coproduction between the United States and Israel is unclear. Several interviewees in Washington claimed that most of the components were now produced and assembled in the United States before being sent to Israel. "It's a bit of a misnomer to think of Iron Dome as a purely Israeli system," concludes Jonathan Lord, a former analyst at the House Armed Services Committee.[61] However, several Israeli former officials disputed that assessment and retorted that Iron Dome was still primarily produced inside Israel.

The vigorous reactions of Israeli officers or engineers against the idea that today most of Iron Dome could be produced in the United States, and not in Israel, reveal the tensions surrounding the national narrative according to which Iron Dome is a purely Israeli system. The evolution of US funding and coproduction suggests that Iron Dome has become a joint enterprise between the two countries after the initial years of research and development. However, coproduction was not the final step taken by Congress. Lawmakers also requested that the Department of Defense consider purchasing Iron Dome for its own needs.

Iron Dome Batteries for the US Army

In 2019, Congress mandated the US Army to procure two Iron Dome batteries.[62] In the defense bill of that year, Congress "directs the Secretary of the Army" to assess the "possible integration of the Iron Dome system into the Army air and missile defense architecture."[63] The decision was more influenced by political

---

[60] Jen Judson, "Raytheon and Rafael to Build Iron Dome in US," *Defense News*, August 4, 2020. https://www.defensenews.com/land/2020/08/03/raytheon-and-rafael-to-build-iron-dome-in-us/.

[61] Interview with Jonathan Lord, former political-military analyst in the US Department of Defense, and professional staff member for the House Armed Services Committee, March 12, 2024.

[62] Jen Judson, "It's Official: US Army Inks Iron Dome Deal," *Defense News*, August 13, 2019. https://www.defensenews.com/digital-show-dailies/smd/2019/08/12/its-official-us-army-inks-iron-dome-deal/.

[63] 115th Congress, "Department of Defense Appropriations Bill 2019," June 21, 2018: 236. https://www.congress.gov/115/crpt/hrpt769/CRPT-115hrpt769.pdf.

factors than by operational considerations. Military experts wondered about the type of scenario that required US forces to consider a system against short-range rockets like those operated by Hamas in Gaza. In fact, following the ordering of those two batteries, the US Army struggled to manage them. After procuring the two batteries, troops were trained to use them at Fort Bliss in Texas, and one battery was deployed to Guam for a military drill in 2021.[64]

For the US Army leadership, the system created logistic headaches. Designed for use by the IDF, Iron Dome did not integrate seamlessly into the US Army's command-and-control system, formally known as the "Integrated Battle Command System." This required guarantees in terms of cybersecurity that involved the US Army's ability to access the original computer program of Iron Dome. However, Israel used its contractual right not to share the source code. In effect, the batteries could not be operated within the air defense architecture of the US Army, questioning their operational relevance. Tom Karako, a Washington-based missile defense expert, assessed in 2023, "Unless Israel permits access to address these concerns, these two batteries will remain a standalone niche capability (. . .) As such, the Army seems not to know what to do with them."[65]

The logic of procuring Iron Dome batteries for the US Army remains unclear. Mick Mulroy, former deputy assistant secretary of defense for the Middle East (2017–19), suggested there was a financial incentive: "My understanding is the Patriot is more expensive to operate continually than Iron Dome . . . I've been in the conversation where that was brought up that (Patriot missiles) are more expensive . . . That's also because we were looking for a system to have redundancy: we're not all relying on one system if the enemy finds a way to deal with one system, we still have another."[66]

Despite the issues surrounding the US Army's procurement of Iron Dome batteries, the Marine Corps followed suit. In 2023, the service revealed plans to order three batteries and deploy them to the Indo-Pacific Command in Hawaii.[67] Yet it is unclear how the Marine Corps intended to address the same issue the

[64] Noah Robertson, Bryant Harris, Jen Judson, "US Agrees to Send Two Iron Dome Batteries to Israel," *Defense News*, October 25, 2023. https://www.defensenews.com/pentagon/2023/10/24/us-agrees-to-send-two-iron-dome-batteries-to-israel/.

[65] Tom Karako, "Why It's Time for the US Army to Divest Iron Dome," *Breaking Defense*, March 27, 2023.

[66] Interview with Mick Mulroy, former deputy assistant secretary of defense for the Middle East (2017–19), March 2, 2024.

[67] Australian Defence Magazine, "US Marines to Deploy Iron Dome in the Pacific in 2025," May 7, 2024. https://www.australiandefence.com.au/news/news/us-marines-to-deploy-iron-dome-in-the-pacific-in-2025.

army encountered with the obstacles to integrating the Iron Dome into its command-and-control system.

Eventually, the army got rid of its Iron Dome batteries. In late October 2023, as the war raged between Israel and Hamas, the Defense Department announced it was planning to send back the two batteries it had bought four years earlier.[68] Facing an unprecedented flow of rocket attacks, Israel requested additional support from the United States. From an American standpoint, it made sense to address the issue with batteries already in service and unused by its armed forces. But the story of the batteries ordered by the US Army, dispatched to Hawaii and then sent back to Israel, also serves as a snapshot of how much Washington's politics shaped the US–Israel military cooperation, sometimes to the point where operational needs were subordinate to congressional considerations.

Iron Dome and Congressional Feuds

The MoU signed in 2016 was meant as a framework for routine military cooperation between the United States and Israel. The Obama administration believed that allocating a specific budget to missile defense, particularly Iron Dome, would end the typical quarrels between the government and Congress over the level of support to Israel. However, an emergency clause was added, leaving some leeway in case Israel faced a war.

The adoption of the MoU coincided with the consolidation of Netanyahu's security concept in the Gaza Strip, discussed in Chapter 3. In the following years, the Israel–Hamas conflict seemed to fade away while US politics kept getting more and more contentious. The election of Donald Trump in November 2016, just a few months after the MoU was signed, ushered in a period of domestic and international turbulence. After years of bitter relations with Obama, Netanyahu welcomed the new President Trump, calling him a "true friend of the State of Israel."[69]

Donald Trump and his administration went on to endorse several of Netanyahu's policy positions. In December 2017, the US president formally recognized Jerusalem as the capital of Israel and ordered the relocation of the US Embassy there. Then, in 2019, he also recognized Israel's sovereignty over the Golan Heights, captured from Syria in the 1967 war. Those decisions gave

---

[68] Noah Robertson, Bryant Harris, Jen Judson, "US Agrees to Send Two Iron Dome Batteries to Israel."

[69] Politico, "Netanyahu Calls Trump 'a True Friend' of Israel," November 9, 2016. https://www.politico.com/story/2016/11/netanyahu-trump-israel-true-friend-231094.

credence to Netanyahu's approach to downplay the importance of the Palestinian issue. Meanwhile, the United States focused its efforts on taming Iran with Trump's idea of a "maximum pressure" that ended the US commitment to the JCPOA signed by President Obama in 2015.

Throughout that period, the MoU worked well; there was no need for emergency funding, as the Gaza Strip seemed contained. But progressively, Israel, and more specifically, US military support to the government of Benjamin Netanyahu, became a partisan issue in Washington. Even before the Gaza War started in October 2023, Democrats were getting frustrated with the US policy in the Israel–Palestine conflict. A Gallup poll published in the spring of 2023 showed that for the first time, Democrats' sympathy was shifting toward the Palestinians. Data indicated an apparent decline in support for Israel, starting in 2016, the year Donald Trump was elected.[70] Questioning the legitimacy of US support to Israel had long seemed inconceivable in Washington. But the turn of events was to come to the forefront when war reappeared in the Middle East, and the US government activated the clause of the MoU for emergency funding.

On September 23, 2021, a few months after the latest IDF operation against Hamas, Guardian of the Walls, the Israeli government requested an extra $1 billion in aid from the US administration of then-President Joe Biden. The envelope was intended to facilitate the procurement of additional Iron Dome batteries. It qualified as an "emergency requirement" under the provisions negotiated by the Obama administration for the 2016 MoU. When the "supplemental appropriations act" was submitted to Congress, everyone anticipated its swift approval. Bipartisan support for Israel had long been one of the few policy issues on which Democrats and Republicans agreed. If there was any uncertainty on US funding, it was on how much Congress would increase the administration's initial request. This was particularly salient within the legislative branch of government. Former Israeli Ambassador to the United States Michael Oren discusses in his memoirs the strong support provided by Congress for Iron Dome, noting, "Behind the Iron Dome stands a marble dome of the Capitol."[71] Likewise, Benjamin Netanyahu regularly praised the role of Congress in his speeches: "Last summer, millions of Israelis were protected from thousands of Hamas rockets because this capital dome helped build our Iron Dome."[72]

[70] Lydia Saad, "Democrats' Sympathies in Middle East Shift to Palestinians," Gallup, March 16, 2023. https://news.gallup.com/poll/472070/democrats-sympathies-middle-east-shift-palestinians.aspx.
[71] Oren, "Invest in Iron Dome for Peace": 334.
[72] Washington Post, "The Complete Transcript of Netanyahu's Address to Congress," March 3, 2015. https://www.washingtonpost.com/news/post-politics/wp/2015/03/03/full-text-netanyahus-address -to-congress/.

For most of the session at the House of Representatives, lawmakers unambiguously supported the emergency fund. Many politicians on the floor explained that the bill supported only an "entirely defensive" system that would "protect millions of civilians." But then, Representative Rashida Tlaib from Michigan took the floor. Tlaib was not only one of the first Muslim women elected to Congress but also the very first Palestinian American, born in Detroit to a mother and father who left the West Bank in the 1970s. Tlaib was a unique symbol of the new American social fabric and the new politics within the Democratic Party. The year she was first elected to the House of Representatives marked the emergence of a new generation of Democrats leaning toward the left. Alongside three other congresswomen, Alessandra Ocasio-Cortez, Ilhan Omar, and Ayanna Pressley, Tlaib was considered a member of the self-declared "squad." Among other things, the group frequently criticized Israel's occupation of Palestinian territories, and through that process challenged the traditional bipartisan nature of congressional debates regarding Israel.[73]

As Tlaib started talking, she "rose in opposition to this supplemental" that would "enable and support war crimes." She argued, "We cannot continue talking only about Israel's need for safety at a time when Palestinians are living under a violent apartheid system." Tlaib questioned the logic behind the "$1 billion in American taxpayer dollars that my colleagues want to give (. . .) an absurd and unjustifiable 140 times increase to U.S. funding for the Iron Dome." Tlaib only talked for one minute, but her statement was fiercely rebuked and depicted by other lawmakers as "anti-Israeli" and "antisemitic." In the final vote, 420 representatives voted "yes," nine voted "nays," including Cori Bush, Ilhan Omar, and Rashida Tlaib. Despite her initial opposition, the other member of the "squad," Ocasio-Cortez, voted "present."[74] Later, the congresswoman wrote a letter to her constituents to clarify her position, explaining that the bill had been approved because of the "reckless decision by House leadership to rush this controversial vote within a matter of hours and without true consideration."[75]

For the majority of the staffers working in Congress, Tlaib's argument was a marginal view that did not threaten US support to Israel in general or to

---

[73] Anna North, "How 4 Congresswomen Came to Be Called 'the Squad'," Vox, July 18, 2019. https://www.vox.com/2019/7/17/20696474/squad-congresswomen-trump-pressley-aoc-omar-tlaib.

[74] All the quotes from this debate are taken from Congressional Record, Proceedings and Debates of the 117th Congress, First Session 167, no. 165 (September 23, 2021). https://www.congress.gov/117/crec/2021/09/23/167/165/CREC-2021-09-23.pdf.

[75] Office of House Representative Alexandria Ocasio-Cortez, "A Note from Rep. Alexandria Ocasio-Cortez," September 24, 2021. https://ocasiocortezforms.house.gov/news/email/show.aspx?ID=55LU2VD3J7CAG.

Iron Dome specifically. One interviewee working at AIPAC insists, "Many of the critics of Israel's use of US weapons continue to strongly support funding defensive systems like Iron Dome."[76]

But beyond the surface, in 2021, an increasing number of analysts and political operatives in Washington were also questioning the amount of the emergency bill. For instance, Dylan Williams was at the time vice president of J Street, an interest group created the same year Obama came to power. Like AIPAC, J Street described itself as a pro-Israel organization, but it grew out of the discomfort of Jewish American liberals with Israel's occupation of Palestinian territories. In 2021, when the draft supplemental act started circulating in congressional offices, Williams

> talked to very senior congressional offices and democratic offices, talking to their staff and asking them questions like, has Israel explained? Not just how it came up with this suspiciously nice round figure of $1 billion but also how it's justifying the notion that it is too much of a burden for Israel to pay for it out of its own public funds the way the United States has to pay for its defense. And what I was getting back from these Democratic offices was no, they haven't even bothered.[77]

From the Israeli perspective, after the war of May 2021, the IDF assessment indicated worrying trends regarding the quantity and quality of Hamas's arsenal. Replenishment of the existing Iron Dome batteries was necessary but not sufficient. There needed to be more. In our interview three years after the events, Williams did not challenge the legitimacy of the military argument, but he questioned the lack of transparency in the diplomatic process:

> Did Israel calculate that the cost of that would be $1 billion, or that the cost of that would be several billion, and they decided that they had a 1 billion budget gap that they just couldn't fill without United States assistance? No, they didn't. They absolutely didn't. They came back to the United States, possibly stretching the meaning of the MoU and saying, another billion should do it. Just give it to us. And that struck even supporters of Iron Dome, even supporters of Israel . . . there was real consternation, even among administration officials and even among Democrats who ended up voting for the extra $1 billion.[78]

[76] Email correspondence with anonymous source at American Israel Public Affairs Committee, March 26, 2024.

[77] Interview with Dylan Williams, former Vice President of J-Street (2009–23), Washington, DC, March 15, 2024.

[78] Interview with Dylan Williams, March 15, 2024.

At the time, Williams wrote an article for the Quincy Institute, a Washington-based think tank, that relayed those doubts. The piece questioned the logic of asking $1 billion from the United States, even though the latter was "already struggling to meet the myriad needs of its citizens in difficult times to pay for it." Later, it added perhaps the most sensitive part of the question: "Those of us who advocate in support of funding for Iron Dome . . . are facing increasing skepticism from a growing number of voters and lawmakers who wonder why Israel needs additional U.S. money when it is spending vast sums building illegal settlements in occupied Palestinian territory."[79]

Other American commentators rejected Williams's argument. Lenny Ben-David, a former consultant for AIPAC, even called for his resignation in a comment for the *Jerusalem Post*.[80] Meanwhile, Nancy Pelosi, then Speaker of the House, praised the approval of the supplemental act, commenting that the "passage of this bill reflects the great unity in Congress, on a bipartisan and bicameral basis, for Israel."[81]

The controversy surrounding the supplemental act in 2021 was not an epiphenomenon. It reflected an underlying current within the US Democratic Party and the coming of age of a new generation of politicians and foreign policy advisers questioning the principle of unconditional US support to Israel. Another illustration of this trend was my conversation with Matt Duss, a former foreign policy adviser to Senator Bernie Sanders. By the time of the interview, Duss was widely seen as an influential voice of the left wing of the Democratic Party. Now a vice president of the Center for International Policy, Duss argues that this new generation no longer tolerates the unconditional nature of that support: "The establishment view has been basically, we just support Israel, whatever Israel wants . . . but there are a lot of Democrats who have fundamental disagreements with what Israel is doing in the occupied territories and their vision, Israel's vision, Netanyahu's vision for the future of the country."[82]

After winning the vote in the House in September 2021, the supplemental act was submitted to the Senate. This time, Senator Bernie Sanders challenged it differently. Contrary to Tlaib and the few other members of the House who

---

[79] Dylan Williams, "Any New US Aid to Israel Should Prioritize Peacebuilding, Not More Weapons," Responsible Statecraft, Quincy Institute, June 17, 2021. https://responsiblestatecraft.org/2021/06/17/any-new-us-aid-to-israel-should-prioritize-peacebuilding-not-more-weapons/.

[80] Lenny Ben-David, "Who Tried to Block US Funding for Iron Dome?," *Jerusalem Post*, August 16, 2022. https://www.jpost.com/opinion/article-714876.

[81] Joe Gould, "House Passes $1 Billion for Israel's Iron Dome System in Blowout Vote," *Defense News*, September 24, 2021. https://www.defensenews.com/congress/2021/09/23/house-passes-1-billion-for-israels-iron-dome-system-in-blowout-vote/.

[82] Interview with Matt Duss, former foreign policy advisor to Senator Bernie Sanders, March 7, 2024.

opposed the additional funding for Iron Dome, Sanders conditioned his approval of the bill on the provision of the same amount—$1 billion—for humanitarian relief to the Gaza Strip. In late September, Sanders addressed a letter to Chuck Schumer, the majority leader in the Senate, in which he acknowledged that Iron Dome "saves civilian lives . . . that is unquestionably a good thing and something I support." But then, he made the case that "for us to provide an additional billion dollars in aid to Israel while ignoring the suffering of people in Gaza would be unconscionable and irresponsible."[83] Chuck Schumer agreed to the principle of humanitarian aid to be supplied to Gaza, and in return, Sanders approved the supplemental act. However, the US government did not allocate $1 billion as Sanders demanded.

Later, acknowledging the drama in Congress, President Joe Biden reportedly told Prime Minister Netanyahu, "Bibi, I gotta tell you, I'm coming under a lot of pressure back here. This is not Scoop Jackson's Democratic Party," a reference to the late Democratic senator who advocated a strong pro-Israel view and influenced many key figures of the neoconservative movement in the 1970s.[84] Overall, the 2021 controversy in Congress was a harbinger of tensions that were to resurface and intensify after the 2023 Gaza War began.

The Fallout of the 2023 Gaza War

The Gaza War that followed the Hamas assault on October 7, 2023, triggered unprecedented tensions within the Democratic Party and the US administration of Joe Biden. More than a dozen administration officials publicly resigned to protest what they perceived to be US support for Israel's offensive, with accusations ranging from "genocide-enabling" to "blind support to atrocities."[85] Those tensions brought about a debate on the need to rethink US military aid to Israel. But even as the relationship between Biden and Netanyahu became openly contentious, the former refused outright to consider suspending US support for Iron Dome.

According to Bob Woodward's account in his book *War*, President Biden asked his Secretary of State Anthony Blinken, in February 2024, to come up

---

[83] Office of Senator Bernard Sanders, "Letter from US Senator Bernard Sanders to the Honorable Charles Schumer," September 29, 2021. https://s3.us-east-1.amazonaws.com/jewish-currents/Sanders-letter.pdf.

[84] Benjamin Netanyahu, *Bibi: My Story* (New York: Threshold Editions, 2022): 646.

[85] Kanishka Singh, Humeyra Pamuk, "Gaza Protests: US Officials Who Have Quit Over Biden's Support of Israel," Reuters, July 3, 2024. https://www.reuters.com/world/middle-east/us-officials-who-have-resigned-protest-over-bidens-gaza-policy-2024-07-02/.

with options to consider if Israel dismissed his call not to attack Rafah, a city in southern Gaza. Blinken detailed three scenarios: "public separation," "something at the United Nations" (*sic*), and "suspending some military assistance to Israel." Biden reportedly responded, "I will not cut off or suspend defensive assistance to Israel, Iron Dome, anything to defend itself. It has to preserve its deterrent against Iran and Hezbollah."[86] Three months later, when President Biden publicly criticized the Israeli offensive in Rafah and threatened to withhold US military aid, he told journalists, "[W]e're walking away from Israel's ability to wage wars in those areas," but he quickly added, "[W]e're going to continue to make sure Israel is secure in terms of Iron Dome."[87]

Some critics of the US security assistance to Israel suggest that there should be a distinction between offensive and defensive military systems. Such a view implies that only support to systems like Iron Dome (or others like David's Sling, and Arrow) should be preserved, but that the US government should review, and if needed suspend, systems that are offensive by design (ammunition, weapons, fighter jets). This distinction is relevant at the political level, but far less so at the operational and legal levels. First, supporting an ally or a partner only on the defensive sends a confusing message to the warring parties. It suggests that the United States solely wants to reduce the damage inflicted on Israel by its opponents but is reluctant to support a counteroffensive. As a result, it could increase the incentive for the aggressor to attack if the latter estimates that it won't suffer a massive retaliation due to US restraint. In other words, drawing a clear line between offensive and defensive military aid might pressure Israel, but it could also unintentionally incite the other side to launch an attack. But it is at the legal level that the offensive–defensive distinction loses its relevance. Asked about the debate, an analyst from the US Congressional Research Service (who preferred to remain anonymous) explains,

> For obvious reasons, missile defense is more politically palatable. But I will tell you this: there is no definition in law of what constitutes an offensive versus a defensive system. That is a purely political construct. It's not a legal construct. The US hasn't a list or a definition that says these precision-guided munitions are offensive weapons, that's something that is just a political construct.[88]

<hr>

86 Bob Woodward, *War* (New York: Simon & Schuster, 2024): 259–260.

87 Kevin Liptak, "Biden Says He Will Stop Sending Bombs and Artillery Shells to Israel If It Launches Major Invasion of Rafah," CNN, May 9, 2024. https://edition.cnn.com/2024/05/08/politics/joe-biden -interview-cnntv/index.html.

88 Interview with anonymous analyst, Congressional Research Service, March 5, 2024.

Iron Dome and the Enduring US–Israel Cooperation

In retrospect, it is telling that most of the controversy surrounding US military support to Israel was defined during the presidency of Barack Obama, who too often was mischaracterized as critical of Israel. In reality, Obama's support to Iron Dome, and more broadly his revamping of US military support through the MoU of 2016, highlights how much the former president followed a traditional posture that considered the security of Israel an unquestionable priority of US policy in the Middle East, even if that meant putting aside US disapproval of Israel's occupation of Palestinian territories or, in the case of Obama, his troubled relations with Israel's Prime Minister Benjamin Netanyahu.

One of the most striking—but not the most surprising—aspects of the US policy discussion on Israel in general, and Iron Dome in particular, is that it often seemed to be driven by Washingtonian perspectives, rather than insights from the Middle East region. In recent years, as Israel increasingly became a partisan issue, the debate surrounding the US military aid to the country was often defined by the fault lines between Democrats and Republicans in the federal capital. Many of the measures adopted for missile defense funding, including the adoption of the MoU in 2016, were not guided by grand strategy but by political tactics between the government and Congress.

One consequence of this politicization was that the numbers behind the amount of US funding to Iron Dome (or to the IDF in general) appeared disconnected from operational needs. It is difficult to see a strategic logic when the budget projected for one year by the Defense Department for Iron Dome nearly doubles after Congress reviews the government's request. As Andrew Exum recalled, the annual allocation for Iron Dome agreed upon within the 2016 MoU was merely the average of past years. Likewise, the supplemental bill voted on in September 2021 provided $1 billion in aid to the Israeli government on top of its annual package, but the controversy surrounding it followed the political logic of Washington, pitting the progressive wing of the Democrats against the rest of Congress. There was no discussion on the exact financial demands of replenishing Iron Dome batteries, nor was there any discussion on whether the amount, as suggested by some critics, was intended to procure additional batteries.

Furthermore, there was no discussion on whether this was a sound strategy against Israel's enemies. All in all, it was not the result of a comprehensive political–military assessment of Israel's future security needs. The US government is plethoric, but somehow, when one external observer asks former officials at the White House, the Defense Department, or the State Department about the strategy behind these amounts, most of the interviewees humbly reply that strategy hardly factored in and that most of the time, decisions were defined by political realities.

At the political level, US support for Iron Dome served different goals. It showed that the US government was helping its Middle Eastern ally against what became the close and immediate challenge of its population during the 2010s. Interestingly, Iron Dome also resonated with a US passion for missile defense that dated to the Reagan administration.

Noticeably, in 2024, the Republican Party platform called to "build a great Iron Dome missile defense shield over our entire country."[89] Then, after his election, President Trump ordered in January 2025 the building of an "Iron Dome missile defense shield" in the United States (later renamed "Golden Dome").[90] From a military standpoint, producing and deploying Iron Dome batteries on American soil did not make much sense. The United States did not face similar rocket threats as Israel, and the sheer size of its territory meant that Iron Dome could not provide credible defensive coverage.[91] But the value of the analogy lay elsewhere. In reality, the program launched by the Trump administration went far beyond Israel's Iron Dome. It included the development of new systems such as space-based sensors and interceptors to destroy ballistic, hypersonic, and cruise missiles. The mention of Iron Dome in the GOP platform and the subsequent executive order signed by Donald Trump in January 2025 underlined how much the Israeli system had captured the political imagination far beyond Israel. Perhaps more than any other system currently in service, Iron Dome had become a symbol that could revive the old Reaganian dreams of securing the homeland against foreign threats.

The Trumpian pledge of an American Iron Dome also signaled that the bipartisan approach to missile defense that emerged during the Obama presidency had come to an end. While Democratic observers derided the terms of the Republican Party's platform as disconnected from reality, Republican pundits praised it. But just like with domestic politics in Israel, the increasing

[89] "2024 Republican Party Platform," July 8, 2024. University of California in Santa Barbara, The American Presidency Project. https://www.presidency.ucsb.edu/documents/2024-republican-party-platform.

[90] White House, "Fact Sheet: President Donald J. Trump Directs the Building of the Iron Dome Missile Defense Shield for America," January 27, 2025. https://www.whitehouse.gov/fact-sheets/2025/01/fact-sheet-president-donald-j-trump-directs-the-building-of-the-iron-dome-missile-defense-shield-for-america/.

[91] Steve Fetter, David Wright, "Can the Iron Dome Be Transmuted Into a Golden Dome?," *The Washington Quarterly* 48, no. 2 (2025): 95–114. https://doi.org/10.1080/0163660X.2025.2514916.

US investment in Israel's missile defense revealed a reluctance in Washington to question the status quo with the Gaza Strip. The steady growth of US funding to replenish Iron Dome, after each war in 2012, 2014, and 2021, was read through the lens of the operational needs of Israel. From time to time, US administration officials and members of Congress argued that Iron Dome was preventing a new escalation and, therefore, was also saving Palestinian lives. There was no desire, no ambition to turn ceasefires into diplomatic processes. The constant rearmament of Hamas, its assertiveness, and the support of Iran surely helped in preventing that. But Washington's disengagement showed that, in practice, US decision-makers had resigned themselves to accepting Netanyahu's idea that the conflict with the Palestinians could not be resolved; it could only be managed. This set of assumptions proved tragically wrong on the morning of October 7, 2023.

5

October 7 and the End
of the Iron Dome Decade

At 6:30 a.m. on October 7, 2023, Israelis heard the familiar sound of the *Tzeva Adom* siren. Suddenly, early birds out for a run and partygoers at the Nova Festival saw myriad rockets piercing the skies. *Tzofar*, one of the Israeli apps providing live feed on rocket threats, started sending hundreds of notifications to mobile phones. The sheer number of attacks quickly indicated that this was no usual incident. For years, the population in the South had become accustomed to the possibility of a sudden rocket attack, forcing them to take shelter and wait patiently for ten minutes before life could return to normal. But on the morning of October 7, the scale of the rocket campaign was unprecedented.

According to Israel's government, a total of thirty-seven hundred rockets were fired in the first four hours. They targeted Sderot, Be'er-Sheva, Tel Aviv, and the center of the country. Then, as people ran and hid in shelters, combatants of Hamas's special unit, the Nukhba ("elite" in Arabic), launched an offensive on the Israel Defense Forces (IDF) security barrier. By 10:00 a.m., they had overrun three military installations around the frontier and raided the town of Sderot and the nearby kibbutzim, such as Be'eri, Kfar Aza, and Nahal Oz. In those areas, shelters that had provided comfort for the past decade turned into death traps. Designed to be accessible from the outside at any time, shelters cannot be locked. As Hamas combatants flooded the Gaza envelope, they attacked those shelters around the kibbutzim of Re'im and Alumim, throwing grenades at them or executing those who were hiding inside.[1]

Today, it is estimated that on the day Hamas launched its surprise attack on Israel, its fighters killed some 1,200 people and kidnapped 240 others. Facing the rocket barrage that morning, Iron Dome initially seemed effective in intercepting the projectiles. In a public address a few months later, Moshe Patel, director of the Israeli Missile Defense Organization, insisted, "Our system was

---

[1] Isabel Kershner, "They Ran Into a Bomb Shelter for Safety. Instead, They Were Slaughtered," *New York Times*, November 11, 2023. https://www.nytimes.com/2023/11/11/world/middleeast/israel-hamas -oct-7-attack-shelter.html.

fully deployed and ready for this attack . . . what we faced is scenarios that we simulated and tested."[2]

Later, government investigations revealed by Israeli media challenged Patel's statement. In February 2025, the IDF acknowledged that the quantity of rockets fired by Hamas overwhelmed its air defense batteries. After a first wave of more than fourteen hundred rockets in the first twenty minutes, Iron Dome batteries reportedly needed immediate replenishment. The continuous rocket attacks and the ground invasion by the Nukhba forces prevented the IDF from resupplying batteries. According to media reports, three IDF personnel were killed while trying to replenish them.[3]

The attacks on October 7 exposed the flaws in the security concept, the "conceptzia," forged over the previous decade. They shattered the illusion of security fed by the technical success of Iron Dome. Reflecting on the events, the former Israeli ambassador to the United States, Michael Oren, writes, "The batteries all but guaranteed that Israelis could continue to live and work normally even as Fajr-5 rockets, each capable of destroying their homes, targeted them . . . I, too, fell for that false sense of security."[4] October 7 was the tragic conclusion of an era. It was the end of the Iron Dome decade that started after the first successful interception of a Hamas rocket in 2011, and that saw Israeli governments embracing a containment policy vis-à-vis Gaza.

Against that backdrop, this chapter investigates how Iron Dome contributed to the evolution of Israeli military strategy during that decade. It first explores the Israeli military debates, showing how, in the 2010s, the IDF adopted a doctrine that lessened the traditional emphasis on offensive strategies in favor of a more balanced approach relying on defensive measures and limited counteroperations. The chapter also shows that Israel was not the only one to evolve. During that period, nonstate rivals like Hezbollah and Hamas also adapted to the new reality brought about by Iron Dome. They fielded new, more sophisticated weapons and developed new tactics to test the resilience of the Israeli system. This fueled tensions within the IDF and led several officers to warn against the security illusion created by Iron Dome, with some going so far as to describe the system as a new "Maginot Line." Furthermore, the new Israeli strategy deepened the country's long-term

2   Center for Strategic and International Studies, "Israel's Missile Defense Engagements Since October 7th," Transcript, July 12, 2024. https://www.csis.org/analysis/israels-missile-defense-engagements -october-7th.

3   Robert Tollast, "Israel's Iron Dome System Overwhelmed on October 7, Inquiry Reveals," *The National*, February 4, 2025. https://www.thenationalnews.com/news/mena/2025/02/04/israels-iron -dome-system-overwhelmed-on-october-7-inquiry-reveals/.

4   Michael Oren, "Iron Dome: Israel's Double-Edged Sword (Part I)," Substack, June 13, 2024. https:// claritywithmichaeloren.substack.com/p/iron-dome-part-one.

dependence on US financial and technological support, which went against its traditional aspirations toward self-reliance. In the early 2020s, the IDF leadership attempted to tackle these issues by introducing a new plan called "Decisive Victory," which aimed to reemphasize the offensive against nonstate enemies, to no avail.

Eventually, the military failure of October 7 leads to a reckoning over the policies adopted in the previous decade. Today, Israel is reemphasizing offensive, and more specifically, preemptive, operations. In the strategic environment after October 7, political decision-makers and military commanders no longer believe that nonstate threats from Gaza or elsewhere can be contained, or that groups like Hamas and Hezbollah can be deterred. Israel's tolerance for vulnerabilities at its borders has dropped, and the IDF aims by all means to reduce the arsenal of potential adversaries before they contemplate orchestrating another event similar to the October 7 attack.

Reshaping the Israeli Military Model

After years of resistance within the IDF, the effectiveness of Iron Dome on the battlefield changed the way Israeli officers thought about war. This was first noticeable regarding recruitment. Suddenly, air defense became a sought-after specialty. Young, conscripted soldiers were now eager to join those units.[5]

The attractiveness of Iron Dome and air defense highlighted a culminating point in the Israeli military's evolution. Starting in the early 1990s, Israel's armed forces adopted a military model that increasingly relied on the most advanced technologies, whether for early warning capabilities (sensors, radars, and unmanned aerial vehicles [UAVs]) or power projection capabilities (the procurement of F-35 fighter jets and the introduction of precision-guided munitions). This evolution was heavily influenced by American military concepts and doctrines, particularly the theories related to the "Revolution in Military Affairs" (RMA).[6]

Developed amid the Gulf War in 1990–1, the RMA posited that advances in communication technologies and firepower were changing warfare, giving a decisive edge to the military that mastered these new technologies. Most of those debates focused on offensive capabilities, but missile defense greatly benefited from the same technological progress. Improvements in detecting and

---

5 Interview with Doron Gavish, former Air Defense Commander, IDF, Tel Aviv, July 10, 2024.
6 Andrew Krepinevich, "Cavalry to Computer: The Pattern of Military Revolutions," *The National Interest* no. 37 (Fall 1994): 30–42.

intercepting missiles and rockets suddenly transformed the Reagan dream of the Strategic Defense Initiative into a viable project.[7]

In the Israeli context, the technological progress brought about by this RMA coincided with an erosion of national service and the reserve as the pillars of the national community. In the 1990s, Ben-Gurion's model of the "people's army" no longer resonated with a new generation of Israelis who had grown more individualistic. If reservists were no longer reporting for duty, the IDF would be unable to plan mass mobilization. The new technologies would compensate for this. The time for large ground units to conquer the Sinai Peninsula was gone. From now on, early warning systems and standoff weapons could allow Israelis to foil attacks from their enemies. By 1998, Eliot Cohen, Michael Eisenstadt, and Andrew Bacevich predicted that this evolution would ultimately transform Israel's military model, with the IDF increasingly focusing on "defensive and counteroffensive rather than offensive operations."[8]

However, this shift was nothing short of a cultural revolution for the IDF, an organization that had fostered a military culture deeply oriented toward the offensive during its initial decades of existence and characterized by a profound distrust of defensive tactics. Israel's military literature is filled with maxims and statements from IDF commanders calling for an offensive posture. Major General Meir Amit, former head of the Mossad in the 1960s, wrote, "The IDF did not excel in defense. We trained solely for a mobile war and transfer of the fighting onto the enemy's territory. Only offensive moves can undermine the enemy, seize the initiative, and throw him off-balance."[9] In a seminal study from the 1980s, Ariel Levite explained, "Only by inflicting such a humiliating defeat (in terms of casualties, destruction, and loss of territory) or succession of defeats, it was maintained, could the Arabs be dissuaded, temporarily or permanently, from launching a war against Israel."[10]

For the generation of Israeli flag officers who advanced through the ranks in the 2000s and 2010s, investing in a defensive strategy also evoked memories of the Bar-Lev Line.[11] This was a chain of fortifications along the eastern bank

[7] Colin Gray, *Strategy for Chaos: Revolutions in Military Affairs and the Evidence of History* (London: Routledge, 2003); Eliot Cohen, "Change and Transformation in Military Affairs," *Journal of Strategic Studies* 27, no. 3 (2004): 395–407. https://doi.org/10.1080/1362369042000283958.

[8] Eliot Cohen, Michael Eisenstadt, Andrew Bacevich, "Israel's Revolution in Security Affairs," *Survival* 40, no. 1 (1998): 48–67, 61. https://doi.org/10.1093/survival/40.1.48.

[9] Quoted in: Moshe Tlamim, Emanuel Sakal, *Soldier in the Sinai: A General's Account of the Yom Kippur War* (Lexington: University Press of Kentucky, 2014): 2.

[10] Ariel Levite, *Offense and Defense in Israeli Military Doctrine* (London: Routledge, 1989): 43.

[11] Yaacov Bar-Siman-Tov, "The Bar-Lev Line Revisited," *Journal of Strategic Studies* 11, no. 2 (1988): 149–176. https://doi.org/10.1080/01402398808437336.

of the Suez Canal, costing around \$300 million in the late 1960s. Regarded as impenetrable, the Egyptian armed forces swiftly overran the Bar-Lev Line during the 1973 war. The project was already controversial before the war, with key figures such as Yisrael Tal, then the IDF's deputy chief of staff, and Ariel Sharon, then commander of the 143rd Armored Division, opposing it from the outset.[12] Tal himself later wrote that the IDF was a "defence force in its mission" but an "army of offense in its essence."[13] The assertion echoed Amir Peretz's first meeting with the IDF chiefs mentioned in Chapter 2, during which he asked them, "Generals, could you tell me if the 'H' in *Tsahal* (Hebrew acronym for the IDF) stands for *Haganah* (defense in Hebrew) or *Hatkafah* (offense in Hebrew)?"[14]

This offensive preference was so internalized that scholars saw it as a cultural trait of the IDF. For Dima Adamsky, a professor at Reichman University, this Israeli "cult of the offensive" is shaped by Jewish history: "The Israeli narrative associated defensive warfare with the victim mentality of the Diaspora Jews, while offense was in accord with such traits of the Israeli personality as dynamism, initiative, and improvisation."[15] This paved the way to a form of "offensive romanticism" that military commanders like Ariel Sharon or Moshe Dayan embodied.

However, technological innovation and the social evolution of Israel in the 1990s questioned the endurance of that "offensive romanticism." In 2011, when Iron Dome first intercepted a rocket from the Gaza Strip, Israel's society had undergone profound changes. Its citizens could not accept the notion that a counteroffensive was the only appropriate response. To defeat aggression from Hamas or Hezbollah, the IDF consolidated its air superiority and reinforced its early warning capabilities. In this context, missile defense systems, particularly Iron Dome, became the focal point. The performance of those systems denied neighbors the ability to inflict severe casualties. As a result, the success of Iron Dome, on the battlefield and in the political arena, led governments to embrace the logic of defense.

In 2016, as Iron Dome was fully integrated into the IDF Strategy, the Israeli government launched another project named the "Iron Wall," a vast fortification aimed at covering an area of 65 kilometers around the Gaza Strip. In addition

---

[12] Zeev Schiff, *October Earthquake: Yom Kippur 1973* (New York: Routledge, 2017): 136–137.

[13] Quoted in Levite, *Offense and Defense in Israeli Military Doctrine*: 43.

[14] Interview with Amir Peretz, former Minister of Defense (2007–8), IAI Headquarters, Lod, July 29, 2024.

[15] Dima Adamsky, "From Israel with Deterrence: Strategic Culture, Intra-war Coercion and Brute Force," *Security Studies* 26, no. 1 (2017): 157–184, 165. https://doi.org/10.1080/09636412.2017.1243923.

to a concrete barrier, it relied on hundreds of cameras, radars, and sensors. Interestingly, the name "Iron Wall" could be read as an explicit reference to the success of Iron Dome, both projects coexisting in the same military universe.[16]

At an ideological level, it also evoked a famous article from the Zionist thinker and influential figure for the Israeli right Ze'ev Jabotinsky. The latter argued in an essay written in 1923 that the future state of Israel could not realistically coexist with its Arab neighbors without defending itself via the construction of an "Iron Wall." In other words, Jabotinsky's expression captured the idea of a fortress under siege.[17] Noticeably, when Prime Minister Benjamin Netanyahu announced the creation of the "Iron Wall" barrier surrounding Gaza, he confidently asserted, "In our neighborhood, we need to protect ourselves from wild beasts. At the end of the day, there will be a fence like this one surrounding Israel entirely."[18] The statement highlighted how the defensive mindset had taken center stage in both political rhetoric and military strategy.

All those measures contributed to the conclusion that a high-intensity offensive campaign involving a *levee en masse* was no longer the most probable scenario to prepare for. As a result, the changes in the IDF model predicted by Cohen, Eisenstadt, and Bacevich in 1998 came to the forefront in the 2010s. This was evident in the defense policies implemented during those years. For instance, the multiyear plan launched by the IDF in 2016, named "Gideon," emphasized the idea of creating lethal but smaller ground forces. The logic was to get fewer but better-trained soldiers.[19] This was based on the belief that future wars would be brief, and their outcomes would be determined by the technological advantage of one side rather than the size of its army.

The IDF Strategy of 2015

The Gideon plan was the product of the then–IDF Chief of General Staff Gadi Eisenkot. During that same period, the latter also acknowledged the changes at the doctrinal level with the publication of the official IDF Strategy in 2015. For

---

16 Reuters, "Israel Announces Completion of Underground Gaza Border Barrier," December 7, 2021. https://www.reuters.com/world/middle-east/israel-announces-completion-underground-gaza-border-barrier-2021-12-07/.

17 Yaacov Shavit, *Jabotinsky and the Revisionist Movement 1925–1948* (London: Routledge, 2013).

18 *The Guardian*, "Netanyahu Plans Fence Around Israel to Protect It from 'Wild Beasts'," February 10, 2016. http://www.theguardian.com/world/2016/feb/10/netanyahu-plans-fence-around-israel-to-protect-it-from-wild-beasts.

19 Yossi Melman, "The Gideon Doctrine: The Changing Middle East and IDF Strategy," *Jerusalem Post*, September 13, 2015. https://www.jpost.com/jerusalem-report/the-gideon-doctrine-412594.

the first time in its history, the IDF released a document explaining its doctrine to the general public.

The role and influence of Eisenkot in shaping this IDF Strategy perfectly illustrate the evolution of Israel's military thinking during that period. Eisenkot is often known outside of Israel for one statement he made in 2008, when he was the Northern Commander. Interviewed by the newspaper *Yedioth Ahronoth* about the likelihood of a new conflict against Hezbollah, Eisenkot stated that "what happened in the Dahya quarter in Beirut in 2006 will happen in every village from which Israel is fired on. We will apply disproportionate force on it and cause great damage and destruction there." He went on to say, "From our standpoint, these are not civilian villages, they are military bases."[20]

Following the statement, foreign observers concluded that Eisenkot had revealed a new military doctrine, which was quickly dubbed the "Dahya doctrine." Dahya (Arabic for "suburbs") refers to a densely populated group of Shia neighborhoods in southern Beirut, where Hezbollah's headquarters are located. During the first days of the 2006 war, it was the target of massive air strikes by the Israeli Air Force. Iron Dome was still under development when Eisenkot made his statement. Still, his assertive tone and the call for massive, openly disproportionate retaliation reminded us that the IDF had no intention of entrenching itself in a defensive posture.[21]

Two years later, the same Eisenkot warned that Israelis needed to curb their enthusiasm for Iron Dome and should not be "under the illusion that someone will open an umbrella over their heads."[22] In that logic, missile defense systems like Iron Dome were not central to the country's defense policy. They were an insurance policy meant to prevent the aggressor from winning the fight with a first wave of attacks and to provide time for a counteroffensive. Eisenkot's stance suggested that missile defense had little effect on Israel's strategy culture. It was not a revolution but a mere complement that widened the options for the decision-maker.

However, Eisenkot had changed by the time he became the IDF chief of general staff and oversaw the new IDF Strategy. The document acknowledged that operations against nonstate actors could not achieve the destruction of the enemy but only the weakening of their capacities: "From time to time, the IDF

20 "Israel Warns Hezbollah War Would Invite Destruction," *Yedioth Ahronoth*, October 3, 2008. http://www.ynetnews.com/articles/0,7340,L-3604893,00.html.

21 Jean-Loup Samaan, "The Dahya Concept and Israeli Military Posture Vis-à-Vis Hezbollah Since 2006," *Comparative Strategy* 32, no. 2 (2013): 146–159. https://doi.org/10.1080/01495933.2013.773728.

22 Ahiya Raved, "Eisenkot: Missile Defense – For IDF Bases," *Yedioth Ahronoth*, January 12, 2010. https://www.ynetnews.com/articles/0,7340,L-3992238,00.html.

will be required to conduct campaigns with limited or delineated achievements. In most cases, these campaigns aimed to restore calm and provide future deterrence will cause limited damage to the enemy."[23] The 2015 Strategy talked of "neutralizing threats as necessary and delaying the next conflict" to create "extended periods of security calm."[24] It differentiated between three scenarios where force may be used: "routine" situations, "emergency," and warfare. Iron Dome's interceptions of sporadic rocket attacks, along with operations like Pillar of Defense (2012) and Protective Edge (2014), were featured in the first two categories. In these situations, the IDF's objective was "to cause damage to the enemy in a limited and delineated manner." This evoked the idea of a "campaign between wars," or, as colloquially described by IDF officers, operations aimed at "mowing the grass."[25] This notion of a "campaign between the wars" (ha-ma'arakha ben ha-milhamot in Hebrew), often attributed to Eisenkot, also contributed to the idea that the IDF had to rebalance its strategy and stop emphasizing decisive offensive campaigns.[26]

The 2015 Strategy also delved into what constitutes Israel's deterrence posture. It was "specific and adapted to each enemy" and entailed "limited offensive actions to signal deviations from the 'rules of the game'" and "disrupting and thwarting capabilities." In essence, the document provided an intellectual framework for thinking about the limited wars fought by the IDF during that decade against nonstate organizations. Ultimately, it argued that those could not be eliminated. Both sides had to accept the status quo. This IDF Strategy remarkably differed from Eisenkot's past statements on the Dahya reprisals or the Iron Dome illusion. As one of his former advisers interviewed in 2024 explained, "Back in 2008, Eisenkot was expressing a prevailing opinion within the IDF, but like everyone else, he changed his mind, or nuanced it, after Iron Dome proved so effective."

Of course, this does not mean the IDF abandoned offensive operations. In carefully worded diplomatic language, the 2015 document stated that the "IDF's fundamental priorities shall continue to be the development of offensive capabilities before defensive capabilities, despite the centrality of defense and the increased threats to the home front." This represented a recalibration between

---

[23] Israel Defense Forces, "The IDF Strategy," July 2016: 21. https://www.inss.org.il/he/wp-content/uploads/sites/2/2017/04/IDF-Strategy.pdf#page9.

[24] Israel Defense Forces, "The IDF Strategy": 10.

[25] Efraim Inbar, Eitan Shamir, "'Mowing the Grass': Israel's Strategy for Protracted Intractable Conflict," *Journal of Strategic Studies* 37, no. 1 (2014): 65–90. https://doi.org/10.1080/01402390.2013.830972.

[26] Amr Yossef, "Military Doctrines in Israel and Iran: A Doctrinal Hybridity," *Middle East Journal* 75, no. 2 (Summer 2021): 243–263, 244. https://doi.org/10.3751/75.2.13.

offensive and defensive strategies within the IDF culture. Such a balance would have been inconceivable a few years earlier and was made possible by the success of Iron Dome. This was not a sudden shift, nor was it a clear-cut move. As scholars Oren Barak, Amit Sheniak, and Assaf Shapira write, this was a "gradual, incremental, improvised, and largely informal" rebalancing. The result did not amount to a full reliance on defense but "rather a new type of 'hybrid' military strategy, one that is characterized by an emphasis on defense yet retains some offensive elements."[27]

This recalibration of Israel's military posture only temporarily addressed the Gaza challenge. Although Iron Dome led political leaders to believe that the rocket threat was under control, many in the IDF remained uncertain about this success. While they questioned the effectiveness of missile defense, hostile groups just across the border, such as Hamas and Hezbollah, were also learning to adapt.

Hamas, Hezbollah, and a Counterrevolution in Military Affairs

In 2020, Eran Ortal, then the head of the IDF Dado Center, wrote an article in an Israeli military journal where he argued that Israel's operations in Gaza "only serve to 'vaccinate' the enemy against IDF power by gradually exposing him to limited doses of our capabilities."[28] The tone was provocative, but Ortal's argument addressed an overlooked issue, that is, the ability of Israel's opponents to absorb the damage inflicted by the IDF and to learn from it. The IDF was exploring new approaches to tackle the challenges posed by nonstate actors, but those actors were also taking stock of the evolving conflict. Military innovation was indeed not Israel's monopoly.

In the 2000s and 2010s, both Hamas and Hezbollah drew lessons from past operations and refined their strategies. Their extensive use of rockets and missiles followed changes in their military organizations and the training of their soldiers. To some extent, this evolution mirrored the reforms of the IDF, although on a much smaller scale. Their reliance on rocket warfare, combined

---

[27] Oren Barak, Amit Sheniak, Assaf Shapira, "The Shift to Defence in Israel's Hybrid Military Strategy," *Journal of Strategic Studies* 46, no. 2 (2020): 345–377. https://doi.org/10.1080/01402390.2020.1770090.

[28] Eran Ortal, "Going on the Attack: The Theoretical Foundation of the Israel Defense Forces' Momentum Plan," *Dado Center Journal* 28 (October 1, 2020). https://www.idf.il/en/mini-sites/dado-center/vol-28-30-military-superiority-and-the-momentum-multi-year-plan/going-on-the-attack-the-theoretical-foundation-of-the-israel-defense-forces-momentum-plan-1/.

with new measures (construction of tunnels, concealment tactics) to protect their arsenal, inside either Gaza or South Lebanon, against IDF operations. Israeli Brigadier General Itai Brun refers to this as "the other revolution in military affairs." According to Brun, those groups define the "absorption" of an IDF offensive as their primary military objective, allowing them to deny the coercive value of Israel's precision-guided munitions.[29]

This process of mutual adaptation is a common phenomenon in military history: Offensive innovation gives rise to defensive innovation, which in turn sparks new offensive innovation. It refers to what the British strategist John Frederick Charles Fuller called "the constant tactical factor." According to Fuller, every improvement in a weapon leads to countermeasures, which render the initial improvement obsolete.[30]

From that perspective, Palestinian and Lebanese organizations learned through different wars, similarly to regular armed forces. They first developed and institutionalized their understanding of Israeli society and its military culture. Both organizations established intelligence units tasked with gathering and analyzing data on Israel. Their leaders became well versed in Israeli culture and politics. Ahmad al Jabari, who led Hamas's military wing until he was killed in 2012, was said to monitor Israeli media every day.[31] Likewise, Yahya Sinwar, the architect of the October 7 attacks, spent his time in Israeli jails learning Hebrew and studying the country's history and Zionist thinkers. Hassan Nasrallah, the charismatic secretary general of Hezbollah, killed in 2024, also frequently boasted about his understanding of the Israeli mindset. In 2000, following the IDF withdrawal from south Lebanon, Nasrallah famously called Israel a "spider's web," a metaphor meant to emphasize the fragility of its social structures and, by extension, the ability of Hezbollah to drain it with its rocket strategy.

Hezbollah, more so than Hamas, demonstrated its ability to adapt to the IDF's evolving tactics. After the emergence of the "Dahya" concept following Gadi Eisenkot's public comments in 2008, Hassan Nasrallah acknowledged in his speeches the Israeli strategy. He went even further by articulating the party's response. As Israel threatened to launch a new operation focused on Hezbollah's positions, the group revamped its footprint in Lebanon. In March 2011, the IDF

---

[29] Itai Brun, "'While You're Busy Making Other Plans' – The 'Other RMA,'" *Journal of Strategic Studies* 33 (4): 535–565. https://doi.org/10.1080/01402390.2010.489708.

[30] J. F. C. Fuller, *Armament and History: The Influence of Armament on History from the Dawn of Classical Warfare to the End of the Second World War* (London: Charles Scribner's Sons, 1945).

[31] Netanel Flamer, "'The Enemy Teaches Us How to Operate': Palestinian Hamas Use of Open-Source Intelligence (OSINT) in Its Intelligence Warfare Against Israel (1987–2012)," *Intelligence and National Security* 38, no. 7 (2023): 1171–1188, 1176. https://doi.org/10.1080/02684527.2023.2212556.

leaked to *The Washington Post* a map that showed a thousand bunkers, hidden weapons storage facilities, and surveillance sites spread all around Lebanon, in the north or the Bekaa Valley.[32] This repositioning of Hezbollah's sites de-emphasized the place of South Lebanon as the center of gravity in a future conflict. It also underlined the growing range of the party's arsenal that could be stationed far from the Israel–Lebanon border.

The messaging strategy of Hezbollah also evolved. The group maintained secrecy regarding the details of its arsenal, but its leaders constantly asserted the enormous scale of their firepower. In 2013, Iron Dome was viewed as a major success story for Israel, suggesting that the country could finally prevent Hezbollah and Hamas from targeting its cities. However, a different narrative spread inside the Lebanese areas controlled by Hezbollah. Inside the Hezbollah-funded Museum of Resistance in Mleeta, visitors would be greeted by a video of Hassan Nasrallah's speech, titled *Khitaab al-Rada'a* (Speech of Deterrence). In this one-hour speech, Nasrallah directly addressed the IDF leaders, saying,

> They think they can demolish Dahya's buildings as we barely "puncture their walls." But I tell them today: You destroy a Dahya building, and we will destroy buildings in Tel Aviv . . . If you target Beirut's Rafik Hariri International Airport, we will strike Tel Aviv's Ben Gurion International Airport. If you target our electricity stations, we will target yours. If you target our plants, we will target yours.[33]

Nasrallah's message mirrored Israeli threats of reprisal. As Daniel Sobelman from the Hebrew University of Jerusalem explains, Hezbollah designed its own red lines and a list of "equations" (*muadalat* in Arabic) that referred to Israel's high-value assets as targets for Hezbollah in the case of an Israeli campaign in Lebanon.[34] Ultimately, the confidence that the leaders of Hamas and Hezbollah had in understanding Israel led them to believe they could successfully devise operations that would undermine the morale of the IDF and the broader Israeli society. Like the Israeli top brass, they believed they could deliver a decisive blow and manage the escalation ladder.

---

[32] Greg Linch, "Israeli Military Maps Hezbollah Bunkers," *Washington Post*, March 30, 2011. http://www.washingtonpost.com/wp-srv/special/world/Israeli-military-information-on-Hezbollah.html.

[33] Hassan Nasrallah, *Khitaab al radaa'* (Speech of Deterrence) DVD Video, Dar Al Manar, Beirut, 2010.

[34] Daniel Sobelman, "Learning to Deter: Deterrence Failure and Success in the Israel-Hezbollah Conflict, 2006–16," *International Security* 41, no. 3 (Winter 2016–17): 151–196, 185. http://dx.doi.org/10.1162/ISEC_a_00259.

Hamas and Hezbollah also made improvements at the operational level, including the expansion of their missile capabilities, the enhancement of combatants' training, and the development of new tactics. An excellent example of Hamas's adaptability was its shift to tunnel warfare after the 2012 war. That year, Operation Pillar of Defense revealed the IDF's mastery in detecting and striking Hamas operatives, such as Ahmed Jabari, on the ground. Consequently, Hamas invested in tunnel networks to relocate most of its command-and-control units. Its fighters improved their ability to remain hidden while launching rockets at Israel.[35] Then, Israel discovered the expansion of those tunnels two years later, during the 2014 war. This prompted another round of military adaptation on the Israeli side, with its Yahalom unit and its special operation soldiers, going through a new learning and training process to combat Hamas's forces inside the tunnels.[36]

Hamas's commanders also carefully studied Iron Dome's performance to identify loopholes. The first rockets fired at Sderot and the Gaza envelope were meant to disrupt civilian life and to create a climate of terror in the area. In the following years, the objective of such attacks also included overwhelming Israel's defense systems. The massive rocket barrage in the first hours of October 7, 2023, illustrates this aim. As mentioned earlier, the IDF later acknowledged that its air defense units failed to replenish some batteries in a timely manner due to the rapid pace of the attacks. But there were many other instances before that.

In 2021, on May 11, the first day of Operation Guardian of the Walls, Hamas and the Palestinian Islamic Jihad (PIJ) reportedly fired 137 rockets at Tel Aviv in just five minutes, calling it "the largest ever barrage" at the time.[37] These salvos did not render Iron Dome irrelevant, but they highlighted a pattern: Hamas had stockpiled enough weapons to use rockets as a means of attrition warfare. Coupled with improved concealment tactics in Gaza, this could prolong the fighting, and the longer the conflict lasted, the more challenging it became for the IDF to protect its territory against these attacks.

Another way to overwhelm Iron Dome was to expand the geographical range of rocket attacks. There is evidence that Hamas rethought its target list after the success of Iron Dome in 2012. By then, most of the Iron Dome batteries were deployed in the south. The IDF had designed a "polygon" area between

---

[35] Nicolo Petrelli, *Israel, Strategic Culture and the Conflict with Hamas: Adaptation and Military Effectiveness* (London: Routledge, 2018): 158.

[36] Raphael D. Marcus, "Learning 'Under Fire': Israel's Improvised Military Adaptation to Hamas Tunnel Warfare," *Journal of Strategic Studies* 42, no. 3–4 (2019): 344–370. https://doi.org/10.1080/01402390.2017.1307744.

[37] Joseph Trevithick, "Largest Rocket Barrage from Gaza Ever Hits Central Israel Amid Fears of An Imminent War," *The Drive*, May 11, 2021. https://www.thedrive.com/the-war-zone/40561/largest-rocket-barrage-from-gaza-ever-hits-central-israel-amid-fears-of-an-imminent-war.

Ashkelon, Ashdod, and Be'er-Sheva to be defended. After Hamas learned of this coverage, it started to test the limits of the batteries. Uzi Rubin, a former missile expert at MAFAT, notes that by 2015, Hamas "tailored their use of rockets for geographic location: short-range rockets to attack Israeli communities near the Gaza border, medium-range rockets to attack Israel's southern cities such as Be'er-Sheva and Ashdod, long-range rockets to attack central Israel and the Tel Aviv metropolitan area, and extra long-range rockets to attack Haifa."[38]

Rubin's point is evident when we study the geography of rocket attacks during the 2014 war. In this fifty-day conflict, half of the rockets were fired at Israeli cities and kibbutzim in the Gaza envelope; one-third focused on Ashdod, Be'er-Sheva, and Ashkelon. Finally, a small portion (approximately 325) targeted central and northern Israel, reaching major urban centers around Tel Aviv, Jerusalem, and Haifa.[39] Iron Dome batteries may have been designed as mobile systems to enable commanders to move them around. But three years after their deployment on the battlefield, the flow of Gaza rockets during Operation Protective Edge suggested that more batteries were needed to build a robust defensive coverage on Israel's territory.

More recently, the strategies of Hamas and Hezbollah also involved the use of armed drones. Palestinian and Lebanese combatants emulated the experience of the Houthi insurgency in Yemen. The Houthis started using "kamikaze" drones in the mid-2010s, targeting specifically the Patriot surface-to-air missile defense batteries of the Saudi-led coalition.[40] In theory, a joint campaign combining drone strikes on the radars of Iron Dome batteries and rocket attacks on urban centers increases the pressure on the defensive means.[41]

Iron Dome already faces a significant issue with drones. This has been repeatedly shown in the conflicts of Gaza and Lebanon since 2023. Hezbollah was able to fly drones several times above Israel's airspace, avoiding detection and occasionally destroying targets. In October 2024, a drone attack by Hezbollah at an army base killed four soldiers. The Houthis have also been able to evade Israel's defense systems. On July 19, 2024, the Yemeni group fired a UAV at a building in

38 Uzi Rubin, "Israel's Air and Missile Defense During the 2014 Gaza War," Begin-Sadat Center for Strategic Studies, 2015: 5. https://besacenter.org/wp-content/uploads/2015/02/111eng_web.pdf.

39 Raphael S. Cohen, David E. Johnson, David E. Thaler, Brenna Allen, Elizabeth M. Bartels, James Cahill, Shira Efron, *From Cast Lead to Protective Edge: Lessons from Israel's Wars in Gaza* (Santa Monica, CA: RAND Corporation, 2017): 134.

40 Conflict Armament Research, "Evolution of UAVs Employed by Houthi Forces in Yemen," February 2020. https://www.conflictarm.com/dispatches/evolution-of-uavs-employed-by-houthi-forces-in-yemen/.

41 Victor Gervais, "Asymmetric Warfare: The Threat of Militant Groups Using Drones in the Middle East," Trends, January 24, 2021. https://trendsresearch.org/insight/asymmetric-warfare-the-threat -of-militant-groups-using-drones-in-the-middle-east/.

Tel Aviv, killing one person and injuring ten others. Those attacks challenged the belief in Israel's invulnerability. Meeting the day after a Houthi drone attack on Tel Aviv, Doron Gavish, former air defense commander, explains, "The issue with UAVs is detection; they have a different trajectory, and when they have a short range, it's difficult to have enough time to detect and to intercept them."

At the same time, Gavish notes, "We have to consider the threat in proportion because at the end of the day, seven kilos of explosive (the payload of the Houthi drone that attacked Tel Aviv a day before) it's not much, but it questions the feeling of security of the people."[42] Gavish's statement recalls the debates inside the IDF in the 1980s concerning the assessments of the missile threat: For many, they were not in essence—and still are not—means of massive destruction, but they challenge the ability of Israel's government to guarantee the safety of its citizens, from Sderot to Haifa. In hindsight, Israel's military assessments surely underestimated the ability of an enemy like Hamas to adapt. As Eran Ortal warned, "We've not really grasped the true nature of rockets. They were not only about the amount of damage they will cause in our cities, but it's also about our enemy deterring you from preventing the threat from growing on the other side."[43]

Noticeably, Hamas or Hezbollah initially relied on Iran to access weaponry. Specifically, the Islamic Revolutionary Guards Corps played a crucial role in the military evolution of these nonstate actors.[44] But in the years preceding the 2023 war, their ability to build their arsenals directly in Gaza or Lebanon increased. By the late 2000s, Hamas had built a rocket research and development center at the Islamic University of Gaza that directly supported the production of Qassam rockets.[45] This was not simply a matter of technology. In the end, the proliferation of rockets, missiles, and drones in the Middle East changed Israel's security equation because Hamas and Hezbollah found effective ways to integrate those capabilities into their military structures and to devise a coherent strategy. As Michael Horowitz from the University of Pennsylvania argues in his book *The Diffusion of Military Power*, military innovation succeeds when the actor invests in financial resources and organizational changes to fully adopt the new technology: "It is the employment of technologies by organizations, rather than the technologies themselves, that most often makes the difference."[46]

---

[42] Interview with Doron Gavish, former Air Defense Commander, IDF, Tel Aviv, July 22, 2024.

[43] Interview with Eran Ortal, former Commander of the Dado Center, Tel Aviv, June 16, 2024.

[44] Jean-Loup Samaan, "Missile Warfare and Violent Non-State Actors: The Case of Hezbollah," *Defence Studies* 17, no. 2 (2017): 156–170. https://doi.org/10.1080/14702436.2017.1295788.

[45] Yoram Cohen, Jeffrey White, *Hamas in Combat: The Military Performance of the Palestinian Islamic Resistance Movement* (Washington, DC: Washington Institute for Near East Policy, October 2009).

[46] Michael Horowitz, *The Diffusion of Military Power: Causes and Consequences for International Politics* (Princeton, NJ: Princeton University Press, 2010): 2.

A Failure of Imagination

In 2015, General Meir Finkel, then commander of the IDF Dado Center, wrote a much-discussed article in the military journal *Maarachot* (Battles in Hebrew) titled "Iron Dome: The New Maginot Line?" The flag officer argued in the essay that "all the shortcomings of the Maginot Line—its astronomical costs at the expense of offensive measures, the creation of a false sense of security, and the decline of the offensive doctrine in the military—can also be seen in the context of Iron Dome."[47]

Finkel's argument ran counter to the prevailing political sentiment. The assertion on a new Maginot Line might have been the dominant view among the top brass a decade earlier, but mentalities inside the defense ministry had changed. The article was published when Iron Dome was widely regarded as a success, having saved many lives during operations in 2012 and 2014. The engineers at Rafael and MAFAT who worked on Iron Dome had just been awarded Israel's prestigious Defense Prize. The new IDF Strategy document and the Gideon plan, led by Gadi Eisenkot, shifted the armed forces toward a new posture that struck a balance between offense and defense.

Several high-level figures of the military establishment opposed Finkel's analogy about the Maginot Line. For instance, during our conversation, General Jacob Amidror, Netanyahu's former national security adviser, was adamant about debunking the comparison when Iron Dome first entered the battlefield. In our discussion, Amidror insists, "The Maginot Line is not a good example; Iron Dome is successful . . . here we have something which succeeded in neutralizing the ability of Hamas and Hezbollah to destroy Israel with rockets and missiles."[48]

Despite Amidror's insistence, the Maginot Line analogy is worth exploring. Many tensions within the IDF during the past decade echo the French military debate of the interwar period. In the 1920s, the French government invested in a vast network of fortifications along its border with Germany. What became known as the Maginot Line—named after French Defense Minister André Maginot, who oversaw its initial construction in 1922—was the result of political and military assumptions.

Governments in Paris assessed that the French population would no longer tolerate the burden of offensive campaigns such as those fought during the First

---

47 Meir Finkel, "Kipat Barzel – Kav Magino Hachadash?" (Iron Dome – The New Maginot Line?), *Maarachot* no. 461 (June 2015): 11. https://www.maarachot.idf.il/media/t13cig4r/כיפת-ברזל-קו-מאזינו-החדש.pdf.

48 Interview with Jacob Amidror, former National Security Adviser (2011–13), Raananah, June 17, 2024.

World War. Between 1914 and 1918, the overreliance of European military leaders on the offensive and their belief in the potential of a single breakthrough on the battlefield to secure a decisive victory led to tragic stalemates: In 1916, 163,000 French troops died during the Battle of Verdun; a year later, the Battle of the Aisne claimed approximately 187,000 French soldiers. In the aftermath of the First World War, France reduced the duration of its national service to one year. Officers also believed France's superiority in fortifications and artillery would deter any German ambition to launch an attack.[49]

Making historical analogies is always a delicate exercise, but their use can reveal how decision-makers view their challenges and frame their options.[50] Despite the many differences between France during the interwar period and Israel over the past fifteen years, there are notable similarities in their policy decisions that warrant our attention: The desire by the political elite to maintain the status quo, the fatigue of the general population regarding the burden of preparing for war, and the confidence of the military establishment that the country's technological superiority can compensate for the reduction in manpower.

It is also worth stressing that, contrary to a long-enduring myth, the French Maginot Line did *work* on the battlefield. It was, from an operational standpoint, a major innovation.[51] The problem with the system was that it became a central, if not the central, element of French defense policy. It shaped the culture of politicians and military leaders, preventing them from imagining other conflict scenarios.

With the benefit of hindsight, Israeli military thinkers now also offer a more critical view of the benefits of Iron Dome. Eado Hecht, a lecturer at the IDF Command and Staff College, concedes that the Maginot Line analogy is correct in describing a "way of thinking... basically that we're allowing the enemy to hit us. Sooner or later, they'll get through if you're passive; it's just a matter of time. No matter how heavy your armor is, sooner or later, they'll find the weak point, and this is what happened on October 7."[52] Likewise, Eran Ortal sees the limits of the IDF's reliance on Iron Dome: "When Peretz invested in air defense, they had in mind the need to protect the population. They did not think of Iron Dome as a strategic framework; what they did was to put a band-aid on a scratch."[53]

---

[49] Jean-Marc Marill, "La doctrine militaire française entre les deux guerres," *Revue historique des Armées* no. 184 (1991): 24–34.

[50] Yuen Foong Khong, *Analogies at War: Korea, Munich, Dien Bien Phu, and the Vietnam Decisions of 1965* (Princeton, NJ: Princeton University Press, 1992).

[51] Judith Hughes, *To the Maginot Line: The Politics of French Military Preparation in the 1920s* (Cambridge, MA: Harvard University Press, 2006).

[52] Interview with Eado Hecht, Tel Aviv, July 25, 2024.

[53] Interview with Eran Ortal, Tel Aviv, June 16, 2024.

Finkel's article in 2015 was not an isolated act. While the political establishment in Jerusalem recognized a clear benefit in a defensive strategy that maintained the status quo in Gaza, thereby avoiding possible concessions to the Palestinians, IDF officers openly expressed their doubts regarding this approach. As the Dado Center wrote in its journal in the summer of 2015, "the debate over the proper balance between IDF's offensive capabilities and the growing dominance of its defensive forces has returned, turning into a stormy conceptual fight."[54]

Officers, reservists, and commentators published articles that supported or challenged the defensive shift. For instance, in February 2021, Shay Shabtai, a colonel from the reserve, wrote a short paper for the Begin-Sadat Center at Bar-Ilan University, portraying the adoption of Iron Dome as "an expression of failure in national decision-making." Shabtai argued specifically that, notwithstanding the technological achievement of Iron Dome, the system reflected the preference of the government "to avoid major decisions" regarding the growth of nonstate actors like Hamas.[55] In other words, analysts and officers feared that Iron Dome embodied a political priority forced on the IDF that would ultimately have negative military consequences.

Some of the tensions within the IDF were also related to how much the military assessed the rocket threat to affect the daily lives of Israelis. As it turned out, the dispute of the 1980s between David Ivry and the military intelligence agency was not over. The belief that rocket attacks did not have a strategic implication lingered within the IDF's top brass. In one of my interviews in Tel Aviv, a retired IDF officer shared a revealing anecdote about a war game convened by the government and the military in 2008:

> We did a war game two years after the Lebanon War where we were fighting against the Syrian army, Olmert (then prime minister) came to the command center, Gaby Ashkenazy was the chief of staff, and he told Olmert "we're in control, we're destroying them" . . . Olmert stayed silent, he looked at the map of rockets fired at Israel and replied, "ok, but they're still shooting at us, they're shooting at Tel Aviv, what do you do about that?" Ashkenazy had no response. He just didn't fully understand the concerns of Olmert for the cities.

54 Eran Ortal, "Editor's Preface," *Dado Center Journal* no. 4 (July 2015). https://www.idf.il/en/mini-sites/dado-center/vol-4-defense-and-home-front/vol-4-defense-and-home-front/.

55 Shay Shabtai, "Hahatztaidot beKipat Barzel Kvitui Lechshel beKablat Hahachaltot Haleumit" (The Acquisition of Iron Dome as an Expression of a Failure in National Decision-Making), Begin-Sadat Center, February 2021. https://besacenter.org/wp-content/uploads/2021/02/הצטיידות-בכיפת-ברזל-תימואלה-תותלחהה-תלבקב-לשכל-יוטיבכ-1924-Shabtai-Hebrew-final.pdf.

IDF commanders also grew frustrated with Iron Dome because its effectiveness reduced their capacity to argue for reprisals in the event of rocket attacks. Several interviewees expressed concerns about how Israel's missile defense performance shifted the international public opinion away from the initial threat posed by rockets. Jacob Amidror lamented, "If you have a good defense, you are losing your legitimacy to attack. Israel can react only when Israel is bleeding. Otherwise, the world is condemning Israel."[56] Michael Oren, former Israeli ambassador to the United States, also wrote,

> When Israelis had access to bomb shelters and early warning systems, why then exact vengeance on the innocent Palestinians who had neither? Interviewing on CNN during the operation, I was asked—twice, without irony—why doesn't Israel provide Iron Dome to Gaza? Israel, it seemed, had the right to defend itself but only passively, shooting Iron Dome until it ran out of interceptors.[57]

The topic also surfaced in the Israeli–US dialogue. Daniel Shapiro, former US ambassador to Israel (2011–17), recalls, "it didn't take long for the Israelis to start raising the question of the downside: they worried 'we might find that we're normalizing rockets being fired at us and reducing the legitimacy to respond, to punish the people attacking us because we have the defenses.'"[58] In other words, Iron Dome increased the role of defense systems among the policy options available to the commander in chief, but it reduced the leeway for the IDF to plan reprisal operations that had been the standard response to Palestinian attacks since the 1950s.[59]

The Decline of Israel's Self-Reliant Aspirations

The increasing reliance on Iron Dome also coincided with greater dependence on the United States. This trend is not new. Since the 1980s, US financial aid has been essential in preserving Israel's military advantage in the region. However, the introduction of Iron Dome and missile defense has magnified this dependence. Iron Dome may have been a system designed and first produced

---

[56] Interview with Jacob Amidror, former National Security Adviser (2011–13), Raananah, June 17, 2024.

[57] Oren, "Iron Dome: Israel's Double-Edged Sword."

[58] Interview with Daniel Shapiro, Washington, DC, February 20, 2025.

[59] Ze'ev Drory, *Israel's Reprisal Policy, 1953–1956. The Dynamics of Military Retaliation* (London: Routledge, 2004).

by Israel, but its endurance was made possible because of the United States' increased involvement in financing and producing parts of it.

This overreliance on the United States would not be an object of contention if Israel considered itself a small state that has no choice but to "bandwagon" with a great power. However, Israeli leaders have always defied Thucydides' rule on small states; that is, "[t]he strong do what they can, and the weak suffer what they must."[60] Since 1948, the sense of permanent insecurity that fed Israel's strategic culture came with the firm belief that self-reliance was the only sustainable course of action. Dependence on an external power was considered perilous. This idea is a recurring theme in the speeches and memoirs of Israel's founding fathers. In his memoirs, Ben-Gurion insists, "We must prepare for war while relying on our own strength and capability. Our fate, the fate of the Yishuv, of the nation, and of the Jewish state, depends first and foremost, and above all, on us."[61] Similarly, Ariel Sharon once told Prime Minister Levi Eshkol, "Every appeal we make to the great powers proves our weakness."[62] The Israeli scholar Zeev Maoz made a similar point when he explained that from an Israeli standpoint, the country "cannot rely on the outside world to ensure its survival and defense. Ultimately, Israeli men and women will have to risk their lives to defend their country. Nobody else will do it for them."[63]

Therefore, the notion of self-help is a key pillar of Israel's national identity, and in many ways, Zionism derived from that proposition. But today, it is more an aspiration than a reality. Over the years, the Israeli–American partnership generated a dependence that was not only diplomatic, in securing the support of one global power, but also military. This Israeli reliance on US security assistance has been on full display throughout the Gaza War after October 2023. This was obvious in both defensive and offensive capabilities, as the administrations of President Biden and then-President Trump approved numerous shipments of additional ammunition needed by the IDF in its operations in Gaza and Lebanon.

However, the case of Iron Dome allows us to grasp how far this overreliance has gone. The initial success of Iron Dome led the Israeli government to expand the territorial coverage of the air defense system. Quickly, Benjamin Netanyahu and Defense Minister Ehud Barak decided they would not stop at three batteries. They

---

[60] Thucydides, *The Peloponnesian War* (London: J. M. Dent, 1910).

[61] Quoted in: Ariel Levite, *Offense and Defense in Israeli Military Doctrine* (Boulder, CO: Westview Press, 1989): 29.

[62] Ariel Ilan Roth, "Reassurance: A Strategic Basis of U.S. Support for Israel," *International Studies Perspectives* no. 10 (2009): 378–393, 382–383. https://www.jstor.org/stable/44218611.

[63] Zeev Maoz, *Defending the Holy Land: A Critical Analysis of Israel's Security and Foreign Policy* (Ann Arbor: University of Michigan Press, 2006): 8.

added three others, then six, and then nine. As seen with the evolution of officials like Gadi Eisenkot, gone was the caution of those within the IDF who considered Iron Dome a protection limited to a few military sites and infrastructures.

This was not just a matter of revising the IDF doctrine. It involved a conscious choice to deepen Israel's reliance on US funding, which amplified the disconnect between the rhetoric of Israel's self-reliance and the reality of that increased dependence on the United States. In the near future, this gap could lead to increased friction. Since the Obama presidency, US administrations have provided Israeli governments with support for Iron Dome to a level that has no equivalent elsewhere. However, they did so because there was—and there still is, as of this writing—a strong belief that Iron Dome prevents conflict escalation because of its defensive purpose. The most optimistic observers in Washington even portray Iron Dome as an instrument of peace.

But suppose the bipartisan consensus on the topic weakens, as foreshadowed in previous congressional disputes in 2021, and suppose financial support can no longer be taken for granted. In that case, it will expose the vulnerabilities of Israel's military posture. As noted by Oren Barak, Amit Sheniak, and Assaf Shapira, the Israeli shift toward defense, and more specifically missile defense, coincided with the decision of its governments to allow for the first time in its history "a constant deployment of foreign military forces in its territory to defend it against potential threats."[64] This deployment included the integration of US AEGIS missile ships patrolling in the Mediterranean, the installation of the US X-band AN/TPY-2 radar, and the connection of Israeli sensors to the US Shared Early Warning satellite missile system.

The addition of a Terminal High Altitude Area Defense (THAAD) battery in October 2024, as Israel prepared for a potential escalation with Iran, also revealed how much this overreliance has been normalized.[65] The US-made THAAD system is designed to intercept short- to medium-range ballistic missiles rather than the rockets targeted by Iron Dome. Its deployment occurred amid the 2024 war between Israel and Hezbollah when military planners in Washington and Tel Aviv feared that the Lebanese organization could use its most advanced arsenal on Israeli cities.

By the time the Biden administration approved this deployment, US air defense capabilities in both Israel and Ukraine faced a risk of shortages. Dana

---

[64] Barak, Sheniak, Shapira, "The Shift to Defence in Israel's Hybrid Military Strategy": 14.

[65] Lolita Baldor, "US to Send Missile Defense System and Troops to Israel," *Military Times*, October 14, 2024. https://www.militarytimes.com/news/your-military/2024/10/14/us-to-send-missile-defense-system-and-troops-to-israel/.

Stroul, a former deputy assistant secretary of defense for the Middle East (2021–3), stated at the time, "The US can't continue supplying Ukraine and Israel at the same pace. We are reaching a tipping point."[66] By extension, it questioned Israel's ability to sustain its operational tempo against Hamas and Hezbollah while guaranteeing the defense of its territory. While the system did not collapse this time, in future conflicts, Israel's reliance on US funding and arms production could reach its limits.

"Decisive Victory": Last Attempt to Transcend the Status Quo

By the end of the 2010s, the issue of Gaza was a policy priority for neither Israel nor the United States. The Netanyahu government was supporting the US administration of President Trump (then in his first term) in promoting a "peace plan" dubbed "the deal of the century," which focused on the West Bank and was perceived as favorable to the Israeli prime minister's views. After the Palestinian Authority rejected the proposal, Israeli and American officials shifted their goal toward normalization efforts with Gulf states, which culminated with the Abraham Accords signed by the UAE and Bahrain in 2020.

In the meantime, frustrations within the IDF kept growing vis-à-vis the Gaza status quo and the 2015 Strategy. The document acknowledged the fact that, for all its formidable military power, Israel could not destroy Hamas. The country would rely on its missile defense batteries to protect citizens and occasionally degrade the enemy's capabilities to "delay" the next war.

However, this new institutional culture went against the ethos of the IDF. Consequently, in January 2019, Aviv Kochavi, who succeeded Gadi Eisenkot as the head of the IDF, introduced a new plan. Upon assuming his new role in January of that year, Kochavi delivered a public speech aimed at shifting the tone of the IDF's message. He stated that the country's army was "all about victory."[67] In the following months, Kochavi's close advisers were eager to highlight that "victory" had been a forgotten word in the IDF lexicon after fifteen years of irregular wars fought in Lebanon and the Gaza Strip. Now, the team surrounding

[66] John Paul Rathbone, "Israel Races to Supply Anti-Missile Shield," *Financial Times*, October 15, 2024. https://www.ft.com/content/5b884be4-c883-421b-89d6-32cf860e97df.

[67] Daniel Pipes, "What Does 'Victory' Really Mean to the Israel Defense Forces," *Jerusalem Post*, November 26, 2020. https://www.jpost.com/opinion/idf-sees-victory-as-rapid-destruction-of -enemy-capabilities-opinion-650265.

the new chief of the general staff was committed to making "victory" the latest buzzword in Israel's military debates. Soon, Kochavi announced the development of a new operational concept called "Decisive Victory."

The concept aimed to initiate a comprehensive reform of the IDF, encompassing procurement, training, and service interoperability. It openly questioned the relevance of the 2015 IDF Strategy. Conversely, the "Decisive Victory" concept represented a return to form. It denied the notion that the IDF should gear up for prolonged and limited operations, essentially implying indecisiveness.[68] Kochavi's plan was built on a series of works and publications published by the IDF Dado Center that described nonstate enemies, namely, Hamas and Hezbollah, as "diffuse, rocket-based terror armies."[69] Kochavi and his team did not refer to these groups as "insurgents" or "guerrillas" but as "organized, well-trained armies, well-equipped for their missions."[70]

Fundamentally, the proponents of "Decisive Victory" considered that the IDF's previous options were flawed. Just as Meir Finkel asserted in his article that Iron Dome was a new Maginot Line, Kochavi and his circle posited that overreliance on defensive means was perilous. In their eyes, previous IDF operations in Gaza failed to achieve their objectives and weakened Israel's deterrence credibility.

Eran Ortal, then head of the IDF Dado Center and a supporter of Kochavi's concept, argued that the new strategy involved the ability "to attack deep into enemy territory, to conquer main nerve centers, and inflict a decisive defeat while suppressing enemy rockets and missiles launched nearby toward Israeli forces and toward the home front."[71] For Gabi Siboni and Yuval Bazak, two retired officers, the primary characteristics of "Decisive Victory" were the shortening of the war's duration and the "overwhelming destruction of enemy capabilities using intelligence assets, precise fire capabilities, and offensive autonomous systems."[72]

As a result, the strategy focused on rapid offensive operations relying on smaller units, backed by massive firepower. In his speeches, Kochavi explained that "at the heart of the multiyear concept is increasing lethality in quantity and

[68] Avi Kober, *Israel's Wars of Attrition: Attrition Challenges to Democratic States* (London: Routledge, 2009).

[69] Ortal, "Going on the Attack: The Theoretical Foundation of the Israel Defense Forces' Momentum Plan."

[70] Ortal, "Going on the Attack: The Theoretical Foundation of the Israel Defense Forces' Momentum Plan."

[71] Eran Ortal, "Turn on the Light, Extinguish the Fire: Israel's New Way of War," War on the Rocks, January 19, 2022. https://warontherocks.com/2022/01/turn-on-the-light-extinguish-the-fire-israels -new-way-of-war/.

[72] Gabi Siboni, Yuval Bazak, "The IDF 'Victory Doctrine': The Need for an Updated Doctrine," Jerusalem Institute for Strategy and Security, June 14, 2021. https://jiss.org.il/en/siboni-idf-victory- doctrine-the-need-for-an-updated-doctrine/.

precision." The IDF would rely on "greatly enhanced ability to expose the enemy, greatly enhanced ability to destroy the enemy and multi-branch operations."[73] In other words, it aimed to escalate very early and very quickly. It emphasized maneuver, standoff fire, joint operations, and heavy reliance on new technology to accelerate decision-making. It was to put greater emphasis on uncrewed systems and precision-guided munitions. Artificial intelligence (AI) was also set to play a significant role in coordinating units, as the platforms and weapon systems used by the IDF increasingly incorporated AI. The general staff established a dedicated department to oversee this digital transformation.

While the Gideon plan followed Eisenkot's 2015 Strategy, "Decisive Victory" paved the way for another four-year plan, called "Momentum" (*Tnufa* in Hebrew), covering the 2020–24 period. According to IDF public statements, the new plan was built upon the scenario of a multifront war and aimed to prepare soldiers for "swift and massive use of force against enemy systems." At the operational level, one ambitious experiment in the *Tnufa* plan called setting up a new outfit called the "Ghost Unit" (*Yikhidat Refaim* in Hebrew). This elite force combined the various capabilities of the armed forces—infantry, armor, artillery, combat engineers, the air force, UAVs, and cyber-operatives, among others—into a single unit described as one "with the human capabilities of a battalion, but with the firepower of a division."[74] To put it another way, a leaner, more agile, and meaner force. This marked a clear departure from the notion that the IDF had become a defensive force, of which Iron Dome was one of its biggest success stories.

At the rhetorical level, the "Decisive Victory" concept was adopted by the successive governments of Benjamin Netanyahu, Naftali Bennett, and Yair Lapid, as its claim of "victory" conveniently aligned with their political discourse. Around the time Kochavi claimed that the Israeli armed forces were "all about victory," Netanyahu also declared that the IDF was "ready for a single goal—victory in war."[75]

Still, other Israeli experts voiced skepticism regarding "Decisive Victory." Gabi Siboni, a reserve colonel and a close adviser to former Chief of General Staff Eisenkot, dismissed the reform as "no more than a PR stunt." In our conversation, he argued, "It takes years, if not decades, to implement the kind of

---

73　Amiram Barkat, "Chief of Staff Launches Plan for 'More Lethal' IDF," *Globes*, February 13, 2020. https://en.globes.co.il/en/article-chief-of-staff-launches-plan-for-more-lethal-idf-1001318466.

74　Udi Shaham, "Drones and Navigation Systems: 'Ghost' Is Moving the IDF to the Next Level," *Jerusalem Post*, March 18, 2021. https://www.jpost.com/israel-news/drones-and-navigation-systems-ghost-is-moving-the-idf-to-the-next-level-662450.

75　Pipes, "What Does 'Victory' Really Mean to the Israel Defense Forces."

reforms that Kochavi and his advisers want to impose."[76] Eado Hecht, a lecturer at Israel's Command & Staff College, saw it as more "marketing hype than a true concept of operations."[77] Likewise, Amos Harel, the defense correspondent for the newspaper *Haaretz*, called "Decisive Victory" a "political speech that has no direct relevance for the battleground."[78]

The implementation of "Decisive Victory" raised questions at the operational level as well. After years of limited wars that had shifted the heroic figure from soldiers to defensive systems like Iron Dome, the new concept proposed an offensive military doctrine. It focused on the idea that an enemy could be defeated if its capabilities were destroyed with massive firepower in the initial hours of the conflict. For Kochavi and his team, new AI technology enhanced the IDF's coverage of potential enemy targets.[79] The claim assumed that a comprehensive intelligence assessment of the enemy's capabilities existed, making a swift and decisive victory possible. Perhaps the riskiest dimension of "Decisive Victory" was that, at its heart, it assumed Israel's ability to control or dominate the logic of military escalation. To put it another way, the IDF would determine when an operation starts and ends. This approach conferred no agency on the part of the enemy.

Ultimately, government instability, characterized by five legislative elections between April 2019 and November 2022, as well as financial difficulties, hindered the implementation of the new concept. Following Hamas's attacks on October 7, 2023, "Decisive Victory" appeared to be the ultimate attempt to confront the "Maginot Line" mindset that dominated the IDF and the political elite. It aimed to change the equation of limited wars with Hamas or Hezbollah by returning to the foundations of Israel's military culture. Consequently, the Palestinian offensive against cities and kibbutzim in the fall of 2023 crystallized a crisis within the IDF that had been developing for many years. For the first time since the 1973 war, it questioned the notion that Israel's armed forces effectively deterred a major attack on the country.

Israel's Deterrence System After October 7

Before October 2023, the idea that Hamas was deterred was largely accepted within the Israeli strategic community. Many statements by government officials

<hr>

[76] Zoom interview with Gabi Siboni, September 14, 2021.
[77] Email correspondence with Eado Hecht, September 17, 2021.
[78] Zoom interview with Amos Harel, September 23, 2021.
[79] Yaakov Lappin, "IDF Identifies 'as Many Targets in a Month as It Did in a Year,'" *Jewish News Syndicate*, December 4, 2022. https://www.jns.org/idf-identifies-as-many-targets-in-a-month-as-it-did-in-a-year/.

indicated a high degree of confidence in that assumption. In July 2022, Brigadier General Nitzan Nuriel, former director of the Counter-Terrorism Bureau in the Prime Minister's Office, asserted that in Gaza, "we created a new level of deterrence . . . Hamas is very disturbed, and it's doing almost everything it can to avoid its organization and its supporters opening fire against us and is also preventing others from doing so." Likewise, National Security Adviser Tzachi Hanegbi also described Hamas as "deterred" by the IDF Strategy.[80] The logic of deterrence also prevailed in the conflict between Israel and Hezbollah. For most IDF planners, both sides had devised military strategies after the 2006 war that deterred each other.[81]

Looking back, one can identify several flaws in the belief in deterrence. It relied on two core assumptions: that the ability to prevent an attack through air defense capabilities such as Iron Dome and the threat of punishment if the attack were to occur were compelling. In theory, both assumptions reflected two distinct mechanisms of deterrence: by denial and by punishment. However, in reality, there was little evidence that Hamas complied with these rules.

First, the frequency of Israel's limited wars against Hamas eroded the notion of deterrence by punishment. The limited campaigns conducted between 2008 and 2023 were intended to "restore" deterrence, but they had the opposite effect: increasing the frequency of war and the predictable outcome of each operation, temporarily weakening Hamas's power, which in turn discounted the cost of punishment. It merely "vaccinated" Hamas, as some IDF officials feared.

Second, the logic of deterrence by denial remained questionable. Although Iron Dome demonstrated impressive technical performance, its deterrence effect against Hamas (or the PIJ) was difficult to prove. In the past decade, each conflict saw a steady increase in the number of rockets fired at Israel and a constant improvement in their accuracy. Hamas was hardly deterred due to the cost imbalance between offense and defense. Deterrence by denial is effective only if the cost of bypassing those defensive measures gets too high.[82] In the case of Iron Dome and the rockets fired from Gaza or Lebanon, the cost imbalance favored the aggressor: A Palestinian rocket costs between US$700 and US$1,000,

80 Quoted in Michel Wyss, "The October 7 Attack: An Assessment of the Intelligence Failings," *CTC Sentinel* 17, no. 9 (October 2024): 4. https://ctc.westpoint.edu/the-october-7-attack-an-assessment-of-the-intelligence-failings/.

81 Sobelman, "Learning to Deter: Deterrence Failure and Success in the Israel-Hezbollah Conflict, 2006–16"; Jean-Loup Samaan, *From War to Deterrence? Israel-Hezbollah Conflict Since 2006* (Carlisle: US Army War College, 2014).

82 Amir Lupovici, "Deterrence Through Inflicting Costs: Between Deterrence by Punishment and Deterrence by Denial," *International Studies Review* 25, no. 3 (2023): 1–21, 6. https://doi.org/10.1093/isr/viad036.

whereas a Tamir interceptor on one of the Iron Dome batteries to shoot it down costs approximately US$40,000. This suggests that the offense would continue to prevail in the long term, thereby diminishing the deterrent effect on Hamas.

Furthermore, other defensive means deployed by the IDF also proved ineffective. The "Iron Wall" may have showcased the excellence of Israel's defense industry and its hefty price—the last barrier upgrade cost $1 billion over three years. But on October 7, Hamas and other groups quickly crossed it; the IDF counted around thirty breaches of the barrier.[83] Israel believed that Hamas possessed neither the capabilities nor the ambition to breach the fortifications. This failure of imagination was primarily driven by the belief that the sophistication of the Iron Wall deterred Hamas.

The war after October 7 shattered all those assumptions. In the subsequent hours and days, most debates that had animated IDF circles for the past decade became obsolete. Concepts like limited wars, "the campaign between the wars," and "mowing the grass" were no longer relevant. They were viewed as fostering the complacency of the IDF. The IDF's move toward a defensive posture was rejected. What Israel's war cabinet implemented in the Gaza Strip during the haste of launching its operation in October 2023 amounted to total war: The enemy, that is, Hamas, was not to be dealt with. It was not to be weakened. It had to be destroyed. The rhetoric of the 2015 IDF Strategy was gone.

At the beginning of the war, Yoav Gallant, then defense minister, detailed a three-phase plan to the Knesset Foreign Affairs and Defense Committee that put a first emphasis on the destruction of Hamas's infrastructures.[84] At the operational level, this translated into a systematic effort to target Hamas's political leaders, eliminate its combatants and commanders, and destroy its arsenal. In this new war environment, the logic that Iron Dome prevented escalation, that it gave time to the Israeli government to respond, and that ultimately it saved lives on both sides was forgotten.

This shift in the IDF's mindset toward Hamas also applied to Hezbollah. After almost a year of gradual escalation at the Israel–Lebanon border, war came back to Beirut eighteen years after the last devastating conflict. In late September 2024, the Israeli Air Force conducted a massive air campaign on Lebanon. Then, on

[83] Jon Swaine, Joyce Sohyun Lee, Sarah Cahlan, Imogen Piper, Brian Monroe, Evan Hill, Meg Kelly, "How Hamas Exploited Israel's Reliance on Tech to Breach Barrier on Oct. 7," *Washington Post*, November 17, 2023. https://www.washingtonpost.com/investigations/2023/11/17/how-hamas -breached-israel-iron-wall/.

[84] Reuters, "Israel Aims to End Its Responsibility for Gaza Strip – Minister," October 20, 2023. https://www.reuters.com/world/middle-east/israel-aims-end-its-responsibility-gaza-strip-minister -2023-10-20/.

the first of October, the IDF launched a ground invasion of southern Lebanon. There, as well, limited war was no longer acceptable. The IDF and the Mossad proceeded to assassinate most of Hezbollah's military and political leaders, including its longtime Secretary General Hassan Nasrallah, who was killed in an air strike on September 27.

Conclusion

In the aftermath of the Gaza War, the concept of Israel's deterrence and the role assigned to Iron Dome surely differ from what they were in the past two decades. Iron Dome was regarded as a tool of deterrence because it presumed the IDF could not—or should not—address the rocket challenge solely through offensive measures. Iron Dome reflected the threshold of what Israel's governments were willing to tolerate at their borders.

New military and political factors will define the future contours of the IDF Strategy, as well as the place conferred to Iron Dome and missile defense within that framework. At the military level, many voices within the IDF blame the October 7 failure on the flawed beliefs fostered by the success of systems like Iron Dome. Retired officials, such as Jacob Amidror, point out that the IDF lost its culture of preventive operations, which aim to eliminate threats before they materialize. In light of the operations in Gaza and Lebanon, the Israeli military posture is once again returning to its inclination toward offensive strategies, and it will continue to do so in the near future.

However, the political reality of Israel and its borders will also constrain the very notion of its defense. As of this writing, the government of Benjamin Netanyahu has kept troops in the Gaza Strip with the intent to reoccupy, at least temporarily, the Palestinian territory. The IDF has also expanded its presence in the West Bank, in southern Lebanon, and in Syria following the fall of Bashar al-Assad. In the short term, these positions may be justified to create "buffer zones" to defend Israel. Still, it raises speculation about the expansionist ambitions of the far-right members of Mr. Netanyahu's government.

This has direct consequences for the application of any defense or deterrence strategy. Deterrence or defense can maintain a status quo, but only if the conditions of that status quo are considered acceptable to both parties. This is why the Israeli scholar Uri-Bar Joseph noted in 1998 the limits of Israel's deterrence model: "Neither military superiority nor unmistakable resolve to use it is enough to ensure the future success of Israel's deterrence strategy; the most important condition to be met is the establishment of a new territorial and political status quo acceptable to the Arab side."[85] David Ivry, the former air force chief who adamantly called for Israel's investments in missile defense, shared a similar conclusion: "If you want to write a concept of defense, you have to decide about your borders, but you cannot get a political coalition, of which everybody will accept the same idea of Israel's borders so you have to design that concept in such a way that everybody can live with it."[86]

This is what each Israeli government did between 2007 and 2023. During this period, Israel's political establishment tolerated a fragile status quo in the Gaza Strip that followed Ariel Sharon's disengagement plan. Since none of the successive governments wanted to challenge this status quo—either by reoccupying the Palestinian territory or by normalizing relations with Hamas— they opted for a containment strategy illustrated by the rise of Iron Dome. This approach transformed political strategy into military action, and due to the tactical success of the system, it allowed each government to avoid difficult decisions. However, changes on the battlefield arose, suggesting an end to this status quo. This does not imply that Iron Dome will disappear; it will continue to play a crucial role in intercepting rockets and missiles. However, its prominence in the political arena will likely diminish as governments and military officials shift back to an offensive stance. From this perspective, it is worthwhile to explore the potential contours of Israel's missile defense in the years to come.

---

[85] Uri Bar-Joseph, "Variations on a Theme: The Conceptualization of Deterrence in Israeli Strategic Thinking," *Security Studies* 7, no. 3 (1998): 145–181, 180. https://doi.org/10.1080/09636419808429353.
[86] Interview with David Ivry, former Chief Israel Air Force, Ramat HaSharon, July 22, 2024.

6

Beyond Iron Dome

The Future of Missile Defense in the Middle East

Late in the evening of Saturday, April 13, 2024, Iran launched an air attack on Israel's territory. Iran's operation was a retaliatory action after the Israel Defense Forces (IDF) bombed the annex of the Iranian embassy in Damascus, killing two generals of the Islamic Revolutionary Guard Corps (IRGC). Following the Israeli strike in Syria, Middle Eastern countries braced for escalation. They closed their airspace, airlines canceled their flights, and governments called—in vain—for restraint.

By all measures, the Iranian response was unprecedented. The offensive combined more than 200 unmanned aerial vehicles (UAVs), 110–130 ballistic missiles, and 30 cruise missiles.[1] For the first time since the Scud attacks by Saddam Hussein in 1991, a Middle Eastern state launched a direct assault on Israel. But whereas Saddam had used 42 Scud missiles, Iranian planners determined that a barrage of over 300 projectiles was necessary to respond to the killing of their military commanders in Damascus. The old illusion of the IDF top brass that enemies would not dare launch missiles at Israel's territory was gone.

Somehow, both Israel and Iran found a way to portray the events positively. Iranian officials promptly hailed their operation as a major success. They claimed that their weapons reached the IDF Air Force Nevatim airbase in the Negev Desert and an IDF intelligence center in Mount Hermon. Subsequently, they warned that if the United States were to support further Israeli attacks against Iran, the next reprisal would include US bases in the Middle East.[2]

From the Israeli perspective, a complex yet successful air defense campaign met the Iranian offensive. No one was killed, and the damage to the military bases

---

[1] Steve Fetter, David Wright, "Can the Iron Dome Be Transmuted Into a Golden Dome?," *The Washington Quarterly* 48, no. 2 (2025): 95–114, 97. https:/doi.org/10.1080/0163660X.2025.2514916.

[2] Andie Parry, Alexandra Braverman, Ashka Jhaveri, Johanna Moore, Peter Mills, Nicholas Carl, "Iran Update," Institute for the Study of War, April 14, 2024. https://www.understandingwar.org/backgrounder/iran-update-april-14-2024.

was limited. This reflected the technical achievements of its various systems and the diplomatic support the country could garner. Indeed, that night, the IDF was not the only one blocking the Iranian barrage. Israel relied on US capabilities and military personnel as well as those of two NATO allies (the UK and France) and Arab states (Jordan, reportedly Saudi Arabia, and the UAE).

Specifically, two US Navy destroyers, USS *Arleigh Burke* and USS *Carney*, shot down six Iranian ballistic missiles from the Mediterranean. US Air Force aircraft destroyed drones on their way to Israel via Jordan, Iraq, and Syria. They were supported by UK Royal Air Force fighter jets operating from bases in Cyprus.[3] French military forces stationed in Jordan also contributed to the operation. However, President Macron downplayed their involvement in his public statement: "Following the demand of Jordanian authorities, we made some interceptions, but strictly to protect and defend ourselves."[4]

The ambivalent message from the French government echoed the unease of the Arab regimes involved in the operation. The Royal Jordanian Air Force directly shot down dozens of Iranian drones that crossed its airspace, but Amman's intervention triggered anger in Arab social media that depicted it as a betrayal of the Palestinian cause. It compelled the Jordanian government to justify its involvement in a cautious statement. Jordan's Foreign Minister Ayman Safadi stated, "There was imminent danger of drones or missiles falling in Jordan, and the Jordanian armed forces dealt with this danger in the appropriate manner . . . We took them yesterday and we will take them in the future, whether the source of the threat is Israel, Iran or any [other] element."[5] Other Arab countries, such as Saudi Arabia and the UAE, reportedly became involved in the operation, although their authorities denied any involvement.[6] At a minimum, Gulf states allowed the United States to use its missile defense capabilities stationed in the Arabian Peninsula to respond to the Iranian attack.

---

[3] Julian Borger, "US and UK Forces Help Shoot Down Iranian Drones Over Jordan, Syria and Iraq," *The Guardian*, April 14, 2024. https://www.theguardian.com/world/2024/apr/14/us-and-uk-forces -help-shoot-down-iranian-drones-over-jordan-syria-and-iraq.

[4] France Info, "Attaque de l'Iran contre Israël: Emmanuel Macron clarifie les annonces d'Israël sur 'l'aide' apportée par la France," April 15, 2024. https://www.francetvinfo.fr/monde/proche-orient /israel-palestine/attaque-de-l-iran-contre-israel-emmanuel-macron-clarifie-les-annonces-d-israel -sur-l-aide-apportee-par-la-france_6488027.html.

[5] Justin Salhani, "Tightrope: Jordan's Balancing Act Between Iran and Israel," *Al Jazeera*, April 21, 2024. https://www.aljazeera.com/news/2024/4/21/tightrope-jordans-balancing-act-between-iran -and-israel.

[6] Summer Said, Stephen Kalin, "Israel-Iran Confrontation Forces Gulf Powers to Choose Sides," *Wall Street Journal*, April 16, 2024. https://www.wsj.com/world/middle-east/israel-iran-confrontation -forces-gulf-powers-to-choose-sides-62649a7a.

Ultimately, the role of Arab states did not amount to an active participation alongside the IDF, like officials and commentators in Israel or the United States may have hoped.[7] But it showed the new operational reality of missile defense in the Middle East. The details of the night of April 13, 2024, as we know them, reveal the complexity of both the offensive and defensive measures. In its offensive, Iran showcased the vast array of weapon systems at its disposal and the challenges they posed for its opponents' militaries. On the defensive side, Israel demonstrated the effectiveness of its missile defense systems and the importance of cooperation among partners, most crucially the United States, in responding to such attacks.

However, the episode also highlights emerging challenges. Iran not only was able to launch an attack of unprecedented sophistication but also set a new threshold for escalation. Eventually, a direct attack on Israel's territory did not trigger a regional war. Other similar events followed: Less than six months later, on October 1, Iran launched another attack with some 200 ballistic missiles in response to the successive killing of Hamas leader Ismail Haniyeh in Tehran, Hezbollah Secretary General Hassan Nasrallah, and IRGC General Abbas Nilforoushan in Beirut.[8] Israeli defensive capabilities worked again in mitigating most of the damage caused by the Iranian attacks, but it is hard to see how this trajectory is sustainable. According to various assessments, the Iranian attack of April 13, 2024, cost Tehran about $80 million, whereas the interception of all those missiles and drones was billed at $1 billion.[9]

The former star of Israel's skies, Iron Dome, played only a supporting role during this war of missiles and countermissiles. Against Iran's advanced arsenal, the system was less relevant than other lesser-known systems, Arrow and David's Sling. It showed how the centrality of Iron Dome throughout the past decade was now getting pushed to the background.

Against that backdrop, this final chapter examines how the landscape of missile proliferation and missile defense continues to evolve and what it means for the future character of war in the Middle East. The chapter explains how the Israeli missile defense posture relies on a multilayered architecture that continues to become more complex as it integrates new systems, such as laser-based weaponry. We then examine how new technologies, such as uncrewed systems,

---

7 John Hannah, "US, Israeli, Arab Coordination in Mideast Against Iran Comes to Fruition," *Defense News*, April 18, 2024. https://www.defensenews.com/opinion/2024/04/18/us-israeli-arab-coordination-in-mideast-against-iran-comes-to-fruition/.

8 Fetter, Wright, "Can the Iron Dome Be Transmuted Into a Golden Dome?": 97.

9 Michael Horowitz, "Battles of Precise Mass," *Foreign Affairs* 103, no. 6 (November–December 2024): 34–40, 38. https://www.foreignaffairs.com/world/battles-precise-mass-technology-war-horowitz.

hypersonic weapons, and artificial intelligence (AI), are driving significant innovations in firepower, speed, and command and control. The introduction of these technologies on the battlefield presents challenges and opportunities for the IDF. But ultimately, they contribute to a new military revolution that will, in time, transform the nature of Israel's conflicts with its adversaries.

As a result, it also affects the concept of strategic stability in the Middle East, amid the risk of military escalation. Given Israel's tendency toward offense since the October 7 attacks, the failure of nonproliferation initiatives in the Middle East, and the benefits that offenders gain from new technologies (e.g., uncrewed systems, AI), regional powers will continue to lean toward offense rather than passively defending. In this context, missile defense systems will play a limited role in mitigating damage, further weakening their deterrent value.

Finally, the evolution of Israel's military race with its close enemies provides lessons for states in the Middle East, as well as in Asia and Europe, which are increasingly investing in missile defense. Israel's missile defense experience serves as an instrument of influence for the country's diplomats and its defense industry. However, as the chapter underlines, the limited sales of Iron Dome show that beyond the international fascination with its success story, this Israeli experience and the nature of the threat the country faces remain, ultimately, unique.

Israel's Missile Defense: A Multilayered Approach

Throughout the past decade, the IDF has come to view its air defense policy as a "multi-layered" approach or "integrated defense."[10] This means that missile defense relies on a variety of systems rather than a single, one-size-fits-all solution. Intercepting short-range rockets or drones requires systems that differ from those used against cruise or midrange ballistic missiles. Though Iron Dome is the most well-known system operated by the IDF, Israel's missile defense strategy already relies on two other "layers" designed to address different threats: David's Sling and Arrow (currently its second and third versions).

As mentioned earlier in the book, Arrow was Israel's first missile defense system. It remains the most ambitious one to date, meant to intercept long-range missiles (up to 2,400 kilometers) such as those stored by Iran. Initially, it benefited from the US Strategic Defense Initiative in the 1980s. As of 2023, the US

[10] Ariel Levite, Shlomo Brom, "From Dream to Reality: Israel and Missile Defense," in: Catherine Kelleher, Peter Dombrowski (eds.), *Regional Missile Defense from a Global Perspective* (Stanford, CA: Stanford University Press, 2015): 137–160.

Congressional Research Service estimated that the US government contributed $4.5 billion (in current US dollars) to the development of Arrow since 1990. Though American administrations provided much of the initial funding, Israel now covers half of the annual costs dedicated to the system.[11]

To date, three versions of Arrow have been developed. The IDF first used it on the battlefield in March 2017, when Arrow 2 intercepted a Syrian surface-to-air missile targeting an Israeli fighter jet on its way back after a raid on Syria.[12] Arrow 3, which entered service that same year, is said to be a "more advanced version in terms of speed, range and altitude."[13] Whereas Iron Dome remains the leading actor against the rockets of Hamas and Hezbollah, Arrow came to the limelight during the war after October 7, 2023, to foil the attacks from the Houthis and Iran. In November 2023, the IDF announced the interception of a ballistic missile fired by the Houthis from Yemen. Using the Arrow 3 system outside Earth's atmosphere, the interception was described as "the first combat ever to take place in space."[14]

David's Sling, the other major system, was launched just a few months after Iron Dome, in August 2008. It intercepts long-range rockets and cruise missiles, whose ranges vary between 40 and 250 kilometers. It focuses on the arsenal stored by Hezbollah, Iran, and Syria, rather than that of groups in the Gaza Strip. From the outset, Israel codeveloped David's Sling with the United States. According to congressional reports, the United States contributed over $2.4 billion between 2006 and 2023 to its development.[15] Just like with Iron Dome, the US company Raytheon (renamed RTX in 2023) teamed up with Rafael to coproduce David's Sling interceptor, the Stunner, in one of its factories in Tucson, Arizona, since 2018. The IDF used the defense system for the first time on July 23, 2018, to intercept two SS-21 Tochka ballistic missiles fired by Syrian regular forces from the Golan.[16]

Iron Dome, David's Sling, and the two most recent versions of Arrow constitute the three pillars of Israel's integrated defense today. But given the

---

[11] Jeremy Sharp, "U.S. Foreign Aid to Israel," *Congressional Research Service*, March 1, 2023: 22. https://www.congress.gov/crs-product/RL33222.

[12] Barbara Opall-Rome, "Israel Explains Arrow Intercept of Syrian SAM," *Defense News*, March 21, 2017. https://www.defensenews.com/land/2017/03/20/israel-explains-arrow-intercept-of-syrian-sam/.

[13] Sharp, "U.S. Foreign Aid to Israel": 23.

[14] Harriet Barber, "How Israel Shot Down a Ballistic Missile in Space for the First Time," *The Telegraph*, November 5, 2023. https://www.telegraph.co.uk/world-news/2023/11/04/how-israel-shot-down -ballistic-missile-in-space-houthis/#:~:text=Israel%20this%20week%20used%20its,to%20take% 20place%20in%20space.

[15] Sharp, "U.S. Foreign Aid to Israel": 22.

[16] Seth Frantzman, "Israel Activated Its David's Sling Missile System for the First Time. Will More Sales Start Booming?," *Defense News*, July 31, 2018. https://www.defensenews.com/smr/space-missile -defense/2018/07/27/davids-sling-missile-system-used-for-first-time-by-israel/.

constantly evolving security environment, other systems are expected to enter service in the near future. The most discussed one uses a high-energy laser. Its name, "Iron Beam," sounds like a sequel or a spin-off from Iron Dome. Designed by Rafael, the same company that built Iron Dome, Iron Beam aims to detect rockets, artillery, mortars, or UAVs and intercept them with two electrically powered high-energy lasers at the target. As of today, Israeli officials claim that it will operate at a range of up to 5 kilometers, making it a possible substitute for Iron Dome, but not for David's Sling or Arrow.[17]

Iron Beam was already a major feature of US President Joe Biden's first visit to Israel in the summer of 2023. In a carefully planned demonstration that resembled Barack Obama's visit a decade earlier, Joe Biden followed then–Prime Minister Yair Lapid and Defense Minister Benny Gantz to a location near the airport, where Chief of General Staff Aviv Kochavi and Danny Gold, then the director of MAFAT, introduced him to Iron Beam.[18]

Biden expressed immediate enthusiasm for Iron Beam.[19] There was no skepticism like the one displayed by the Bush administration when Amir Peretz first requested financial support for Iron Dome. In April 2024, the US government submitted a bill titled "the Israel Security Supplemental Appropriations Act," which included no less than $1.2 billion for the procurement of Iron Beam. Just as with Iron Dome, US funding for Iron Beam sparked discussions about the US Army procuring the new system and RTX becoming involved in its production.[20]

As of this writing, the IDF used prototypes of Iron Beam during the Gaza War. Rafael claimed in May 2025 that the system was used for the first time "to intercept aerial threats in combat."[21] Following these tests, the IDF planned to deploy the final version of the system in 2026.[22]

<hr>

[17] Jean-Loup Samaan, "Iron Beam: A New Chapter in Israel's Missile Defence Saga," S. Rajaratnam School of International Studies, Commentary no. 91, June 26, 2023. https://rsis.edu.sg/wp-content/uploads/2023/06/CO23091.pdf.

[18] Emanuel Fabian, "Biden Views Defense Tech at Airport, Including Iron Dome, New Laser-Based Iron Beam," *Times of Israel*, July 13, 2022. https://www.timesofisrael.com/biden-views-defense-tech-at-airport-including-iron-dome-new-laser-based-iron-beam/.

[19] US Embassy in Israel, "Remarks by Former President Biden at Arrival Ceremony," July 13, 2022. https://bidenwhitehouse.archives.gov/briefing-room/speeches-remarks/2022/07/13/remarks-by-president-biden-at-arrival-ceremony/.

[20] Jen Judson, "US Seeks to Fund Israeli Laser as Army Considers Iron Beam's Potential," C4ISRNET, November 13, 2023. https://www.c4isrnet.com/battlefield-tech/directed-energy/2023/11/13/us-seeks-to-fund-israeli-laser-as-army-considers-iron-beams-potential/.

[21] Rafael Advanced Defense Systems (@RAFAELdefense), "A World First—Combat-Proven Laser Defense, Powered by Rafael," X, May 29, 2025. https://x.com/RAFAELdefense/status/1927767382002487624.

[22] Steven Scheer, "Israeli Anti-Missile Laser System 'Iron Beam' Ready for Military Use This Year," Reuters, September 18, 2025. https://www.reuters.com/business/aerospace-defense/israeli-anti-missile-laser-system-iron-beam-ready-military-use-this-year-2025-09-17/.

At first sight, Iron Beam's biggest asset is the financial affordability it promises in the long term. Because laser-based missile defense uses energy instead of a traditional interceptor to destroy targets, it could be much more cost-effective than the current Iron Dome batteries. Iron Beam could then ease reliance on other systems.

The technical expectations surrounding Iron Beam may recall the discussions about Skyguard (formerly Nautilus) in the 2000s, before it was abandoned in favor of Iron Dome. However, from a scientific standpoint, Iron Beam's application of the laser differs from that of Skyguard. Iron Beam is based on solid-state lasers that use special crystals to convert electrical energy into photons. Skyguard relied on a chemical laser, specifically a reaction generated from chemicals (in this case, deuterium fluoride) to create a continuous output.[23] In comparison, scientists contend that solid-state laser technology is less complex than chemical lasers.[24]

At the political level, the hopes inspired by Iron Beam also resonate with those from the time of Iron Dome. The most enthusiastic supporters of the laser-based system believe that today, the new technology will offset the imbalance between the costs of offense and defense that has favored the aggressor until now. This led former Prime Minister Naftali Bennett to declare in 2022, "This is a game-changer: (the enemy) can invest tens of thousands of dollars in a rocket and we can invest two dollars to cover the cost of the electricity in shooting down the rocket."[25]

Iron Beam is unlikely to replace Iron Dome, though. At best, it is a system that will complement and add a new layer to Israel's missile defense architecture. Moreover, it still faces technological issues that constrain its operational relevance. First, weather conditions significantly affect its ability to operate. Iron Beam's sensors are said to work effectively in optimal conditions, such as a sunny and cloudless day, but less so in cases of rain and clouds. This questions the decision to rely on a system that could be made suddenly—and quite randomly—inefficient. This limitation, inherent with laser technology, was already one of the reasons why Skyguard had been canceled. The then–Defense Minister Amir Peretz explained, "[I]t means that Hamas just has to check the weather to know

---

23 Interview with Yehoshua Kalisky, senior researcher at the Institute for National Security Studies, Tel Aviv, July 16, 2024.

24 Iain Boyd, "High-Energy Laser Weapons: A Defense Expert Explains How They Work and What They Are Used For," *The Conversation*, March 7, 2024. https://theconversation.com/high-energy-laser-weapons-a-defense-expert-explains-how-they-work-and-what-they-are-used-for-225071.

25 Paul Iddon, "Is the Iron Beam Laser Defense System a Military and Economic Game-Changer for Israel?," *Forbes*, June 9, 2022. https://www.forbes.com/sites/pauliddon/2022/06/09/is-the-iron-beam-laser-defense-system-a-military-and-economic-game-changer-for-israel/?sh=22acd0581f5d.

if it can attack us or not."[26] In Israel, due to the Mediterranean climate, one might argue that this issue is mostly prevalent during the winter season.

The second technical challenge relates to the interception range. As the laser beam travels through the air, its energy is absorbed by molecules and aerosols in the atmosphere and eventually loses power. Here, the difference between the solid-state laser generated by Iron Beam and the chemical laser of Skyguard becomes an issue. Scientists acknowledge that because a solid-state laser produces less power, its potential interception range is also smaller.[27] This means that the system could only destroy rockets at short range (reportedly less than 10 kilometers).

Finally, another significant limitation pertains to the pace of intervention: Generating a laser beam may take only a few seconds, but that makes the system slower than Iron Dome and less effective when facing a salvo of rockets. Israeli engineers have acknowledged these shortcomings and have been working on ways to address them. It suggests that research and development costs will soar before they become advantageous compared to Iron Dome. It also means that Israel crucially needs the financial and scientific support of the United States for new upgrades on Iron Beam.

Despite these issues, Iron Beam's supporters argue that criticism of the laser technology misunderstands the nature of missile defense. They insist that only a wide range of different technologies will ensure Israel's security. From that perspective, Iron Beam is a new item that complements, but does not substitute for, the systems already in service. Gabi Siboni, a retired colonel from the IDF, insists, "It can only be complementary, and we need to ensure we have the right balance between offense and defense."[28] Likewise, Doron Gavish, former commander of the air defense unit, speculates, "I could see a decision made in the engagement control center, 'do we shoot with the laser or do we shoot with Iron Dome?' Probably the decision would be, 'let's shoot first with the laser if we can, it's cheaper, it causes less damage in terms of debris.'"[29] Looking at the most recent developments with Iron Beam and more broadly missile defense, David Ivry, former director general of Israel's defense ministry, argues, "you need to have a comprehensive concept if you can't have one unique answer to all the threats, (laser) won't be the major component of defense, it's one of many

---

26 Interview with Amir Peretz, former Minister of Defense (2007–8), IAI Headquarters, Lod, July 29, 2024.
27 Boyd, "High-Energy Laser Weapons."
28 Interview with Gabi Siboni, Senior Consultant to the IDF, Tel Aviv, July 18, 2024.
29 Interview with Doron Gavish, Tel Aviv, July 10, 2024.

different answers."[30] In other words, new "layers" of Israel's missile defense will demand greater consideration of their overall coherence.

The Difficult Diplomacy of Missile Defense in the Middle East

While technology is a key factor driving the complexity of Israel's multilayered architecture, regional diplomacy is another one. Missile attacks launched by Iran, Hamas in the Gaza Strip, Hezbollah in Lebanon, or the Houthis in Yemen require a defense strategy that involves consultations with various regional stakeholders. The geography of Middle Eastern rivalries means that to protect Israel's territory, its government needs to cooperate with other countries closer to Iran. It enables them to share radar data for early warning purposes or to coordinate joint interceptions.

However, defense diplomacy between Israel and its Arab neighbors has always been complicated by the latter's reluctance to publicize these exchanges. The normalization of relations between Israel and a majority of the Arab world is still contingent upon Israel's cessation of its occupation of Palestinian territories. This was a significant aspect of the tensions surrounding Saddam Hussein's Scud attacks on Israel in 1991, namely, the possibility that Israel's involvement could trigger a collapse of the US-led coalition.

In April 2024, Arab officials expressed embarrassment after the involvement of some of those countries in defending Israel against Iran's missiles. It reflected the enduring taboo of Arab Israeli relations, despite some achievements made with the Abraham Accords that normalized relations between Israel, the UAE, and Bahrain in 2020. The agreement paved the way for greater cooperation at the trade and security levels. It led the US Department of Defense to integrate Israel into the area of responsibility of its Central Command (CENTCOM). Such a decision allowed greater coordination between CENTCOM and US allies and partners in the Middle East. Seen from Washington, a regional missile defense architecture relying on Israel and Gulf states serves US regional interests. Most US partners in the region, such as Saudi Arabia, Bahrain, Kuwait, the UAE, and Qatar, already operate American systems for various purposes, including early warning, command and control, and interceptors.[31]

---

[30] Interview with David Ivry, Ramat HaSharon, July 22, 2024.
[31] International Institute for Strategic Studies, "Missile-Defence Cooperation in the Gulf," Strategic Dossier, 2016.

As a result, in 2022, the Biden administration began exploring the idea of a new regional framework for cooperation in missile defense. Since the mid-1990s, each US administration has urged the Gulf states to collaborate on a regional air defense structure.[32] However, this time, it explicitly included Israel in the discussion. In January of that year, Israel's then–Defense Minister Benny Gantz stated that his country was now contributing to a "Middle East Air Defense Alliance" alongside the United States and Gulf states.[33] None of the Arab governments involved commented on Gantz's statement. A year later, the onset of the Gaza War heightened the unease among Arab officials regarding such a rapprochement.

True, those states have had no issue cooperating with CENTCOM and the IDF against Iran's missile attacks of April 14, 2024. But the Gulf contribution in this case was limited to sharing their radar data with American counterparts, while the Jordanian air defense unit intercepted Iranian drones that violated the kingdom's airspace.[34] Overall, Arab partners downplayed their contribution (and in the Saudi case, even denied it).[35]

Given the level of discontent generated by the Gaza War among Arab populations, this diplomatic deadlock is unlikely to disappear in the short term. Furthermore, the Israeli air strikes on Qatar in September 2025, presumably to kill political leaders of Hamas, led Gulf leaders to condemn the aggression and express their solidarity with Doha swiftly. This will leave only room for ad hoc, discrete cooperation between Israel and Arab states. As a result, it will also constrain the ability of Israel, or the United States, to build robust processes and mechanisms to coordinate missile defense efforts at the regional level.

A New Military Revolution in the Making?

Iron Dome also loses its central role because of the emergence of new technologies on the battlefield. Specifically, uncrewed systems are becoming more accessible and

---

[32] Jean-Loup Samaan, "The Gulf Cooperation Council and the Elusiveness of Defense Cooperation: The Revealing Effect of the 2017–2021 Crisis," *Middle East Journal* 76, no. 2 (Summer 2022): 179–198. https://doi.org/10.3751/76.2.12.

[33] Dan Williams, Aziz El Yaakoubi, "Israel Says It's Building Regional Air Defence Alliance Under U.S.," Reuters, June 20, 2022. https://www.reuters.com/world/middle-east/israel-says-building-regional-air-defence-alliance-under-us-2022-06-20/.

[34] Suleiman Khalidi, "Jordan Airforce Shoots Down Iranian Drones Flying Over to Israel," Reuters, April 14, 2024. https://www.reuters.com/world/middle-east/jordans-air-defence-ready-shoot-down-any-iranian-aircraft-that-violate-its-2024-04-13/.

[35] Al-Arabiya, "Saudi Arabia Not Involved in Intercepting Iran Missiles, Drones at Israel," April 15, 2024. https://english.alarabiya.net/News/saudi-arabia/2024/04/15/saudi-arabia-didn-t-take-part-in-intercepting-iranian-attacks-on-israel-sources.

affordable; AI is enhancing the ability of military commanders to detect and strike targets; and tomorrow, the introduction of hypersonic missiles could render current missile defense systems obsolete. Altogether, these trends shape a new military revolution combining speed and scale, quality and quantity, precision and mass.[36]

For the IDF, this represents both a challenge and an opportunity. Uncrewed systems and AI can help improve Israel's ability to defend its territory or foil an adversary's attack. However, following Fuller's "constant tactical factor," the proliferation of these technologies also provides Iran and its allied nonstate groups like Hezbollah or Hamas with new ways to overcome their conventional inferiority against the IDF.

Drones Against Iron Dome

The exploitation of uncrewed systems has grown exponentially since their appearance on the battlefield four decades ago. Back in the 1980s, the IDF would use them to detect Hezbollah's leaders in south Lebanon.[37] Initially, armed forces employed drones for limited objectives, but in recent years, their use has taken center stage in most conflicts worldwide. In the Nagorno-Karabakh war of 2020, drone attacks played a decisive role in enabling the victory of Azerbaijan's armed forces over Armenian troops.[38] Then, amid the Russia–Ukraine conflict, drone warfare reached a new milestone in terms of scale and sophistication. By 2024, Ukraine was reportedly producing four million drones annually.[39] Offensives on both sides were disrupted, supply lines were destroyed, and sometimes targets located hundreds of kilometers away from the battlefield were hit, all thanks to the extensive use of drones by Russian and Ukrainian soldiers.[40]

In the Middle East, Israel, Turkey, and Iran have been the most prominent investors in UAVs. The armed forces of Ukraine, Azerbaijan, and Ethiopia have

[36] Michael Horowitz, Joshua Schwartz, "To Compete or Strategically Retreat? The Global Diffusion of Reconnaissance Strike," *Journal of Peace Research* 62, no. 4 (2024): 847–862. https://doi.org/10.1177/00223433241261566.

[37] Ronen Bergman, *Rise and Kill First: The Secret History of Israel's Assassinations* (London: John Murray, 2018): 382–383.

[38] Chris Whelan, "The 2020 Nagorno Karabakh War: Unmanned Combat Aerial Vehicles in Modern Warfare," *Air and Space Power Review* 25, no. 2 (2023): 48–70. https://www.raf.mod.uk/what-we-do/centre-for-air-and-space-power-studies/aspr/aspr-vol25-iss2-3-pdf/.

[39] Joanna Kakissis, Claire Harbage, "Ukraine Is Amping Up Drone Production to Get an Edge in the War Against Russia," NPR, October 15, 2024. https://www.npr.org/2024/10/13/nx-s1-5147284/ukraine-drones-russia-war.

[40] Mariano Zafra, Max Hunder, Anurag Rao, Sudev Kiyada, "How Drone Combat in Ukraine Is Changing Warfare," Reuters, March 26, 2024. https://www.reuters.com/graphics/UKRAINE-CRISIS/DRONES/dwpkeyjwkpm/.

used Turkey's Bayraktar TB2 drones. In Libya, the government's forces in Tripoli have used them. At the same time, those of Marshal Khalifa Haftar relied on Chinese-made UAVs provided by the UAE during the clashes between 2019 and 2020. Meanwhile, Iran's Revolutionary Guards have developed their indigenous capabilities with armed systems, including the Shahed-136, the Mohajer-6, and the Ababil-3. Tehran is also a significant exporter of those capabilities: In the first two years of the Ukraine war, Russian forces fired nearly 4,000 Shahed-136 drones.[41]

The absence of regulatory mechanisms for drone production and technology transfer has enabled a massive proliferation of these systems among states and nonstate actors. As a result, after investing for years in offensive uncrewed capabilities, Israel must find a way to defend against those same technologies. In recent years, nonstate actors have been effective at exploiting Israel's difficulties in countering UAVs. Just like rockets and ballistic missiles in previous decades, UAVs enable Iran and its proxies to compensate for their shortcomings in conventional capabilities and to build low-cost proto-air forces.

The Houthis inside Yemen are a revealing case in point. Before the start of the war against the Saudi-led coalition in 2015, the Houthis were a militia made of poorly trained and poorly equipped combatants.[42] But a decade later, they have become a group capable of launching missiles in the Red Sea or crashing drones in the center of Tel Aviv. The Houthis have proven themselves skilled in the use of so-called kamikaze drones (otherwise known as loitering munitions). On several occasions, the organization sent Qasef-1 drones (derived from the Iranian Ababil-T) to attack the Saudi coalition's Patriot missile batteries.[43] In January 2022, the Houthis also used a combination of UAVs and ballistic missiles when they attacked the industrial area of Abu Dhabi Airport, killing three civilians and wounding six others.[44] Since 2024, they have repeatedly fired drones at Israeli ports and cities that, in some cases, escaped detection. Houthis' ability to maintain a robust inventory and train fighters suggests a significant acceleration in the operational learning process of nonstate actors.[45]

---

[41] David Albright, Igor Anokhin, Spenger Faragasso, "Update: Alabuga's Production Rate of Shahed 136 Drones," Institute for Science and International Security, September 26, 2024. https://isis-online.org/uploads/isis-reports/documents/Alabuga_Production_Rate_update_Sept_26_2024_FINAL.pdf.

[42] Marieke Brandt, *Tribes and Politics in Yemen: A History of the Houthi Conflict* (London: Hurst, 2024).

[43] Conflict Armament Research, *Iranian Technology Transfers to Yemen: "Kamikaze" Drones Used by Houthi Forces to Attack Coalition Missile Defence Systems*, Frontline Perspectives (London: Conflict Armament Research, March 2017).

[44] Aya Batrawy, "Drone Attack in Abu Dhabi Claimed by Yemen's Rebels Kills 3," Associated Press, January 18, 2022. https://apnews.com/article/business-dubai-united-arab-emirates-abu-dhabi-yemen-8bdefdf900ce46a6fd6c7bc685bf838a.

[45] Jean-Loup Samaan, "Missiles, Drones, and the Houthis in Yemen," *Parameters* 50, no. 1 (Spring 2020): 51–64.

Hezbollah has also defied Israel's Iron Dome. Despite suffering a significant blow from the IDF during the 2024 war, the Lebanese organization made some crucial breakthroughs thanks to its fleet of drones. In October 2024, it targeted Prime Minister Netanyahu's private home in Caesarea and an IDF training base in the town of Binyamina (killing four soldiers).[46]

Using kamikaze drones allows nonstate actors to evade radars and loiter in the airspace before suddenly and rapidly engaging a target. For the defense forces, the challenge pertains to both detection and interception. During my visit to an Iron Dome battery in the southern part of the country in July 2024, the commanding officer's primary concern was UAVs. "Countering the UAV threat is a critical national priority," stated Eyal Zamir, the director general of Israel's defense ministry, around the same time.[47] Like rockets, their modest cost (estimated at US$20,000) incentivizes militant organizations. Even if Iron Dome interceptors could destroy them (the exact interception rate of Iron Dome against UAVs is unknown), the imbalance between the cost of the attack and the interception undermines the logic of deterrence by denial.

In March 2025, the IDF announced a new upgrade to Iron Dome, reportedly designed to better address the challenge of drones.[48] Iron Beam, the laser-based system, is also meant to intercept UAVs according to official Israeli reports.[49] Meanwhile, Israeli defense industries initiated several projects to find a longer-term solution. Following these drone attacks, the Ministry of Defense launched a new competition to solicit technologies for countering UAVs. According to the official statement, the objective was to "deploy the new operational capabilities within months."[50]

Elbit Systems showcased a system called "Iron Hawk" that employs interceptor drones to counter hostile ones. Israel Aerospace Industries (IAI) presented its solution named "Precise Falcon," and Rafael launched a project codenamed "Typhoon." Start-up companies also joined the bid. For instance, R2 Wireless, a tech company founded in 2019 by an electrical engineer, claimed it could develop

46 Wyre Davies, Aleks Phillips, Adam Durbin, "Hezbollah Drone Attack Kills Four Israeli Soldiers and Injures 58," BBC, October 14, 2024. https://www.bbc.com/news/articles/c9dy294gweyo.

47 Ellie Cook, "Israel Trials Drone Defenses in 'Groundbreaking Event'," *Newsweek*, October 15, 2024. https://www.newsweek.com/israel-counter-drone-technology-trial-hezbollah-lebanon-iran-1969322.

48 Yuval Azulay, "Iron Dome Gets Drone and Cruise Missile Upgrade," CTech, March 23, 2025. https://www.calcalistech.com/ctechnews/article/rjegtba3jl.

49 Marissa Newman, "Israel Says It's Developed Laser Weapon to Stop Missiles, Drones," *Bloomberg*, September 18, 2025. https://www.bloomberg.com/news/articles/2025-09-17/israel-says-it-s-developed -laser-weapon-to-stop-missiles-drones?embedded-checkout=true.

50 Steven Scheer, "Israel Asks Its Defence Sector to Help Foil Drone Attacks," Reuters, October 15, 2024. https://www.reuters.com/world/middle-east/israel-asks-its-defence-sector-help-foil-drone-attacks -2024-10-15/.

a system using machine learning algorithms to detect incoming drones.[51] Such competition echoes the one initiated almost two decades earlier for Iron Dome. Beyond the technical aspects, counterdrone measures add another layer to the complex maze that has become Israel's missile defense architecture. It has further implications for the governance of these systems, including ensuring interoperability and training air defense personnel.

Moreover, the volume of UAV attacks could be more devastating if coupled with innovative tactics such as the so-called drone swarming technology.[52] Such a tactic enables armed forces to integrate multiple drones into a single fleet, allowing them to communicate and operate together. That technology is increasingly accessible and affordable thanks to progress in AI. In 2016, engineering students at MIT designed a drone swarming program named "Perdix," which is run by the US Defense Department. The unit comprised 100 drones flying at 50 miles per hour.[53] So far, this innovation has remained the exclusive domain of state actors. In June 2025, Ukraine launched operation Spiderweb, using 117 drones and relying on AI to destroy between 10 and 20 Russian aircraft.[54] The IDF itself used drone swarming tactics for the first time in the 2021 Gaza War.[55] It is a matter of time before these technologies get into the hands of nonstate actors too. If MIT students could build a fleet of drones working together a decade ago, it is not a stretch to imagine that militias in the Middle East could eventually master the technique.

The Advent of AI on the Battlefield

Drone swarming is a notable example of how AI influences the field of air defense. Today, AI is changing military strategies in at least three ways: by tracking the likely patterns of the enemy's behavior on the battlefield; by enhancing the

[51] Sharon Wrobel, "Israeli Startup Says It Can Help Detect Deadly Terror Drones with Smart Signal Tech," *Times of Israel*, October 28, 2024. https://www.timesofisrael.com/israeli-startup-says-it-can-help-detect-deadly-terror-drones-with-smart-signal-tech/.

[52] James Johnson, "Artificial Intelligence, Drone Swarming and Escalation Risks in Future Warfare," *The RUSI Journal* 165, no. 2 (2020): 26–36. https://doi.org/10.1080/03071847.2020.1752026.

[53] Zachary Kallenborn, "The Plague Beckons: On the Proliferation of Drone Swarms," in: Rajeswari Pillai Rajagopalan Sameer Patil (eds.), *Future Warfare and Critical Technologies: Evolving Tactics and Strategies* (New Delhi: Observer Research Foundation, 2024): 13–14.

[54] Phil Stewart, Idrees Ali, "Ukraine Hit Fewer Russian Planes Than It Estimated, US Officials Say," Reuters, June 5, 2025. https://www.reuters.com/business/aerospace-defense/ukraine-hit-fewer-russian-planes-than-it-estimated-us-officials-say-2025-06-04/; Harry Law, "Ukraine Just Demonstrated What AGI War Could Look Like," *Time*, June 6, 2025. https://time.com/7291455/ukraine-demonstrated-agi-war/.

[55] David Hambling, "Israel Used World's First AI-Guided Combat Drone Swarm in Gaza Attacks," *New Scientist*, June 30, 2021. https://www.newscientist.com/article/2282656-israel-used-worlds-first-ai-guided-combat-drone-swarm-in-gaza-attacks/.

performance and autonomy of uncrewed systems; and by providing technical support to commanders on major battlefield decisions.[56]

Given the centrality of technological innovation in the Israeli military culture, it is no surprise that the IDF is already among the most advanced armed forces in the application of AI.[57] The last Gaza War revealed the first implications of using AI on the battlefield. In early 2024, an Israeli online media outlet, *+972 Magazine*, reported that the IDF had relied on AI programs to conduct its operation in Gaza. Specifically, the journalists claimed that Israeli officers used systems named "Lavender" and "Gospel" to build a list of targets for their air campaign. Reports suggested that by compiling data from Israel's intelligence services, the list included "as many as 37,000 Palestinians as suspected militants."[58]

The exact extent to which AI was used in the Israeli air campaign is unclear. The IDF rejected the depiction by journalists that the air force was merely executing a list established by an AI process.[59] In one official statement, the government replied, "Information systems are merely tools for analysts in the target identification process."[60] However, no one within the Israeli military establishment denies the use of AI on the battlefield. Even before the Gaza War, the IDF had indicated its ambition to use AI across its organization. The digital transformation was already part of the Tnufa plan, which was pushed by former Chief of Staff Aviv Kochavi in 2020. AI was then used to build the target list for the Israeli Air Force during the May 2021 operation, albeit on a smaller scale.[61] In 2022, the IDF also acknowledged the existence of an official strategy aimed at integrating AI into each of its branches.[62]

[56] Shashank Joshi, "AI on the Battlefield: A Fait Accompli?," *Survival* 67, no. 2 (2005): 115–122. https://doi.org/10.1080/00396338.2025.2481775; Michael Raska, Richard Bitzinger (eds.), *The AI Wave in Defence Innovation: Assessing Military Artificial Intelligence Strategies, Capabilities, and Trajectories* (London: Routledge, 2023).

[57] Eliot Cohen, Michael Eisenstadt, Andrew Bacevich, *Knives, Tanks, and Missiles: Israel's Security Revolution* (Washington, DC: Washington Institute for Near East Policy, 1998); Dima Adamsky, *The Culture of Military Innovation: The Impact of Cultural Factors on the Revolution in Military Affairs in Russia, the US, and Israel* (Stanford, CA: Stanford University Press, 2010).

[58] Yuval Abraham, "'Lavender': The AI Machine Directing Israel's Bombing Spree in Gaza," *+972 Magazine*, April 3, 2024. https://www.972mag.com/lavender-ai-israeli-army-gaza/.

[59] Noah Sylvia, "The Israel Defense Forces' Use of AI in Gaza: A Case of Misplaced Purpose," Royal United Services Institute, July 4, 2024. https://www.rusi.org/explore-our-research/publications/commentary/israel-defense-forces-use-ai-gaza-case-misplaced-purpose.

[60] The Guardian, "Israel Defence Forces' Response to Claims About Use of 'Lavender' AI Database in Gaza," April 3, 2024. https://www.theguardian.com/world/2024/apr/03/israel-defence-forces-response-to-claims-about-use-of-lavender-ai-database-in-gaza.

[61] Yonah Jeremy Bob, "IDF Unit 8200 Commander Reveals Cyber Use to Target Hamas Commander," *Jerusalem Post*, February 13, 2023. https://www.jpost.com/israel-news/article-731443.

[62] Seth Frantzman, "Israel Unveils Artificial Intelligence Strategy for Armed Forces," C4ISRNET, February 11, 2022. https://www.c4isrnet.com/artificial-intelligence/2022/02/11/israel-unveils-artificial-intelligence-strategy-for-armed-forces/.

Much of the discussion regarding the IDF's use of AI has focused on its reliance on offensive tactics, such as air strikes, and on the implications for law and military ethics. But there are also significant implications of AI for defensive measures, some of which could, if successful, change the way Israel conceives its air defense against Palestinian rockets.

In 2023, a few months before the Gaza War started, Reuters reported on the first use of a software named "Knowledge Well" by IDF commanders.[63] The new system aims to identify patterns in Palestinian rocket launches by compiling data on their range, frequency, and location. The ultimate goal is to predict when and where the next salvos will occur. In military jargon, this means enhancing "situational awareness," but in essence, it is following an old dream of military commanders: transcending the "fog of war" and predicting its outcome.[64] Using AI for its layered missile defense architecture could support its commanders when facing swarming attacks or barrages involving different weapon systems fired from various locations. AI could also decide whether to use Iron Dome or Iron Beam.

Overall, the IDF and the Israeli government have embraced AI as a game changer. Israeli officials assert that "our mission is to turn the State of Israel into an AI superpower."[65] In the first half of 2024, the Netanyahu government launched a tender to establish Israel's first supercomputer, a move aimed at maintaining the country's competitive edge in the field. The head of its national Innovation Authority, Dror Bin, later claimed that around a third of the 9,000 start-ups based in Israel already use AI, making the country host to the "third most generative AI firms in the world."[66] Many of those start-ups focus on defensive technologies, and just as with the development of Iron Dome two decades ago, they rely on reservists who know precisely the needs of the IDF.

However, AI's progress could also weaken Israel's defense over the long term. Iran is investing in this area too. There is currently limited evidence that the Iranian armed forces or the IRGC rely on AI for military operations; however, in

63 Dan Williams, "From Rockets to Recruitment, Israel's Military Refocuses on AI," *Reuters*, June 13, 2023. https://www.reuters.com/business/aerospace-defense/rockets-recruitment-israels-military-refocuses-ai-2023-06-13/.

64 Hendrik Huelss, "Transcending the Fog of War? US Military 'AI', Vision, and the Emergent Post-Scopic Regime," *European Journal of International Security* 10, no. 2 (2025): 190–210. https://doi.org/10.1017/eis.2024.21.

65 Reuters, "Israel Aims to Be 'AI Superpower', Advance Autonomous Warfare," May 22, 2023. https://www.reuters.com/world/middle-east/israel-aims-be-ai-superpower-advance-autonomous-warfare-2023-05-22.

66 Steven Scheer, "Israel to Build Supercomputer to Keep Pace in Global AI Race," *Reuters*, June 26, 2024. https://www.reuters.com/technology/artificial-intelligence/israel-build-supercomputer-keep-pace-global-ai-race-2024-06-26/.

October 2023, IRGC Commander General Hossein Salami stated that Iran was integrating AI into its drone fleets.[67] There have been reports that Tehran has used AI for influence campaigns, for instance, during the 2024 US presidential election.[68] As AI technologies improve and their access becomes easier, Iran will likely follow Israel's example in adopting these technologies for military processes, just as it does with uncrewed systems. The use of AI in missile campaigns such as those launched by Iran on Israel in April and October 2024 could significantly enhance the ability of IRGC commanders to find holes in the air defense coverage of Israel's territory or to determine a pacing of salvos that exhausts the capabilities of Israel's systems. When combined with techniques such as drone swarming, this would make scenarios such as the Iranian missile campaign of April 2024 even more difficult to stop.

The Emerging Challenge of Hypersonic Missiles

The development of hypersonic weapons could put additional pressure on Israel's missile defense systems. The term "hypersonic weapon" refers to the ability of maneuvering a vehicle flying at least Mach 5 (meaning five times the speed of sound or approximately 6,000 kilometers per hour). Given their speed, these projectiles would bypass current air and missile defense systems. There is an operational value to these new technologies, but many uncertainties come along.

There exists a degree of confusion among the general public regarding the novelty of hypersonic technology. Ballistic missiles already fly at hypersonic speeds during their reentry phase. For instance, when it reaches its target, a ballistic missile can go as high as Mach 23.[69] This explains why even the Houthis in Yemen now claim they fire "hypersonic missiles" at Israel.

Introducing hypersonic weapons acts more like a threat multiplier, adding new difficulties to defensive strategies.[70] The real innovation lies in the fact

---

[67] Michael Rubin, "Iran Announces Integration of Artificial Intelligence Into Drone Fleet," US Army Training and Doctrine Command, January 3, 2024. https://fmso.tradoc.army.mil/2024/iran-announces-integration-of-artificial-intelligence-into-drone-fleet/.

[68] Joseph Menn, "Russia, Iran Use AI to Boost Anti-U.S. Influence Campaigns, Officials Say," *Washington Post*, September 23, 2024. https://www.washingtonpost.com/technology/2024/09/23/us-election-foreign-influence-russia-china-iran-ai/.

[69] Joseph Henrotin, "Armes hypersoniques: Quels enjeux pour les armées," French Institute for International Relations, June 18, 2021. https://www.ifri.org/fr/publications/briefings-de-lifri/armes-hypersoniques-enjeux-armees.

[70] Ivan Oelrich, "Cool Your Jets: Some Perspective on the Hyping of Hypersonic Weapons," *Bulletin of the Atomic Scientists* 76, no. 1 (January 2020): 37–45. https://thebulletin.org/premium/2020-01/cool-your-jets-some-perspective-on-the-hyping-of-hypersonic-weapons/.

that the hypersonic weapons currently under development do not follow the ballistic trajectory. Instead, they would fly at the Earth's surface and maintain their hypersonic speed throughout the flight. Currently, two specific systems are being developed: a hypersonic glide vehicle, the most advanced type available today, and a hypersonic cruise missile. The first type designates a projectile launched into space by a rocket. Still, instead of following the extra-atmospheric trajectory at midcourse (like most ballistic missiles would do), it is released and it "glides" in the upper atmosphere.

Meanwhile, hypersonic cruise missiles are upgraded versions of current cruise missiles that utilize advanced jet engines, such as scramjets or ramjets, for propulsion.[71] In both cases, the ultimate goal is to combine the advantages of ballistic and cruise missiles. This means enabling the weapon to be faster than a cruise missile, more maneuverable than a ballistic missile, and therefore less predictable in terms of trajectory.

This combination of speed and maneuverability would make hypersonic weapons highly challenging for defense systems. If a hypersonic weapon does not follow a ballistic trajectory, it can maneuver to conceal its target, making it more difficult for radars to calculate and predict its path. Meanwhile, the speed poses a challenge at the decision-making level by reducing the time governments have to respond to an attack. In this scenario, launching a hypersonic missile allows very little time for early warning (a matter of a few minutes, depending on the distance between attacker and defender). It could then force governments to anticipate and transfer direct responsibility to military commanders—a decision that creates additional issues regarding civil-military relations in times of crisis. At the operational level, this suggests a significant advantage for the offensive. In an initial salvo of hypersonic weapons, the attacker could eliminate another country's military and civilian infrastructures without air and missile defense systems being able to prevent it.

However, there are two reasons to be wary of the extent of the revolution instigated by hypersonic weapons. First, the technology involved in their development is not yet fully mature. According to scientists, significant uncertainties remain about the exact ability of these weapons to combine speed and maneuverability. For instance, the heat generated by hypersonic speed within the atmosphere ionizes the air. It forms a plasma, which creates technical challenges regarding the thermal protection and the vehicle's guidance.[72] As

---

[71] Kelley Sayler, "Hypersonic Weapons: Background and Issues for Congress," Congressional Research Service, February 11, 2025. https://sgp.fas.org/crs/weapons/R45811.pdf.
[72] Oelrich, "Cool Your Jets."

a result, addressing the technological challenges associated with hypersonic weapons necessitates expensive experimentation and tests. This explains why, at present, only a few countries can afford it.

So far, the hypersonic competition has primarily been a race among the United States, Russia, and China (though other countries like India, Japan, or North Korea have made investments too). Public details on those programs remain limited, and there are uncertainties about the progress made by those countries. The United States and Russia have been investing in hypersonic technologies for some time. The USSR worked on a hypersonic weapon program, Meteorit, as early as the 1970s. However, these efforts grew in earnest in the early 2000s after the US administration of George W. Bush withdrew from the Anti-Ballistic Missile Treaty. Washington subsequently launched its conventional prompt global strike program before refocusing resources on the two types of systems previously mentioned (hypersonic glide vehicles and hypersonic cruise missiles).[73]

Russia has been the most vocal country in the domain. In 2018, President Putin described the arsenal as "invulnerable to US defenses" and claimed the country's primacy in the domain a year later.[74] That same year, Russia announced it would deploy a missile regiment armed with hypersonic weapons. It reportedly used hypersonic missiles several times in Ukraine since the war started in February 2022.[75]

Against that backdrop, the introduction of hypersonic weapons won't mean the end of missile defense. Once again, hypersonic weapons follow a long-standing military strategy rule: Offensive technologies always find a way to circumvent defensive measures. The deployment and employment of hypersonic weapons will undoubtedly lead to the upgrading of defensive systems or the design of new ones.[76] According to US and Israeli statements, Arrow 4, whose development started in 2021, is meant to intercept hypersonic missiles.[77] The fourth version of the missile defense system will gradually replace the current

73 Kelley Sayler, "Hypersonic Weapons: Background and Issues for Congress," *Congressional Research Service*, May 5, 2025. https://www.congress.gov/crs-product/R45811.

74 Vladimir Isachenkov, "Putin Says Russia Is Leading World in Hypersonic Weapons," *Associated Press*, December 25, 2019. https://apnews.com/article/vladimir-putin-ap-top-news-international-news-technology-russia-d4e05956217d895594bcef491083e950.

75 *The Economist*, "What Are the 'Hypersonic' Missiles Russia Says It Used in Ukraine?," March 22, 2022. https://www.economist.com/what-are-the-hypersonic-missiles-russia-says-it-used-in-ukraine.

76 Tom Karako, Masao Dahlgren, *Complex Air Defense: Countering the Hypersonic Missile Threat* (Lanham, MD: Rowman & Littlefield, 2022).

77 Arie Egozi, "Israel, US Unveil Arrow 4, Missile Defense with Eye on Hypersonic Threats," *Breaking Defense*, February 19, 2021. https://breakingdefense.com/2021/02/israel-us-unveil-arrow-4-missile-defense-with-eye-on-hypersonic-threats/.

Arrow 2 interceptors, targeting short- and medium-range ballistic missiles. There have also been reports that this new version of Arrow will be designed to counter "missiles that release multiple submunitions, known as MRVs, or MIRVs."[78]

As of today, there are no countries in the Middle East that are deploying or known to be developing hypersonic weapons, but both Israel and Iran are suspected of investing resources in small programs.[79] Both have hypersonic wind tunnel facilities that allow them to test technologies independently, and both have reportedly conducted "foundational research on hypersonic airflows and propulsion systems."[80] In June 2023, Iran declared it had developed a "hypersonic" missile named the "Fattah" that was later used in the 2025 conflict with Israel. Notwithstanding the speed factor, it is doubtful that the new Iranian missile offers the maneuverability necessary to make it a true breakthrough against Israel's missile defense.[81]

Overall, the history of proliferation in the Middle East, be it of ballistic missiles, nuclear technology, or drones, teaches us that states in the region eventually find a way to access these capabilities as production increases and the international diffusion of new technology accelerates. In 2018, when asked about the scenario of Iran and North Korea acquiring hypersonic weapons, Lieutenant General Samuel Greaves, then director of the US Missile Defense Agency, answered, "I assess that risk as extremely high. I don't see what will prevent it from happening."[82]

At the moment, Israel and Iran may find it technically challenging or financially unfeasible to master hypersonic capabilities. However, they could benefit from cooperation with external partners in the coming years. Iran could turn to Russia for greater military cooperation in the field.[83] At the same time, Israel might do so through collaboration with the United States. Introducing

[78] Sebastien Roblin, "Israel and U.S. to Develop New Arrow 4 Missile to Defeat Hypersonic Weapons," *The National Interest*, September 7, 2021. https://nationalinterest.org/blog/buzz/israel-and-us-develop-new-arrow-4-missile-defeat-hypersonic-weapons-192669.

[79] Richard H. Speier, George Nacouzi, Carrie A. Lee, Richard M. Moore, *Hypersonic Missile Nonproliferation Hindering the Spread of a New Class of Weapons* (Santa Monica, CA: RAND Corporation, 2017): 76–78.

[80] Sayler, "Hypersonic Weapons: Background": 22.

[81] Fabian Hinz, "Removing the Hype from Iran's 'Hypersonic' Conqueror," International Institute for Strategic Studies, July 14, 2023. https://www.iiss.org/online-analysis/military-balance/2023/07/removing-the-hype-from-irans-hypersonic-conqueror/.

[82] Zachary Keck, "Iran and North Korea: Soon to Build Hypersonic Missiles?," *The National Interest*, September 15, 2019. https://nationalinterest.org/blog/buzz/iran-and-north-korea-soon-build-hypersonic-missiles-80836.

[83] Isaac Seitz, "Iran's Hypersonic Missiles Summed Up in 4 Words," *National Security Journal*, June 4, 2025. https://nationalsecurityjournal.org/irans-hypersonic-missiles-summed-up-in-4-words/.

hypersonic weapons in the Middle East would then aggravate current security trends. Tehran would likely see hypersonic weapons as a way to reinforce its assertive posture in the Strait of Hormuz. In the long term, Iran's possession of such capabilities would also raise concerns over the hypothetical transfer of its arsenal to proxies in the Middle East, such as Hezbollah in Lebanon and the Houthis in Yemen.

These various innovations demonstrate that the battlefield is constantly evolving and that success stories such as Iron Dome are transient. One cannot yet precisely foresee how uncrewed systems, AI, or hypersonic technology will alter the security environment in the Middle East. Recent conflicts have shown a significant leap forward in both offensive and defensive capabilities, with the Israel–Iran missile exchange in April and October 2024 being a notable example.

However, the biggest unknown lies not in the technical improvements these systems offer but in how they enable new strategies. On the one hand, the proliferation of uncrewed systems creates an issue of mass (or volume of interceptions required). On the other hand, AI and hypersonic technologies affect the tempo of operations. Under those circumstances, facing the risk of massive casualties, commanders on the battlefield may feel greater pressure to act rapidly. During this period of great uncertainty, military organizations like the IDF may consider defensive measures, such as Iron Dome, to be no longer reliable. This could further undermine the idea of strategic stability in the Middle East.

Missile Defense, Strategic Stability, and Nonproliferation Efforts in the Middle East

Technologies like uncrewed systems, AI, or hypersonic missiles will create new incentives for the attacker. The latter can view them as an opportunity to inflict severe damage on the enemy and possibly secure a victory on the battlefield. Conversely, it challenges the viability of defensive strategies. The inefficiency of current missile defense systems in defeating these new technologies raises the level of vulnerability and the financial cost of deploying new defenses. It then undermines the argument for Iron Dome and other defense systems, emphasizing instead offensive and preventive strategies.

At the regional level, this foreshadows a turbulent period for the Middle East and the notion of "strategic stability." In theory, strategic stability refers to a situation in which the status quo prevails between competing forces due to the mechanisms of deterrence.[84] It differs from a state of peace. Hostility continues to shape relationships among the various actors, but it prevents the occurrence of war by deciding that it is too costly for any side to initiate it.

Although imperfect, strategic stability prevailed until the 2023 Gaza War. It did so because, at the political level, Iran and Israel refrained from attacking each other directly. Even though Tehran's nonstate partners fired rockets, these were consistently intercepted by Iron Dome, thus preserving the status quo. Ultimately, this state of strategic stability began to unravel partly because the deterrence value of missile defense throughout the conflict proved limited. This may seem paradoxical: How can the successful display of Israel's missile defense erode its stabilizing effect? How can the enhancement of these systems coincide with a diminished ability to deter adversaries?

The concept of missile defense as a deterrent has long been a contentious issue. It presupposed that adversaries would abandon their offensive plans due to the overwhelming superiority of missile defense. Nevertheless, the Gaza War demonstrated that this assumption did not hold in the context of the Israel–Iran conflict. As shown in the previous chapters, Iron Dome may have worked at intercepting most rockets coming from Gaza, but it did not deter Hamas or the Palestinian Islamic Jihad (PIJ) from investing more and launching more of them.

Additionally, Iran's and Israel's repeated attacks on each other's territory indicate that they are no longer deterred. The events in April and October 2024 marked the first instances of a Middle Eastern state attacking the Jewish state since Saddam Hussein launched Scud missiles at Israel in 1991. In hindsight, the Iraqi attack seems minor compared to the scale of the Iranian missile attacks. In the recent Israel–Iran conflict, both countries crossed one another's mutual red lines. The performance of Israel's missile defense system may have been impressive, but it did not pressure Tehran into scaling down or abandoning its attack. Arguably, the Israeli counterstrikes a few weeks later against Iran served this purpose instead, highlighting the stronger incentive to opt for offensive tactics.

The fact that missile defense is not a deterrent does not render it irrelevant: When necessary, intercepting ballistic missiles and other projectiles still saves lives, and it buys time for decision-makers to prepare their response. However, no one should be under the illusion that missile defense progress, such as improvements in interception rates or better coordination with regional allies

---

[84] Thomas C. Schelling, *The Strategy of Conflict* (Cambridge, MA: Harvard University Press, 1960): 207–229; James M. Acton, "Reclaiming Strategic Stability," in: Elbridge A. Colby, Michael S. Gerson (eds.), *Strategic Stability: Contending Interpretations* (Carlisle: US Army War College, 2013): 117–146.

and partners, creates regional stability on its own. After the multiple clashes between Iran and Israel since October 2023, regional military planners will remain focused on offensive rather than defensive strategies.

If missile defense cannot save strategic stability, one may argue that diplomacy could. In theory, one of the best ways to prevent military escalation is to focus diplomatic efforts on curbing the arms race. Should you fail to address the hostility between two actors, you may at the very least try to prevent them from acquiring the means to express those sentiments on the battlefield. The logic goes that if the international community regulates the flow of arms and constrains the employment of new military technologies, it can reduce the advantage of offensive tactics and preserve strategic stability. This was the intended purpose of nonproliferation efforts during the Cold War.

However, arms control mechanisms in the Middle East have traditionally failed: No country in the region is a member of the Missile Technology Control Regime (MTCR), and only three (Iraq, Jordan, and Libya) adhere to the Hague Code of Conduct against Ballistic Missile Proliferation (HCOC). The MTCR was established by the Group of Seven in April 1987 and was considered "the brainchild" of President Ronald Reagan.[85] It was initially designed to prevent the proliferation of nuclear-capable missiles by demanding transparency from its signatory members and emphasizing their accountability regarding arms sales. It only covers systems traveling at least 300 kilometers, so even if regional actors were to follow the current rules, they could still transfer a significant portion of their low-range inventories, which groups like Hamas, Hezbollah, or the Houthis could use. The MTCR remains constrained by its nonbinding design: It is a regime that provides guidelines and good practices on preventing proliferation, but it has no mandate to interfere in the export licensing decisions of sovereign states. Its framework is also not adapted to the Middle East context, where many of the proliferation flows involve nonstate actors.[86]

The HCOC is a more recent mechanism that entered into force in 2002. It is a multilateral instrument meant to complement the MTCR. Working on a voluntary basis, the code establishes principles and good practices to reduce ballistic proliferation. It promotes transparency in the procurement of ballistic missiles and space-launch vehicles by requiring annual declarations.

---

85 Francesca Fogarty, "A Goliath and David Partnership: U.S.-Israel Missile Defense Collaboration from 1983 to 2016," MA Thesis, Creighton University, 2017: 57.

86 Kolja Brockmann, Mark Bromley, Lauriane Héau, "Adapting the Missile Technology Control Regime for Current and Future Challenges," SIPRI Policy Brief, December 2022. https://www.sipri.org/publications/2022/sipri-policy-briefs/adapting-missile-technology-control-regime-current-and-future-challenges.

It also asks its 145 members to provide prelaunch notifications if they are to conduct tests.[87] A year after the creation of the HCOC, the US administration of President George W. Bush also launched the Proliferation Security Initiative (PSI), a multilateral program designed to disrupt the trade in weapons of mass destruction, delivery systems, and related materials. As of 2024, 114 countries have endorsed the initiative (including Israel, Iraq, and all Gulf states, but excluding Iran). It focuses on cooperation among port authorities to track and prevent vessels carrying illicit materials.

Multilateral tools, such as the PSI, the HCOC, and the MTCR, cannot constrain the national security decisions of their members. If one violates the principle of those agreements, there is no mechanism to impose international sanctions. At best, they serve as diplomatic instruments designed to foster trust among their members. It would be unrealistic to expect countries in the Middle East, particularly Iran and Israel, to sign them without any prerequisites addressing their security concerns. Unsurprisingly, the current regional environment does not favor multilateral security arrangements such as those.

In the absence of a stable deterrence environment between Israel and Iran, initiatives aimed at containing the conflict's escalation, rather than resolving it, are still worth exploring. Under these circumstances, the most feasible goal would be to establish a regional arrangement to prevent the proliferation of weapons systems to nonstate actors. Strengthening instruments like the MTCR could reduce missile proliferation to groups such as Hezbollah and the Houthis. However, even then, it will only slow down the pace of the arms race. Given the trends in missile technologies, these organizations will find ways to acquire them. Over time, it will allow them to maintain their grip on conquered territories and raise the risks of external interventions. In other words, the IDF will continue to rely on offensive options vis-à-vis Iran, while missile defense systems will only partially contribute to maintaining regional strategic stability.

Missile Defense Beyond the Middle East: An Israeli Model?

The threat posed by missiles, rockets, and uncrewed systems will continue to influence the security environment, which is significant for countries beyond

---

[87] Dinshaw Mistry, Mark Smith, "The Missile Technology Control Regime, the Hague Code of Conduct, and missile proliferation," in: Bernd Kubbig, Sven-Eric Fikenscher (eds.), *Arms Control and Missile Proliferation in the Middle East* (London: Routledge, 2012).

Israel. The spread of these technologies to both state and nonstate actors makes the Israeli experience a forewarning of potential conflicts elsewhere. This partly explains why many governments worldwide have closely studied the history of Israel's missile defense enterprise.

As discussed in this book, the story of Iron Dome transcends the technical value of a new military system. Iron Dome has become a quasi-artifact of popular culture. Donald Trump's promise during the 2024 presidential campaign to build an Iron Dome for the entire US territory had no clear operational implications—the US Defense Department later renamed it Golden Dome and defined it as a shift to space-based missile defense systems—but the analogy reflected the unique aura Israel had gained thanks to its system.[88] As a result, the Israeli experience in missile defense has become a key instrument in the country's strategic dialogue with many of its global partners, including Asian countries such as Singapore and India, as well as the Gulf states like the UAE. Still, a closer look suggests that although Israel's experience with Iron Dome captivates interest, this rarely translates into operational cooperation or sales of the system to other countries.

For instance, in March 2022, a few weeks after Russian President Vladimir Putin launched a so-called special operation to invade Ukraine, its leader, Volodymyr Zelensky, urged the Israeli government to provide the Eastern European country with Iron Dome batteries. In a video call to the Knesset, President Zelensky, who is of Jewish descent, said, "Everybody knows that your missile defense systems are the best . . . and that you can definitely help our people, save the lives of Ukrainians, of Ukrainian Jews."[89] For several weeks, Ukrainian officials repeated the request, but to no avail.

Different reasons explain Israel's decision not to transfer Iron Dome batteries to Ukraine.[90] The first reason relates to Israel's own security needs. The government of then–Prime Minister Naftali Bennett feared that delivering Iron Dome batteries abroad could compromise the defensive coverage of Israel's territory. This explanation might have appeared as a convenient justification not to support Ukrainian forces, but just a year and a half later, the IDF faced a shortage of Iron Dome batteries amid the surprise attack of Hamas.

[88] White House, "The Iron Dome for America," January 27, 2025. https://www.whitehouse.gov/presidential-actions/2025/01/the-iron-dome-for-america/.

[89] Reuters, "Israel Will Help Ukrainians 'As Much As We Can', Foreign Minister Says," March 21, 2022. https://www.reuters.com/world/israel-must-live-with-choices-helping-ukraine-zelenskiy-tells-knesset-2022-03-20/.

[90] Steve Hendrix, "As Missiles Strike Ukraine, Israel Won't Sell Its Vaunted Air Defense," *Washington Post*, October 12, 2022. https://www.washingtonpost.com/world/2022/10/12/ukraine-russia-israel-iron-dome/.

Another explanation lies in the Israeli desire not to antagonize Russia. In the past decade, governments in Jerusalem have maintained cordial relations with Moscow, primarily due to the Syrian issue. As the IDF increased its air strikes on Iran and Hezbollah positions inside Syria, it worked hard to prevent escalation with Damascus's leading supporter—namely, Russia. As a result, Israeli and Russian armed forces maintained a discreet channel of communication to deconflict their respective operations inside Syria.[91] In that perspective, transferring Iron Dome batteries to Kiev could have jeopardized the IDF's talks with Russia within Syria.

But there is another, less discussed reason why transferring Iron Dome was dismissed: The system was ill-suited to address the threat faced by Ukraine's air defense. Iron Dome was designed to intercept short-range rockets fired by Hamas and Hezbollah, not the much more advanced missiles Russia possesses.

The Ukrainian case reveals a paradox of Iron Dome: The system may be extremely popular, but its operational relevance remains limited beyond Israeli territory. The types of threats Israel faces, along with the nature and proximity of its opponents, constitute a unique combination that does not materialize elsewhere. For instance, Saudi Arabia may face a security challenge from the Houthis, when the latter fire rockets and missiles from Yemen, but the depth of the Saudi territory is such that the daily life of its citizens is not disrupted in the same way as it is in Israel.

Following the signing of the Abraham Accords with the UAE and Bahrain in 2020, Israeli defense industries felt confident that they would gain access to the large Gulf arms markets. Officials from Rafael and IAI believed that Arrow, David's Sling, and Iron Dome could naturally appeal to Gulf decision-makers.[92] The UAE was by far the Gulf state most comfortable discussing arms trade publicly with Israel. In the fall of 2022, Reuters and *Haaretz* confirmed that the Israeli government approved a deal for Rafael to supply the UAE Armed Forces with SPYDER mobile interceptors.[93] The SPYDER system is reportedly designed to counter drones and cruise missiles. Rafael also used the 2023 edition of IDEX—Abu Dhabi's arms fair—to showcase the latest developments in its

91 Dima Course, "What Russian-Israeli Cooperation in Syria," NATO Defense College, Policy Brief no. 14, September 2021. https://www.ndc.nato.int/news/news.php?icode=1603.

92 Seth Frantzman, "The Gulf Is Getting the Air Defense It Needs," *Jerusalem Post*, August 3, 2022. https://www.jpost.com/middle-east/article-713809.

93 Reuters, Haaretz, "UAE to Buy Israeli Air Defense Tech in First Deal Since Accords, Sources Say," September 22, 2022. https://www.haaretz.com/israel-news/2022-09-22/ty-article/uae-to-buy-israeli-air-defense-tech-in-first-deal-since-accords-sources-say/00000183-65b6-dce0-a3ff-f5beff780000.

Iron Beam project.[94] Then, rumors circulated that the UAE would purchase Iron Dome. Those rumors increased in 2022 after Abu Dhabi suffered, for the first time, drone and missile attacks from the Houthis.

However, talks of an Iron Dome order to the UAE petered out for different reasons. At the operational level, the system failed to address the security challenges Abu Dhabi faced. The Houthi threat to the UAE was significant, but the range of the projectiles fired from Yemen to reach the Emirati territory made Iron Dome irrelevant. Moreover, at the political level, after October 2023, the Gaza War forced the Emirati government to recalibrate its relations with Israel. Several industrial projects were put on hold, and officials in Abu Dhabi grew reluctant about their publicization because of the growing anger from the local population regarding the humanitarian crisis in Gaza.

In India, supporters of Israel's Iron Dome also encountered obstacles. In the late 2010s, speculations grew that the Indian government would procure Iron Dome. For years, the country has faced militias operating from inside Pakistan. At the same time, Israel–India relations deepened.[95] Following Narendra Modi's election in 2014, both governments consolidated their rapprochement, with defense cooperation and arms sales becoming key pillars of this new partnership. Since then, Israel has become the third arms supplier of the Indian armed forces. Among the various projects between the two countries, Rafael and Elta codeveloped the Barak-8 system with Indian partners, including Bharat Dynamics, Kalyani Rafael, and Tata Advanced Systems. The Barak-8, which entered service in 2016, is designed to intercept antiship missiles, UAVs, cruise missiles, and fighter jets.

Therefore, it seemed natural for Delhi to consider procuring the Iron Dome batteries. Still, the Modi government formally declined the offer. The Indian Army expressed skepticism about the value of Iron Dome. Its chief of air staff, Marshal AP Singh, stated in a press conference, "There is no need for an Iron Dome-type system from Israel. We have much more capable systems in our force."[96] The Modi government announced that it would choose an indigenous program instead, focusing on the development of the Kusha missile defense

94 Seth Frantzman, "Rafael to Show Off Laser Weapon at IDEX, Opens New Facility in UAE," *Defense News*, February 17, 2023. https://www.defensenews.com/global/mideast-africa/2023/02/17/rafael-to-show-of-laser-weapon-at-idex-opens-new-facility-in-uae/.

95 Nicolas Blarel, *The Evolution of India's Israel Policy: Continuity, Change, and Compromise Since 1922* (Delhi: Oxford University Press, 2014).

96 Raghav Patel, "India Has More Capable Tech Than Israel's 'Iron Dome' to Saturate Missile Salvos, But Number Needs to be Increased, Asserts New IAF Chief," *Defence News India*, October 5, 2024. https://defence.in/threads/india-has-more-capable-tech-than-israels-iron-dome-to-saturate-missile-salvos-but-number-needs-to-be-increased-asserts-new-iaf-chief.10408/.

system.[97] Expected to enter service by the end of the 2020s, the Kusha system differs from Iron Dome. It will deploy interceptors of a much greater range than the Tamir interceptors, and its engineers claim it will destroy cruise missiles, fighter jets, and UAVs up to a 250-kilometer range. In effect, this is more akin to the Arrow family of missile defense systems than to Iron Dome.

Still in Asia, South Korea had once expressed interest in exploring the opportunity to procure the system. However, like India, it ultimately preferred a local alternative that was better suited to Seoul's security needs. A spokesperson of the South Korean Ministry of Defense explained in 2021 that "Iron Dome responds to rockets fired by militant groups, such as Hamas and irregular forces sporadically . . . Some parts of the system will bear similarities, but what we are going to build is designed to intercept long-range artillery pieces by North Korea, which requires a higher level of technologies, given the current security situation."[98]

Despite those difficulties, several countries acquired specific components of Iron Dome. Singapore, a Southeast Asian state with close military ties to Israel, was initially rumored to be considering the purchase of Iron Dome batteries. Eventually, its defense ministry announced in 2016 the purchase of Iron Dome's radar component, the ELM-2084, built by Elta.[99] Other countries like Finland, Slovakia, and the Czech Republic have also procured the radar. Meanwhile, the UK ordered the command-and-control unit (the one designed by the start-up mPrest) to build its own Sky Sabre system (also known as the "Land Ceptor") that entered service in 2020.[100] Notably, Romania became the first European country and NATO member to procure Iron Dome when its Minister of National Defense, Ionut Mosteanu, confirmed the sale in an interview in July 2025.[101]

Israel also won a sale of Iron Dome batteries in Azerbaijan. In May 2021, the Azerbaijani Defense Industry Minister confirmed the deal to the local media.[102] The transfer of Iron Dome batteries to Baku put the ties between Israel and

[97] Rajat Pandit, "India Aims to Deploy Indigenous Long-Range Air Defence System by 2028–2029," *Times of India*, October 31, 2023. https://timesofindia.indiatimes.com/india/india-aims-to-deploy-desi-iron-dome-by-2028-2029/articleshow/104806572.cms.

[98] Frank Smith, "Why Is South Korea Developing an Israeli-Style Iron Dome?," *Al Jazeera*, July 16, 2021. https://www.aljazeera.com/news/2021/7/16/why-is-south-korea-developing-an-israeli-style-iron-dome.

[99] Singapore Ministry of Defence, "Reply to Media Queries on RSAF's MMR," April 11, 2016. https://www.mindef.gov.sg/news-and-events/latest-releases/2016apr11-Media-Queries-00002.

[100] Ami Rojkes Dombe, "The UK Unveils Sky Sabre Air Defense System with Rafael's BMC4I System," *Israel Defense*, February 13, 2018. https://www.israeldefense.co.il/en/node/33059.

[101] Yuval Peso, "Romania to Become First European Country to Procure Israel's Iron Dome," *Jerusalem Post*, July 21, 2025. https://www.jpost.com/international/article-861770.

[102] Herb Keinon, "Azerbaijan: 'We Have Closed Deal to Buy Israel's Iron Dome Missile System,'" *Jerusalem Post*, December 18, 2016. https://www.jpost.com/israel-news/politics-and-diplomacy/azerbaijan-we-have-closed-deal-to-buy-israels-iron-dome-missile-system-475732.

Azerbaijan in the limelight. Amid the conflict between Armenia and Azerbaijan, Israel kept supplying military systems to the latter. For years, Azerbaijan has bought drones, missiles, and air defense systems from Israeli defense companies. The rapprochement intensified in the 2010s, manifesting in various forms, including trade, oil, and military sales.[103] From an Israeli standpoint, ties to the autocratic republic of Azerbaijan aimed to balance against Iran. "Each country finds it easy to identify with the other's geopolitical difficulties and both rank Iran as an essential security threat," stated a diplomatic cable from the US Embassy in Baku back in 2009.[104] However, Baku's interest in Iron Dome was less driven by Iran than by Armenia's capabilities, particularly its Russian Iskander short-range ballistic missiles.

Overall, a sobering reality emerges: Iron Dome has not been a major item in Israel's arms transfer. In fact, beyond the hype surrounding the system, the biggest sale made by Israel in the field of missile defense involved the Arrow system, not Iron Dome. In June 2023, the German government, led by former Chancellor Olaf Scholz, confirmed the procurement of the Arrow 3.[105] The $3.5 billion deal involves launchers, interceptors, and radars, marking the largest foreign sale in the Israeli defense industry's history.

The transfer is meant to support Berlin's ambitious project, Sky Shield, proposed by Scholz in August 2022 in response to the escalation of Russian missile strikes on Ukraine. Sky Shield is designed as an air defense architecture for the German territory and the European continent. The German selection of an Israeli system did not go without tensions within NATO. For years, countries like France have pushed for enhancing European capabilities in the missile defense domain. Paris has lobbied for programs developed by the French defense industry, such as the SAMP-T interceptor built by MBDA, to be selected. The government of Emmanuel Macron even made a counterproposal after Berlin selected Arrow.[106] In the long term, the German decision will have major implications, as it ties European defense policies closer to Israel, particularly in terms of industrial and technological cooperation.

---

[103] Jean-Loup Samaan, *Israel's Foreign Policy Beyond the Arab World: Engaging the Periphery* (New York: Routledge, 2017).

[104] US Embassy in Azerbaijan, "Azerbaijan's Discreet Symbiosis with Israel," US Diplomatic Cable 09BAKU20_a, January 13, 2009. https://wikileaks.org/plusd/cables/09BAKU20_a.html.

[105] Sebastian Sprenger, "Israel's IAI Plugging Away at German Arrow-3 Order Amid Gaza War," *Defense News*, July 24, 2024. https://www.defensenews.com/global/europe/2024/07/24/israels-iai-plugging-away-at-german-arrow-3-order-amid-gaza-war/.

[106] Elise Vincent, Philippe Ricard, "France Outlines Counter-Offer to Germany's Anti-Missile Defense Project," *Le Monde*, June 19, 2023. https://www.lemonde.fr/en/international/article/2023/06/19/france-outlines-counter-offer-to-germany-s-anti-missile-defense-project_6034034_4.html.

Conclusion

Ultimately, this final chapter revealed that the story of Iron Dome over the past two decades may have been a success, but it was merely one part in a larger narrative that is continually evolving. Many challenges, such as the emergence of new uncrewed systems and the tactics surrounding them, already question the future role of Iron Dome. New technologies can also create opportunities: Counterdrone measures, laser-based defense, and the integration of AI into command-and-control systems could ensure that the IDF maintains its qualitative edge against its rivals.

Overall, Israel's experience with Iron Dome—specifically, the story of a country capable of developing a system to counter the constant threat of rockets—remains a source of fascination worldwide. However, it offers only limited operational lessons for other nations, whose armed forces often face different threats than those posed by the rockets launched by Hamas, Hezbollah, or the PIJ. This distinction explains the contrast between the fame of Iron Dome and its underwhelming record in the global arms market. Ultimately, the success of Iron Dome was, and still is, a unique story intimately linked to the specificities of the Israel–Palestine conflict, its geography, and its key players.

Conclusion

In late July 2024, as I ended a one-day trip to Sderot, the city in southern Israel, I noticed a few social activists drinking coffee near the police station that had been destroyed after the attacks on October 7. The two workers in their mid-thirties were intrigued by the presence of a foreigner going around, asking people questions about their "Iron Dome stories." One of them looked at me with an air of defiance and bluntly said, "Iron Dome is our curse!" Surprised by the sudden anger emanating from the woman, I asked her to elaborate on her feelings. She said, "It's our curse because it has allowed the government in Jerusalem to abandon us, to let the situation with Hamas rot! October 7 would never have happened if there had not been Iron Dome; if it hadn't, they would have been forced to deal with Hamas a long time ago."

The complaint sounded like a contradiction. It was because of the endless rocket attacks suffered by the people of border cities like Sderot that Iron Dome came into existence. It was from Sderot that Amir Peretz, its former mayor, rose to power and became the defense minister who, against all odds, launched the development of this military system. It was from Sderot that the senator soon to become US president, Barack Obama, vowed to support the security of Israelis against those rockets. But the complaint also revealed the anger toward the illusion of security that Iron Dome allowed Israelis to cultivate.

Rise and Fall of an Israeli Hero

For most of the decade that followed Barack Obama's visit, Sderot and the south were associated with the success story of Iron Dome. It was a story meant to capture some of the essential traits of Israel's national identity: its resilience in the face of constant vulnerability and its audacity to innovate despite the opinions of the majority. But by July 2024, the success story of Iron Dome had faded away. As I spoke to those social activists, the ruins of Sderot Police Station, which had been the site of a brutal battle on October 7 that killed about fifty civilians and twenty police officers, were a stark reminder that Iron Dome, and more broadly the Israel Defense Forces (IDF), had failed to come to the rescue.

Calling Iron Dome a "curse" was surely an overreaction that revealed the lingering trauma of October 7 among the local people. When I asked Amir Peretz, the former defense minister as much as the son of Sderot, to comment the quote, he soberly replied, "I can understand where that person is coming from, but it makes no sense: if we didn't have Iron Dome, it would be the Blitz on London during the Second World War on all Israeli cities."[1]

Iron Dome allowed residents, first in Israel's border areas but eventually across the entire country, to avoid being at the constant mercy of rocket attacks. As Peretz suggested, it is hard to imagine what the human casualties and damage might have been if a system like Iron Dome had not been developed. As the previous chapter exposed, the quantity and quality of rockets, missiles, and unmanned aerial vehicles (UAVs) proliferating in the Middle East put tremendous pressure on the defensive capabilities of the IDF.

Military and technological innovations so far have allowed Israel to foil most of the aggressions against its population. But it also enabled its political class to avoid engaging in a painful, yet inevitable, discussion on the future of their relations with the Palestinians. A weapons system is no political program, but as we saw in this book, the development of Iron Dome coincided with the collapse of the peace process, the consolidation of Hamas's power in Gaza, and the disillusionment of the Israeli society regarding the very notion of coexistence with Palestinians.

Against that backdrop, this book tells the story of one military system that, for good and bad reasons, became much more than a military system. Almost two decades after its introduction, Iron Dome joined a small group of defense platforms, such as the formidable Tomahawk cruise missile and the iconic Spitfire fighter jet, whose names are recognized far beyond the realm of military affairs.

Military systems convey a narrative about technological innovation, and the case of Iron Dome is a prime example. In the mid-2000s, the Israeli government could no longer claim that its territory was immune to attacks from its neighbors. The conventional threat from Arab states like Syria and Egypt had faded away, but rockets and missiles now provided nonstate actors with a new ability to reach the cities and the villages, just like David Ivry and his team at the Ministry of Defense had feared in the 1980s.

---

[1] Interview with Amir Peretz, Lod, July 29, 2024.

The creation of Iron Dome reflected some of the key components of Israel's strategic culture. The story of its development involved characters like Amir Peretz, a civilian defense minister who defied most of the military establishment, and Danny Gold, a military engineer criticized by the state comptroller for disregarding legal and administrative procedures in the name of strategic urgency. It was also an illustration of the unique nature of Israel's military–industrial complex. The two major local companies, Rafael and IAI, joined forces to design the various components of the system. They relied on Elta (a subsidiary of IAI) to build the radar, and they had no problem selecting the young start-up company mPrest Systems to design the command and control (C2) system. The engineers working for the private industry were also the reservists in the air force who could identify the operational needs of the IDF. After years of despair for the Israelis living near the borders with Lebanon or the Gaza Strip, Iron Dome truly looked like a new hero. All in all, this was a case study in Israel's ability to adapt and to do so fast. As Eliot Cohen, professor emeritus of strategy at Johns Hopkins School of Advanced International Studies, once wrote, "the history of the Israel Defense Forces is a history of failure followed by exceptionally rapid recovery."[2]

The initial success that accompanied the deployment of Iron Dome brought about new hopes: the hope that the Israeli population along its frontiers would no longer face the constant threat of rocket attacks—the hope that future governments in Jerusalem would not be compelled to respond to any aggression from Hamas, and that they could set the tempo of military intervention on their own terms. The promises of preventing another round of war in Gaza also appealed to the decision-makers in Washington, particularly the administration of President Barack Obama, who personally saw in Iron Dome a noble enterprise that should become an integral part of the US–Israel military cooperation. In the following years, US officials often repeated the belief that Iron Dome served to prevent a new conflict. By extension, they also believed that it protected not only Israeli but also Palestinian lives. Those became talking points used by government officials as well as Congress members. It became a central argument in Washington's political debates. Consequently, questioning the value of US financial support to Iron Dome amounted to questioning US solidarity with Israel and endangering its population. US aid to Iron Dome was, in effect, largely immune to congressional disputes, even the most contentious ones, when the

---

[2] Eliot Cohen, "This Debacle Will Transform Israel," *The Atlantic*, October 9, 2023. https://www.theatlantic.com/ideas/archive/2023/10/how-israel-adapts-after-failure/675588/.

Senate and the House of Representatives reviewed US military aid to Israel amid the Gaza War after October 7.

In hindsight, it is easy to see all the expectations in Israel and the United States around Iron Dome as naive or delusional. The technical disputes of its early years, regarding its performance and added value compared to laser-based systems, went away, but the conflict did not. War came back in 2012, 2014, 2021, and eventually in 2023. Many indicators on the battlefield raised questions about Iron Dome's ability to deter enemies. Hamas, Hezbollah, or the Palestinian Islamic Jihad all found ways to adapt to Iron Dome, building more rockets, adding ballistic missiles, or increasing drones that kept the pressure on Israel's defensive capabilities.

The equilibrium on the military front remained precarious. Frustrations brewed within the IDF among officers fearing a new "Maginot Line mindset." Overall, the Israeli armed forces did not adopt an entirely defensive posture, in terms of either procurement or force structure. However, the success of Iron Dome constrained the strategic options of its commanders due to the preferences of civilian decision-makers. Politically, Iron Dome served the objectives of the successive governments: In the absence of a political solution between Israel and the Palestinians, Iron Dome consolidated the status quo. Increasingly, it played a role in building a new, sophisticated fortress that protected Israelis from the Gaza Strip and eventually led most of the population to grow desensitized to the plight of the Gazans. As Israelis grew tired of the conflict, Iron Dome, and more broadly missile defense, became an obvious solution, but all along, this was a technical remedy to a political predicament.

Another Brick in the Wall

In those years, Iron Dome reflected the bias of its political elite toward the status quo and the tendency of its armed forces to make technological innovations sacrosanct. However, it can also be argued that, at a deeper level, the resort to Iron Dome echoed the ancient idea of Vladimir Jabotinsky, who advocated for an "Iron Wall."

Living in the first half of the twentieth century, Jabotinsky was a leader of the so-called revisionist Zionist movement who vehemently opposed the attempts of Jewish leaders to find an agreement with Palestinian Arabs. In a much-discussed article titled "The Iron Wall," written in Russian in 1923, Jabotinsky stated that peaceful coexistence was conceivable but only after an "Iron Wall" had been established and had deterred the Arabs from attacking Israel. Cooperation will be possible tomorrow if you show your strength today, or as Jabotinsky wrote, "the only way for us to an agreement in the future is absolute rejection of all attempts at an agreement in the present."[3] Jabotinsky may have been sidelined in his time by the more powerful figures of the Zionist movement, such as Chaim Weizmann and David Ben-Gurion. Still, his thinking and the image of Israel protecting itself with an "Iron Wall" endured.[4] As Shmuel Bar explains, "despite the acrimony and rivalry between Jabotinsky and . . . David Ben Gurion, the latter adopted the Jabotinsky paradigm without attribution to its author."[5]

Jabotinsky's ideas fueled the perception of the country as a fortress under siege, which, in recent periods, necessitated reliance on systems like Iron Dome to survive. One of Jabotinsky's research assistants in his final years was Benzion Netanyahu, a scholar of Jewish history and the father of Israel's longest-serving prime minister. The latter frequently declared his admiration for Jabotinsky. On July 18, 2023, just two months before the surprise attacks of Hamas, Benjamin Netanyahu stated during a state memorial ceremony for Jabotinsky, "One hundred years after the 'iron wall' was stamped in Jabotinsky's writings, we are continuing to successfully implement these principles. I say 'continuing' because the need to stand as a powerful iron wall against our enemies has been adopted by every Government of Israel, from the right and the left."[6]

The use of "Iron" to name the dome was not an explicit reference to Jabotinsky. According to several interviewees, the first name tested was actually the "golden dome," but it was dismissed because it was considered too close to the name of the project leader at the defense ministry, Danny Gold.

Despite the coincidence, one is also tempted to explore the symbolism of iron in Jewish culture. Iron is a metal that symbolizes power in the Old Testament. In Deuteronomy, it is used to reflect an unyielding hardness. In the Bible, iron is repeatedly associated with the strength of the Land of Israel and its leaders. But there is also a more obscure and lesser-known interpretation of iron. Isaac Luria,

3   Eran Kaplan, Derek Penslar (eds.), *The Origins of Israel, 1882–1948: A Documentary History* (Madison: University of Wisconsin Press, 2011): 263.

4   Colin Shindler, *The Triumph of Military Zionism: Nationalism and the Origins of the Israeli Right* (London: I.B. Tauris, 2009); Ya'acov Shavit, *Jabotinsky and the Revisionist Movement, 1925–1948* (London: Frank Cass, 1988); Eran Kaplan, *The Jewish Radical Right: Revisionist Zionism and Its Ideological Legacy* (Madison: University of Wisconsin Press, 2005); Joseph Schechtman, Yehuda Benari, *History of the Revisionist Movement* (Tel Aviv: Hadar, 1970); Schechtman, *The Life and Times of Vladimir Jabotinsky: Rebel and Statesman* (Silver Spring, MD: Eshel Books, 1986).

5   Shmuel Bar, "Israeli Strategic Deterrence Doctrine and Practice," *Comparative Strategy* 39, no. 4 (2020): 321–353, 324. https://doi.org/10.1080/01495933.2020.1772624.

6   Israel's Prime Minister's Office, "Excerpt from PM Netanyahu's Remarks at the State Memorial Ceremony for Ze'ev Jabotinsky," July 18, 2023. https://www.gov.il/en/pages/event-ceremony180723.

a sixteenth-century rabbi regarded as one of the fathers of modern Kabbalah, suggests that the roots of the Hebrew word for iron, *barzel*, can be interpreted as the acronym for the four wives of Jacob—Bilhah, Rachel, Zilpah, and Leah— the four wives, the four matriarchs. Through this lens, iron also refers to the protection that mothers instinctively provide for their children. This symbolism could easily be dismissed as an out-of-touch interpretation, but it is tempting to view Iron Dome as a motherly figure that, for a decade, seemed to protect Israelis from rockets.[7]

Today, one may wonder how to reassess the story of Iron Dome after Hamas's surprise attack on October 7 and the ensuing war in Gaza. Israel's biggest defensive failure triggered its most intensive, and by far most controversial, offensive on Gaza—and later Lebanon. The scale of destruction and the humanitarian catastrophe that followed triggered unprecedented condemnations of Israel across the world; arguably, the war will remain as the darkest chapter in the country's history. Those events now eclipse past discussions on the risk of an Israeli Maginot Line. But Iron Dome and all the other defense systems operated by the IDF today and tomorrow (Arrow, David's Sling, Iron Beam, etc.) will not go away. Air and missile defense has never been as vital as it is today for the IDF procurement and its force structure. Many of the officers interviewed for this book questioned whether Israel was deceived by its own success with Iron Dome, but none of them believed that the system had to be abandoned. In fact, this was the reason why one of them, Jacob Amidror, a former national security advisor, rejected the analogy with the Maginot Line.

Iron Dome will remain a key component of Israel's security strategy for its home front. But several unknowns will also shape the fate of Israel's missile defense. First, military competition in the Middle East will continue unabated. Defensive measures are followed by new offensive countermeasures, advanced defensive technologies are upset by new offensive technologies and tactics, and so on. Israel's defense industrial base remains one of the most active and innovative in the world, such that the success of Iron Dome in the past two decades can surely be replicated in future defense systems, whether through laser-based technology, counterdrone measures, or the integration of AI into the C2 system.

But technology is only one part of this story. Before October 7, the precarious status quo between Israel, Hamas, and Hezbollah relied on a set of beliefs about

---

[7] I owe an intellectual debt to Mordechai Miller from the Department of Jewish Thought at Ben-Gurion University for helping me understand the different interpretations of iron in Hebrew language and Jewish tradition.

the ability of the IDF to deter attacks from its opponents. The subsequent wars in Gaza and Lebanon were not only a response to the surprise attack of October 7. More profoundly, they indicated that the very logic of deterrence against those nonstate actors was considered obsolete. At the risk of stating the obvious, it also highlights the limitations of using a purely military response to a problem of political essence. Iron Dome, like so many chapters of Israel's military history, is a tale of victory against all odds, but one that does not fundamentally solve the initial conundrum—that is, the peaceful coexistence between Israelis and Palestinians.

Select Bibliography

Books

Abrams, Elliot. *Tested by Zion: The Bush Administration and the Israeli-Palestinian Conflict* (Cambridge: Cambridge University Press, 2013).

Adamsky, Dima. *The Culture of Military Innovation: The Impact of Cultural Factors on the Revolution in Military Affairs in Russia, the US, and Israel* (Stanford, CA: Stanford University Press, 2010).

Baconi, Tareq. *Hamas Contained: The Rise and Pacification of Palestinian Resistance* (Stanford, CA: Stanford University Press, 2018).

Barak, Ehud. *My Country, My Life: Fighting for Israel, Searching for Peace* (New York: MacMillan, 2018).

Ben-Horin, Yoav, Posen, Barry. *Israel's Strategic Doctrine* (Santa Monica, CA: RAND Corporation, 1981).

Bergman, Ronen. *Rise and Kill First: The Secret History of Israel's Targeted Assassinations* (London: John Murray Publishers, 2019).

Biddle, Stephen. *Nonstate Warfare: The Military Methods of Guerillas, Warlords, and Militias* (Princeton, NJ: Princeton University Press, 2021).

Blanford, Nicholas. *Warriors of God: Inside Hezbollah's Thirty-Year Struggle Against Israel* (New York: Random House, 2011).

Blarel, Nicolas. *The Evolution of India's Israel Policy: Continuity, Change, and Compromise Since 1922* (Delhi: Oxford University Press, 2014).

Brandt, Marieke. *Tribes and Politics in Yemen: A History of the Houthi Conflict* (London: Hurst, 2024).

Bregman, Ahron (ed.). *Warfare in the Middle East Since 1945* (London: Routledge, 2017).

Byman, Daniel. *A High Price: The Triumphs and Failures of Israeli Counterterrorism* (New York: Oxford University Press, 2011).

Carter, Ash. *Inside the Five-Sided Box: Lessons from a Lifetime of Leadership in the Pentagon* (New York: Random House, 2019).

Cohen, Eliot, Eisenstadt, Michael, Bacevich, Andrew. *Knives, Tanks, and Missiles: Israel's Security Revolution* (Washington, DC: Washington Institute for Near East Policy, 1998).

Cohen, Raphael S., Johnson, David E., Thaler, David E., Allen, Brenna, Bartels, Elizabeth M., Cahill, James, Efron, Shira. *From Cast Lead to Protective Edge: Lessons from Israel's Wars in Gaza* (Santa Monica, CA: RAND Corporation, 2017).

Cohen, Stuart. *Israel and Its Army: From Cohesion to Confusion* (London: Routledge, 2008).

Colby, Elbridge A., Gerson, Michael S. (eds.). *Strategic Stability: Contending Interpretations* (Carlisle: US Army War College, 2013).

Daher, Aurelie. *Hezbollah: Mobilisation and Power* (London: Hurst, 2019).

Delaney, William. *Perspectives on Defense Systems Analysis: The What, the Why, and the Who, but Mostly the How of Broad Defense System Analysis* (Cambridge: MIT Press, 2015).

Drory, Ze'ev. *Israel's Reprisal Policy, 1953–1956. The Dynamics of Military Retaliation* (London: Routledge, 2004).

Eilam, Uzi. *Eilam's Arc: How Israel Became a Military Technology Powerhouse* (Brighton: Sussex Academic Press, 2011).

Filiu, Jean-Pierre. *Gaza: A History* (London: Hurst, 2014).

Finkelstein, Norman. *Gaza: An Inquest Into Its Martyrdom* (Oakland: University of California Press, 2018).

Fuller, J.F.C. *Armament and History: The Influence of Armament on History from the Dawn of Classical Warfare to the End of the Second World War* (London: Charles Scribner's Sons, 1945).

Futter, Andrew. *Ballistic Missile Defence and US National Security Policy: Normalisation and Acceptance after the Cold War* (London: Routledge, 2013).

Gates, Robert. *Duty: Memoirs of a Secretary at War* (New York: Alfred Knopf, 2014).

Gleis, Joshua, Berti, Benedetta. *Hezbollah and Hamas: A Comparative Study* (Baltimore, MD: Johns Hopkins University Press, 2012).

Goodman, Micah. *Catch-67: The Left, the Right, and the Legacy of the Six-Day War* (New Haven, CT: Yale University Press, 2019).

Gordon, Michael, Trainor, Bernard. *The Generals' War. The Inside Story of the Conflict in the Gulf* (New York: Little Brown and Company, 1995).

Gray, Colin. *Strategy for Chaos: Revolutions in Military Affairs and the Evidence of History* (London: Routledge, 2003).

Horowitz, Michael. *The Diffusion of Military Power: Causes and Consequences for International Politics* (Princeton, NJ: Princeton University Press, 2010).

Hroub, Khaled. *Hamas: Political Thought and Practice* (Washington, DC: Institute for Palestine Studies, 2010).

Hughes, Judith. *To the Maginot Line: The Politics of French Military Preparation in the 1920s* (Cambridge, MA: Harvard University Press, 2006).

Johnson, David. *Hard Fighting: Israel in Lebanon and Gaza* (Santa Monica, CA: RAND Corporation, 2011).

Kaplan, Eran. *The Jewish Radical Right: Revisionist Zionism and Its Ideological Legacy* (Madison: University of Wisconsin Press, 2005).

Kaplan, Eran, Penslar, Derek (eds.). *The Origins of Israel, 1882–1948: A Documentary History* (Madison: University of Wisconsin Press, 2011).

Karako, Tom, Dahlgren, Masao. *Complex Air Defense: Countering the Hypersonic Missile Threat* (Lanham, MD: Rowman & Littlefield, 2022).

Kelleher, Catherine, Dombrowski, Peter (eds.). *Regional Missile Defense from a Global Perspective* (Stanford, CA: Stanford University Press, 2015).

Khong, Yuen Foong. *Analogies at War: Korea, Munich, Dien Bien Phu, and the Vietnam Decisions of 1965* (Princeton, NJ: Princeton University Press, 1992).

Kober, Avi. *Israel's Wars of Attrition: Attrition Challenges to Democratic States* (London: Routledge, 2009).

Krotz, Ulrich. *Flying Tiger: International Relations Theory and the Politics of Advanced Weapons* (Oxford: Oxford University Press, 2011).

Kubbig, Bernd, Fikenscher, Sven-Eric (eds.). *Arms Control and Missile Proliferation in the Middle East* (London: Routledge, 2012).

Levite, Ariel. *Offense and Defense in Israeli Military Doctrine* (Boulder, CO: Westview Press, 1989).

Levitt, Matthew. *Hezbollah: The Global Footprint of Lebanon's Party of God* (Washington, DC: Georgetown University Press, 2012).

Luttwak, Edward, Shamir, Eitan. *The Art of Military Innovation: Lessons from the Israel Defense Forces* (Cambridge, MA: Harvard University Press, 2023).

Maoz, Zeev. *Defending the Holy Land: A Critical Analysis of Israel's Security and Foreign Policy* (Ann Arbor: University of Michigan Press, 2006).

Mervin, Sabrina (ed.). *Le Hezbollah, état des lieux* (Paris: Actes Sud, 2008).

Moghadam, Assaf (ed.). *Militancy and Political Violence in Shiism: Trends and Patterns* (New York: Routledge, 2012).

Muller, Harald (ed.). *WMD Arms Control in the Middle East: Prospects, Obstacles and Options* (London: Routledge, 2015).

Murray, Williamson, Knox, MacGregor, Bernstein, Alvin. *The Making of Strategy: Rulers, States, and War* (Cambridge: Cambridge University Press, 1996).

Netanyahu, Benjamin. *Bibi: My Story* (New York: Threshold Editions, 2022).

Noe, Nicholas (ed.). *Voice of Hezbollah: The Statements of Sayyed Hassan Nasrallah* (London: Verso, 2007).

Norton, Augustus Richard. *Hezbollah: A Short History*, 3rd ed. (Princeton, NJ: Princeton University Press, 2018).

Oren, Michael. *Ally: My Journey Across the American-Israeli Divide* (New York: Random House, 2015).

Palmer Harik, Judith. *Hezbollah: The Changing Face of Terrorism* (London: I.B. Tauris, 2005).

Panetta, Leon, Newton, Jim. *Worthy Fights: A Memoir of Leadership in War and Peace* (New York: Penguin Press, 2014).

Payne, Keith. *Missile Defense in the 21st Century: Protection Against Limited Threats* (New York: Westview Press, 1991).

Peri, Yoram. *Generals in the Cabinet Room: How the Military Shapes Israeli Policy* (Washington, DC: US Institute of Peace Press, 2006).

Peters, Joel, Newman, David (eds.). *Routledge Handbook on the Israeli-Palestinian Conflict* (London: Routledge, 2012).

Petrelli, Niccolo. *Israel, Strategic Culture and the Conflict with Hamas: Adaptation and Military Effectiveness* (London: Routledge, 2018).

Raska, Michael, Bitzinger, Richard (eds.). *The AI Wave in Defence Innovation: Assessing Military Artificial Intelligence Strategies, Capabilities, and Trajectories* (London: Routledge, 2023).

Razoux, Pierre. *The Iran-Iraq War* (Cambridge, MA: Belknap Press of Harvard University Press, 2015).

Samaan, Jean-Loup. *From War to Deterrence? Israel-Hezbollah Conflict Since 2006* (Carlisle: US Army War College, 2014).

Samaan, Jean-Loup. *Israel's Foreign Policy Beyond the Arab World: Engaging the Periphery* (New York: Routledge, 2017).

Schechtman, Joseph. *The Life and Times of Vladimir Jabotinsky: Rebel and Statesman* (Silver Spring, MD: Eshel Books, 1986).

Schechtman, Joseph, Benari, Yehuda. *History of the Revisionist Movement* (Tel Aviv: Hadar, 1970).

Schelling, Thomas. *The Strategy of Conflict* (Cambridge, MA: Harvard University Press, 1960).

Schiff, Zeev. *October Earthquake: Yom Kippur 1973* (New York: Routledge, 2017).

Senor, Dan, Singer, Saul. *Start-Up Nation: The Story of Israel's Economic Miracle* (New York: Twelve, 2009).

Shavit, Ya'acov. *Jabotinsky and the Revisionist Movement, 1925–1948* (London: Frank Cass, 1988).

Shindler, Colin. *The Triumph of Military Zionism: Nationalism and the Origins of the Israeli Right* (London: I.B. Tauris, 2009).

Speier, Richard H., Nacouzi, George, Lee, Carrie A., Moore, Richard. *Hypersonic Missile Nonproliferation: Hindering the Spread of a New Class of Weapons* (Santa Monica, CA: RAND Corporation, 2017).

Tlamim, Moshe, Sakal, Emanuel. *Soldier in the Sinai: A General's Account of the Yom Kippur War* (Lexington: University Press of Kentucky, 2014).

Waldman, Harry. *The Dictionary of Strategic Defense Initiative* (New York: Wilmington, 1988).

Walt, Stephen, Mearsheimer, John. *The Israel Lobby and U.S. Foreign Policy* (New York: Farrar, Straus and Giroux, 2007).

Woods, Kevin, Palkki, David, Stout, Mark (eds.). *A Survey of Saddam's Audio Files, 1978–2001: Toward an Understanding of Authoritarian Regimes* (Alexandria: Institute for Defense Analyses, 2010).

Woodward, Bob. *War* (New York: Simon & Schuster, 2024).

Zakheim, Dov. *Flight of the Lavi: Inside a US-Israeli Crisis* (Washington, DC: Potomac Books, 1996).

Journal Articles

Adamsky, Dima. "From Israel with Deterrence: Strategic Culture, Intra-war Coercion and Brute Force," *Security Studies* 26, no. 1 (2017): 157–184, 165. https://doi.org/10.1080/09636412.2017.1243923.

Al-Aloosy, Massaab. "Hezbollah in Syria: An Insurgent's Ideology, Interest, and Survival," *Middle East Policy* 29, no. 1 (2022): 125–138. https://doi.org/10.1111/mepo.12608.

Ali, Javed. "Chemical Weapons and the Iran-Iraq War: A Case Study in Noncompliance," *Nonproliferation Review* 8, no. 1 (Spring 2001): 43–58. https://doi.org/10.1080/10736700108436837.

Arazi, Yossi, Perel, Gal. "Integrating Technologies to Protect the Home Front Against Ballistic Threats and Cruise Missiles," *Military and Strategic Affairs* 5, no. 3 (December 2013): 89–110. https://www.inss.org.il/publication/integrating-technologies-to-protect-the-home-front-against-ballistic-threats-and-cruise-missiles/.

Armstrong, Michael J. "The Effectiveness of Rocket Attacks and Defenses in Israel," *Journal of Global Security Studies* 3, no. 2 (2018): 113–132. https://doi.org/10.1093/jogss/ogx028.

Bar-Joseph, Uri. "Variations on a Theme: The Conceptualization of Deterrence in Israeli Strategic Thinking," *Security Studies* 7, no. 3 (1998): 145–181. https://doi.org/10.1080/09636419808429353.

Bar-Siman-Tov, Yaacov. "The Bar-Lev Line Revisited," *Journal of Strategic Studies* 11, no. 2 (1988): 149–176. https://doi.org/10.1080/01402398808437336.

Bar, Shmuel. "Israeli strategic deterrence doctrine and practice," *Comparative Strategy* 39, no. 4 (2020): 321–353, 324. https://doi.org/10.1080/01495933.2020.1772624.

Barak, Oren, Sheniak, Amit, Shapira, Assaf. "The Shift to Defence in Israel's Hybrid Military Strategy," *Journal of Strategic Studies* 46, no. 2 (2023): 345–377. https://doi.org/10.1080/01402390.2020.1770090.

Ben Dor, Rachel, Lieberfeld, Daniel. "Mission Accomplished?: Israel's Four Mothers and the Legacies of Successful Antiwar Movements," *International Journal of Peace Studies* 13, no. 1 (Spring–Summer 2008): 85–97. https://www.jstor.org/stable/41852970.

Bermudez, Joseph. "Ballistic Missiles in the Third World: Egypt and the 1973 Arab-Israeli War," *Jane's Intelligence Review* 3, no. 12 (December 1991): 531–537.

Besser, Avi, Neria, Yuval, Haynes, Maggie. "Adult Attachment, Perceived Stress, and PTSD Among Civilians Exposed to Ongoing Terrorist Attacks in Southern Israel," *Personality and Individual Differences* 47, no. 47 (2009): 851–857. https://doi.org/10.1016/j.paid.2009.07.003.

Brun, Itai. "'While You're Busy Making Other Plans'—The 'Other RMA'," *Journal of Strategic Studies* 33(4): 535–565. https://doi.org/10.1080/01402390.2010.489708.

Clarke, Duncan L. "The Arrow Missile: The United States, Israel and Strategic Cooperation," *Middle East Journal* 48, no. 3 (Summer 1994): 475–491. https://www.jstor.org/stable/4328717.

Cohen, Eliot. "Change and Transformation in Military Affairs," *Journal of Strategic Studies* 27, no. 3 (2004): 395–407. https://doi.org/10.1080/1362369042000283958.

Cohen, Eliot, Eisenstadt, Michael, Bacevich, Andrew. "Israel's Revolution in Security Affairs," *Survival* 40, no. 1 (1998): 48–67. https://doi.org/10.1093/survival/40.1.48.

Dombrowski, Peter, Kelleher, Catherine, Auner, Eric. "Demystifying Iron Dome," *The National Interest* no. 126 (July–August 2013): 49–59. https://www.jstor.org/stable/42896501.

Etzioni-Halevy, Eva. "Civil-Military Relations and Democracy: The Case of the Military-Political Elites' Connection in Israel," *Armed Forces & Society* 22, no. 3 (1996): 401–417. https://www.jstor.org/stable/45346755.

Fetter, Steve, Wright, David. "Can the Iron Dome Be Transmuted Into a Golden Dome?," *The Washington Quarterly* 48, no. 2 (2025): 95–114. https://doi.org/10.1080/0163660X.2025.2514916.

Finkel, Meir. "Kipat Barzel—Kav Magino Hakhadasha?" (Iron Dome—The New Maginot Line?), *Maarachot* no. 461 (June 2015). https://www.maarachot.idf.il/media/t13cig4r/שדחה-וניזאמ-וק-לזרב-תפיכ.pdf.

Flamer, Netanel. "The Enemy Teaches Us How to Operate: Palestinian Hamas Use of Open-Source Intelligence (OSINT) in Its Intelligence Warfare Against Israel (1987–2012)," *Intelligence and National Security* 38, no. 7 (2023): 1171–1188. https://doi.org/10.1080/02684527.2023.2212556.

Gigi, Moti. "Relations Between Development Towns and Kibbutzim: Sderot and Sha'ar Hanegev," *Israel Studies Review* 33, no. 3 (Winter 2018): 121–139. https://doi.org/10.3167/isr.2018.330308.

Horowitz, Michael. "Battles of Precise Mass," *Foreign Affairs* 103, no. 6 (November–December 2024): 34–40. https://www.foreignaffairs.com/world/battles-precise-mass-technology-war-horowitz.

Horowitz, Michael, Schwartz, Joshua. "To Compete or Strategically Retreat? The Global Diffusion of Reconnaisance Strike," *Journal of Peace Research* 62, no. 4 (2025): 847–862. https://doi.org/10.1177/00223433241261566.

Huelss, Hendrik. "Transcending the Fog of War? US Military 'AI', Vision, and the Emergent Post-Scopic Regime," *European Journal of International Security* 10, no. 2 (2025): 190–210. https://doi.org/10.1017/eis.2024.21.

Hussein, Ahmed Qasem. "The Evolution of the Military Action of the Izz al-Din al-Qassam Brigades: How Hamas Established its Army in Gaza," *Al Muntaqa: New Perspectives on Arab Studies* 4, no. 1 (September–October 2021): 78–97. https://www.jstor.org/stable/10.31430/almuntaqa.4.1.0078.

Inbar, Efraim, Shamir, Eitan. "Mowing the Grass: Israel's Strategy for Protracted Intractable Conflict," *Journal of Strategic Studies* 37, no. 1 (2014): 65–90. https://doi.org/10.1080/01402390.2013.830972.

Joana, Jean, Smith, Andy. "Changing French Military Procurement Policy: The State, Industry and 'Europe' in the Case of the A400M," *West European Politics* 29, no. 1 (2000): 70–89. https://doi.org/10.1080/01402380500389257.

Johnson, James. "Artificial intelligence, Drone Swarming and Escalation Risks in Future Warfare," *The RUSI Journal* 165, no. 2 (2020): 26–36. https://doi.org/10.1080/03071847.2020.1752026.

Joshi, Shashank. "AI on the Battlefield: A Fait Accompli?," *Survival* 67, no. 2 (2005): 115–122. https://doi.org/10.1080/00396338.2025.2481775.

Kober, Avi. "From Heroic to Post-Heroic Warfare: Israel's Way of War in Asymmetrical Conflicts," *Armed Forces & Society* 4, no. 1 (2015): 96–122. https://www.jstor.org/stable/48609200.

Koplow, Michael J. "Value Judgment: Why Do Americans Support Israel?," *Security Studies* 20, no. 2 (2011): 266–302. https://doi.org/10.1080/09636412.2011.572690.

Krepinevich, Andrew. "Cavalry to Computer: The Pattern of Military Revolutions," *The National Interest*, no. 37 (Fall 1994): 30–42. https://www.jstor.org/stable/42896863.

Lambeth, Benjamin. "Israel's Second Lebanon War Reconsidered," *Military and Strategic Affairs* 4, no. 3 (December 2012): 45–63. https://www.inss.org.il/wp-content/uploads/sites/2/systemfiles/MASA4-3Engc_Lambeth.pdf.

Libel, Tamir. "Explaining the Security Paradigm Shift: Strategic Culture, Epistemic Communities, and Israel's Changing National Security Policy," *Defence Studies* 16, no. 2 (2016): 137–156. https://doi.org/10.1080/14702436.2016.1165595.

Marcus, Raphael D. "Learning 'Under Fire': Israel's Improvised Military Adaptation to Hamas Tunnel Warfare," *Journal of Strategic Studies* 42, no. 3–4 (2019): 344–370. https://doi.org/10.1080/01402390.2017.1307744.

Marill, Jean-Marc. "La doctrine militaire française entre les deux guerres," *Revue historique des Armées* no. 184 (1991): 24–34.

Oelrich, Ivan. "Cool Your Jets: Some Perspective on the Hyping of Hypersonic Weapons," *Bulletin of the Atomic Scientists* 76, no. 1 (January 2020): 37–45. https://thebulletin.org/premium/2020-01/cool-your-jets-some-perspective-on-the-hyping-of-hypersonic-weapons/.

Ortal, Eran. "Editor's Preface", *Dado Center Journal*, no. 4 (July 2015). https://www.idf.il/en/mini-sites/dado-center/vol-4-defense-and-home-front/vol-4-defense-and-home-front/.

Ortal, Eran. "Going on the Attack: The Theoretical Foundation of the IDF Momentum Plan," *Dado Center Journal*, no. 28 (2020, October 1). https://www.idf.il/en/mini-sites/dado-center/vol-28-30-military-superiority-and-the-momentum-multi-year-plan/going-on-the-attack-the-theoretical-foundation-of-the-israel-defense-forces-momentum-plan-1/.

Postol, Theodore. "Lessons of the Gulf War Experience with Patriot," *International Security* 16, no. 3 (Winter 1991–1992): 119–171. https://doi.org/10.2307/2539090.

Rabinowitz, Or. "'Arrow' Mythology Revisited: The Curious Case of the Reagan Administration, Israel and SDI Cooperation," *The International History Review* 43, no. 6 (2021): 1312–1329. https://doi.org/10.1080/07075332.2021.1883094.

Roth, Ariel Ilan. "Reassurance: A Strategic Basis of U.S. Support for Israel," *International Studies Perspectives* no. 10 (2009): 378–393. https://www.jstor.org/stable/44218611.

Saada-Ophir, Galit. "Mizrahi Subaltern Counterpoints: Sderot's Alternative Bands," *Anthropological Quarterly* 80, no. 3 (Summer, 2007): 711–736. https://www.jstor.org/stable/30052721.

Samaan, Jean-Loup. "The 'Dahya Concept' and Israeli Military Posture vis-à-vis Hezbollah Since 2006," *Comparative Strategy* 32, no. 2 (2013): 146–159. https://doi.org/10.1080/01495933.2013.773728.

Samaan, Jean-Loup. "The Gulf Cooperation Council and the Elusiveness of Defense Cooperation: The Revealing Effect of the 2017–2021 Crisis," *Middle East Journal* 76, no. 2 (Summer 2022): 179–198. https://doi.org/10.3751/76.2.12.

Samaan, Jean-Loup. "Missile Warfare and Violent Non-State Actors: The Case of Hezbollah," *Defence Studies* 17, no. 2 (2017): 156–170. https://doi.org/10.1080/14702436.2017.1295788.

Samaan, Jean-Loup. "Missiles, Drones, and the Houthis in Yemen," *Parameters* 50, no. 1 (Spring 2020): 51–64.

Shamir, Eitan. "Israel's Post-Heroic Wars: Exploring the Influence of American Military Concepts on Israel's Adaptation of Post-Heroic Warfare," *Israel Affairs* 24 (June 2018): 686–706. https://doi.org/10.1080/13537121.2018.1478788.

Sobelman, Daniel. "Learning to Deter. Deterrence Failure and Success in the Israel-Hezbollah Conflict, 2006–16," *International Security* 41, no. 3 (Winter 2016/17): 151–196. https://doi.org/10.1162/ISEC_a_00259.

Sullivan, Jeremiah, Fenstermacher, Dan, Fisher, Daniel, Howes, Ruth, Juff, O'Dean, Speed, Roger. "Technical Debate over Patriot Performance in the Gulf War," *Science & Global Security* 8, no. 1 (1999): 41–98. https://doi.org/10.1080/08929889908426469.

Whelan, Chris. "The 2020 Nagorno Karabakh War: Unmanned Combat Aerial Vehicles in Modern Warfare," *Air and Space Power Review* 25, no. 2 (2023): 48–70. https://www.raf.mod.uk/what-we-do/centre-for-air-and-space-power-studies/aspr/aspr-vol25-iss2-3-pdf/.

Wyss, Michel. "The October 7 Attack: An Assessment of the Intelligence Failings," *CTC Sentinel* 17, no. 9 (October 2024): 1–9. https://ctc.westpoint.edu/the-october-7-attack-an-assessment-of-the-intelligence-failings/.

Yogev, Haim, Cohen, Ronen, Lewin, Eyal. "Revolution in Military Affairs—The Operation Mole Cricket 19 as a Case Study for the Technological Race During the Cold War," *International Area Studies Review* 25, no. 2 (2022): 138–156. https://doi.org/10.1177/22338659221075806.

Yossef, Amr. "Military Doctrines in Israel and Iran: A Doctrinal Hybridity," *Middle East Journal* 75, no. 2 (Summer 2021): 243–263. https://doi.org/10.3751/75.2.13.

Newspaper Articles

Abraham, Yuval. "Lavender: The AI Machine Directing Israel's Bombing Spree in Gaza," *+972 Magazine*, April 3, 2024. https://www.972mag.com/lavender-ai-israeli-army-gaza/.

Armstrong, Michael J. "Gaza's Enhanced Rocket Technology Challenges Israel's Defences," *The Conversation*, May 17, 2021. https://theconversation.com/gazas-enhanced-rocket-technology-challenges-israels-defences-160853.

Australian Defence Magazine, "US Marines to Deploy Iron Dome in the Pacific in 2025," May 7, 2024. https://www.australiandefence.com.au/news/news/us-marines-to-deploy-iron-dome-in-the-pacific-in-2025.

Bahur Nir, Diana, Orbach, Meir. "A Buchris Story: The Rise, Fall, and Comeback of an Israeli Hero," *CTECH*, December 16, 2022. https://www.calcalistech.com/ctechnews/article/1wigv8m1o#:~:text=Raised%20in%20a%20large%2C%20poor,wound%20up%20in%20a%20coma.

Barkat, Amiram. "Chief of Staff Launches Plan for 'More Lethal' IDF," *Globes*, February 13, 2020. https://en.globes.co.il/en/article-chief-of-staff-launches-plan-for-more-lethal-idf-1001318466.

Bassok, Moti. "2006 GDP Growth: 5.1%," *Haaretz*, March 15, 2007. https://www.haaretz.com/2007-03-15/ty-article/2006-gdp-growth-5-1/0000017f-df30-df7c-a5ff-df7a300a0000.

Ben-David, Lenny. "Who Tried to Block US Funding for Iron Dome?," *Jerusalem Post*, August 16, 2022. https://www.jpost.com/opinion/article-714876.

Bob, Yonah Jeremy. "Getting the US to Fund Iron Dome Against All Odds," *Jerusalem Post*, October 24, 2017. https://www.jpost.com/israel-news/senior-defense-official-tells-jpost-how-he-convinced-white-house-to-fund-iron-dome-508254#google_vignette.

Bob, Yonah Jeremy. "IDF Unit 8200 Commander Reveals Cyber Use to Target Hamas Commander," *Jerusalem Post*, February 13, 2023. https://www.jpost.com/israel-news/article-731443.

Borger, Julian. "Lebanon War Cost Israel $1.6bn," *The Guardian*, August 15, 2006. https://www.theguardian.com/world/2006/aug/15/israelandthepalestinians.lebanon.

Borger, Julian. "US and UK Forces Help Shoot Down Iranian Drones over Jordan, Syria and Iraq," *The Guardian*, April 14, 2024. https://www.theguardian.com/world/2024/apr/14/us-and-uk-forces-help-shoot-down-iranian-drones-over-jordan-syria-and-iraq.

Boyd, Iain. "High-Energy Laser Weapons: A Defense Expert Explains How They Work and What They Are Used For," *The Conversation*, March 7, 2024. https://theconversation.com/high-energy-laser-weapons-a-defense-expert-explains-how-they-work-and-what-they-are-used-for-225071.

Broad, William. "Weapons Experts Raise Doubts About Israel's Antimissile System," *New York Times*, March 20, 2013. https://www.nytimes.com/2013/03/21/world/middleeast/israels-iron-dome-system-is-at-center-of-debate.html.

Cirincione, Joe. "Can Donald Trump Really Build an Iron Dome over America?," *Defense One*, July 29, 2024. https://www.defenseone.com/ideas/2024/07/can-donald-trump-really-build-iron-dome-over-america/398394/.

Cohen, Eliot. "This Debacle Will Transform Israel," *The Atlantic*, October 9, 2023. https://www.theatlantic.com/ideas/archive/2023/10/how-israel-adapts-after-failure/675588/.

Cohen, Raphael. "The Inevitable, Ongoing Failure of Israel's Gaza Strategy," *Los Angeles Times*, October 19, 2023. https://www.rand.org/pubs/commentary/2023/10/the-inevitable-ongoing-failure-of-israels-gaza-strategy.html.

Cooper, Michael. "McCain Visits Israeli Town That Rockets Often Strike," *New York Times*, March 20, 2008. https://www.nytimes.com/2008/03/20/us/politics/20mccain.html.

Dadon, Tova. "Barak: Iron Dome Not Perfect," *Yedioth Ahronoth*, March 31, 2011. https://www.ynetnews.com/articles/0,7340,L-4050394,00.html.

Eyadat, Fadi. "Obama Tours Sderot, and Says All the Right Things," *Haaretz*, July 24, 2008. https://www.haaretz.com/2008-07-24/ty-article/obama-tours-sderot-and-says-all-the-right-things/0000017f-dee5-d856-a37f-ffe5fa210000.

Fabian, Emanuel. "Biden Views Defense Tech at Airport, Including Iron Dome, New Laser-Based Iron Beam," *Times of Israel*, July 13, 2022. https://www.timesofisrael.com/biden-views-defense-tech-at-airport-including-iron-dome-new-laser-based-iron-beam/.

Frantzman, Seth. "Israel Activated Its David's Sling Missile System for the First Time. Will More Sales Start Booming?," *Defense News*, July 31, 2018. https://www.defensenews.com/smr/space-missile-defense/2018/07/27/davids-sling-missile-system-used-for-first-time-by-israel/.

Ginsburg, Mitch. "Chinks Remain in Israel's Air Defense Armor, Despite Iron Dome," *Times of Israel*, March 14, 2012. https://www.timesofisrael.com/the-chinks-in-our-missile-defense-armor/.

Ginsburg, Mitch. "In Sderot, the Bomb-Shelter Capital of the World," *Times of Israel*, July 11, 2014. https://www.timesofisrael.com/in-sderot-the-bomb-shelter-capital-of-the-world/.

Ginsburg, Mitch. "Iron Dome—The Newly Beloved Missile Defense System That Nobody Wanted," *Times of Israel*, March 11, 2012. https://www.timesofisrael.com/iron-dome-the-newly-beloved-missile-defense-system-that-nobody-wanted/.

Goldstone, Richard. "Reconsidering the Goldstone Report on Israel and War Crimes," *Washington Post*, April 1, 2011.

Gould, Joe. "House Passes $1 Billion for Israel's Iron Dome System in Blowout Vote," *Defense News*, September 24, 2021. https://www.defensenews.com/congress/2021/09/23/house-passes-1-billion-for-israels-iron-dome-system-in-blowout-vote/.

Greenberg, Hanan. "Peretz to IDF: Develop Anti-Rocket System," *Yedioth Ahronoth*, August 24, 2006. https://www.ynetnews.com/articles/0,7340,L-3295448,00.html.

Greenberg, Hanan. "Sderot: Red Dawn Changed to Color Red," *Yedioth Ahronoth*, September 7, 2006. https://www.ynetnews.com/articles/0,7340,L-3273135,00.html.

Gritten, David. "Israel-Gaza: Shaky Start to Ceasefire Ending Five Days of Fighting," BBC, May 14, 2023. https://www.bbc.com/news/world-middle-east-65585950.

Gross, Judah Ari. "A Wall of Iron, Sensors and Concrete: IDF Completes Tunnel-Busting Gaza Barrier," *Times of Israel*, December 7, 2021. https://www.timesofisrael.com/a-wall-of-iron-sensors-and-concrete-idf-completes-tunnel-busting-gaza-barrier/.

Hannah, John. "US, Israeli, Arab Coordination in Mideast Against Iran Comes to Fruition," *Defense News*, April 18, 2024. https://www.defensenews.com/opinion/2024/04/18/us-israeli-arab-coordination-in-mideast-against-iran-comes-to-fruition/.

Harding, Thomas. "How Iran's Latest Drones Tested Israel's Iron Dome Defence System," *The National*, May 21, 2021. https://www.thenationalnews.com/world/asia/how-iran-s-latest-drones-tested-israel-s-iron-dome-defence-system-1.1227133.

Hendrix, Steve. "As Missiles Strike Ukraine, Israel Won't Sell Its Vaunted Air Defense," *Washington Post*, October 12, 2022. https://www.washingtonpost.com/world/2022/10/12/ukraine-russia-israel-iron-dome/.

Iddon, Paul. "Is The Iron Beam Laser Defense System a Military and Economic Game-Changer For Israel?," *Forbes*, June 9, 2022. https://www.forbes.com/sites/pauliddon/2022/06/09/is-the-iron-beam-laser-defense-system-a-military-and-economic-game-changer-for-israel/?sh=22acd0581f5d.

Judson, Jen. "It's Official: US Army Inks Iron Dome Deal," *Defense News*, August 13, 2019. https://www.defensenews.com/digital-show-dailies/smd/2019/08/12/its-official-us-army-inks-iron-dome-deal/.

Judson, Jen. "Raytheon and Rafael to Build Iron Dome in US," *Defense News*, August 4, 2020. https://www.defensenews.com/land/2020/08/03/raytheon-and-rafael-to-build-iron-dome-in-us/.

Judson, Jen. "US Seeks to Fund Israeli Laser as Army Considers Iron Beam's Potential," *C4ISRNET*, November 13, 2023. https://www.c4isrnet.com/battlefield-tech/directed-energy/2023/11/13/us-seeks-to-fund-israeli-laser-as-army-considers-iron-beams-potential/.

Karako, Tom. "Why It's Time for the US Army to Divest Iron Dome," *Breaking Defense*, March 27, 2023.

Katz, Yaakov. "In Test, Iron Dome Successfully Intercepts Rockets," *Jerusalem Post*, January 6, 2010. https://www.jpost.com/israel/in-test-iron-dome-successfully-intercepts-rockets.

Katz, Yaakov. "3 More Iron Dome Batteries to Arrive by 2012," *Jerusalem Post*, August 21, 2011. https://www.jpost.com/defense/3-more-iron-dome-batteries-to-arrive-by-2012.

Keck, Zachary. "Iran and North Korea: Soon to Build Hypersonic Missiles?," *The National Interest*, September 15, 2019. https://nationalinterest.org/blog/buzz/iran-and-north-korea-soon-build-hypersonic-missiles-80836.

Keinon, Herb. "Azerbaijan: 'We Have Closed Deal to Buy Israel's Iron Dome Missile System," *Jerusalem Post*, December 18, 2016. https://www.jpost.com/israel-news/politics-and-diplomacy/azerbaijan-we-have-closed-deal-to-buy-israels-iron-dome-missile-system-475732.

Kershner, Isabel. "They Ran Into a Bomb Shelter for Safety. Instead, They Were Slaughtered," *New York Times*, November 11, 2023. https://www.nytimes.com/2023/11/11/world/middleeast/israel-hamas-oct-7-attack-shelter.html.

Klein Leichman, Abigail. "The Maverick Thinker Behind Iron Dome," *Israel21C*, August 3, 2014. https://archive.israel21c.org/the-maverick-thinker-behind-iron-dome/.

Kra-Oz, Tal. "A Look at Israeli Life Just Outside the Gaza Strip," *Tablet*, July 11, 2014. https://www.tabletmag.com/sections/news/articles/a-look-at-israeli-life-just-outside-the-gaza-strip.

Kubovich, Yaniv. "Mortars, Rockets and Drones: A Look at Hamas' Arsenal," *Haaretz*, May 5, 2019.

Lappin, Yaakov. "IDF Identifies 'As Many Targets in a Month as It Did in a Year,'" *Jewish News Syndicate*, December 4, 2022. https://www.jns.org/idf-identifies-as-many -targets-in-a-month-as-it-did-in-a-year/.

Levin, Doron. "Barack Obama and the Legacy of Iron Dome," *The Detroit Jewish News*, June 2, 2021. https://www.thejewishnews.com/opinion/guest-column-barack-obama -and-the-legacy-of-iron-dome/article_85eade1b-6a96-5737-98de-ad06755b5899.html.

Levinson, Charles, Entous, Adam. "Israel's Iron Dome Defense Battled to Get Off Ground," *The Wall Street Journal*, November 26, 2012. https://www.wsj.com/articles /SB10001424127887324712504578136931078468210.

Levinson, Charles, Solomon, Jay, "Syria Gave Scuds to Hezbollah, U.S. Says," *The Wall Street Journal*, April 14, 2010. https://www.wsj.com/articles/SB1000142405270230460 4204575182290135333282.

Linch, Greg. "Israeli Military Maps Hezbollah Bunkers," *Washington Post*, March 30, 2011. https://www.wsj.com/articles/SB10001424052702304604204575182290135333282.

Machold, Rhys. "The Iron Dome System Is a Monument to Israel's Hubris," *Jacobin*, May 28, 2021. https://jacobin.com/2021/05/israel-military-iron-dome-system-high-tech -hubris-missile-defense-palestine.

Maital, Shlomo. "Iron Dome: The Inside Story," *Jerusalem Report*, July 15, 2021. https:// www.jpost.com/jerusalem-report/iron-dome-the-inside-story-673995.

Makovsky, David. "The Collapse of Israel's Hamas 'Conceptzia,'" *The National Interest*, October 26, 2023. https://nationalinterest.org/feature/collapse-israels-hamas -conceptzia-207058.

McCarthy, Rory. "Barak in Run-Off for Israeli Labour Party Leadership," *The Guardian*, May 29, 2007. https://www.theguardian.com/world/2007/may/29/israel1.

McCarthy, Rory. "Hizbullah Leader: We Regret the Two Kidnappings That Led to War with Israel," *The Guardian*, August 28, 2006. https://www.theguardian.com/world/2006 /aug/28/syria.israel.

Melman, Yossi. "The Gideon Doctrine: The Changing Middle East and IDF Strategy," *Jerusalem Post*, September 13, 2015. https://www.jpost.com/jerusalem-report/the -gideon-doctrine-412594.

Melman, Yossi. "Romania Looks Set to Be First European Country to Buy Israel's Iron Dome," *Haaretz*, September 20, 2022. https://www.haaretz.com/israel-news/2022-09 -20/ty-article-magazine/.premium/romania-looks-set-to-be-first-european-country-to -buy-israels-iron-dome/00000183-5b1f-d9c4-a1e3-df9f7ca60000.

Menn, Joseph. "Russia, Iran Use AI to Boost Anti-U.S. Influence Campaigns, Officials Say," *Washington Post*, September 23, 2024. https://www.washingtonpost.com /technology/2024/09/23/us-election-foreign-influence-russia-china-iran-ai/.

Moore, Molly. "Rocket Attack Kills 2 Children in Israel," *Washington Post*, September 29, 2004. https://www.washingtonpost.com/archive/politics/2004/09/30/rocket -attack-kills-2-children-in-israel/6f0988d1-8d94-42b5-80e9-15eecb432934/.

Nagel, Jacob, Shohat, Shachar. "Iron Dome Developers Set the Record Straight on Its Evolution," *Jerusalem Post*, April 8, 2021. https://www.jpost.com/arab-israeli -conflict/iron-dome-developers-set-the-record-straight-on-its-evolution-664542.

Opall-Rome, Barbara. "Israel Explains Arrow Intercept of Syrian SAM," *Defense News*, March 21, 2017. https://www.defensenews.com/land/2017/03/20/israel-explains -arrow-intercept-of-syrian-sam/.

Oren, Michael. "Invest in Iron Dome for Peace," *Politico*, March 18, 2012. https://www .politico.com/story/2012/03/investment-in-iron-domeis-investment-in-peace-074149.

Oren, Michael. "Iron Dome: Israel's Double-Edged Sword (Part I)," Substack, June 13, 2024. https://claritywithmichaeloren.substack.com/p/iron-dome-part-one.

Ortal, Eran. "Turn on the Light, Extinguish the Fire: Israel's New Way of War," *War on the Rocks*, January 19, 2022. https://warontherocks.com/2022/01/turn-on-the-light -extinguish-the-fire-israels-new-way-of-war/.

Patel, Raghav. "India Has More Capable Tech Than Israel's 'Iron Dome' to Saturate Missile Salvos, But Number Needs to be Increased, Asserts New IAF Chief," *Defence News India*, October 5, 2024. https://defence.in/threads/india-has-more-capable -tech-than-israels-iron-dome-to-saturate-missile-salvos-but-number-needs-to-be -increased-asserts-new-iaf-chief.10408/.

Pedatzur, Reuven. "How Many Rockets Has Iron Dom Really Intercepted?," *Haaretz*, March 9, 2013. https://www.haaretz.com/opinion/2013-03-09/ty-article/.premium /reuven-pedatzur-does-iron-dome-really-work/0000017f-e3eb-df7c-a5ff-e3fb57020000.

Pedatzur, Reuven. "Iron Dome Is Not Enough," *Haaretz*, November 13, 2012. https:// www.haaretz.com/opinion/2012-11-13/ty-article/.premium/reuven-pedatzur-add -iron-to-the-dome/0000017f-e812-dea7-adff-f9fbe5060000.

Pedatzur, Reuven. "Iron Dome System Found to Be Helpless Against Qassams," *Haaretz*, February 22, 2008. https://www.haaretz.com/2008-02-22/ty-article/iron-dome-system -found-to-be-helpless-against-qassams/0000017f-dc43-db5a-a57f-dc6b41ca0000.

Pedatzur, Reuven. "Why Did Israel Kill Jabari?," *Haaretz*, December 4, 2012. https:// www.haaretz.com/opinion/2012-12-04/ty-article/.premium/reuven-pedatzur-why -kill-jabari/0000017f-ded6-db5a-a57f-defe58f00000.

Pipes, Daniel. "What Does 'Victory' Really Mean to the Israel Defense Forces," *Jerusalem Post*, November 26, 2020. https://www.jpost.com/opinion/idf-sees-victory-as-rapid -destruction-of-enemy-capabilities-opinion-650265.

Politico. "Netanyahu Calls Trump 'A True Friend' of Israel," November 9, 2016. https:// www.politico.com/story/2016/11/netanyahu-trump-israel-true-friend-231094.

Postol, Theodore. "An Explanation of the Evidence of Weaknesses in the Iron Dome Defense System," *MIT Technology Review*, July 15, 2014. https://www.technologyreview .com/2014/07/15/172055/an-explanation-of-the-evidence-of-weaknesses-in-the-iron -dome-defense-system/.

Rathbone, John Paul. "Israel Races to Supply Anti-Missile Shield," *Financial Times*, October 15, 2024. https://www.ft.com/content/5b884be4-c883-421b-89d6 -32cf860e97df.

Raved, Ahiya. "Eisenkot: Missile defense—For IDF Bases," *Yedioth Ahronoth*, January 12, 2010. https://www.ynetnews.com/articles/0,7340,L-3992238,00.html.

Raviv, Dan. "Inside the Iron Dome," *Moment Magazine*, July–August 2018. https:// momentmag.com/inside-the-iron-dome/.

Remnick, David. "Notes from Underground; The life of Yahya Sinwar, the Leader of Hamas in Gaza," *The New Yorker*, August 3, 2024. https://www.newyorker.com /magazine/2024/08/12/yahya-sinwar-profile-hamas-gaza-war-israel.

Robertson, Noah, Harris, Bryant, Judson, Jen. "US Agrees to Send Two Iron Dome Batteries to Israel," *Defense News*, October 25, 2023. https://www.defensenews.com /pentagon/2023/10/24/us-agrees-to-send-two-iron-dome-batteries-to-israel/.

Roblin, Sebastien. "Israel and U.S. to Develop New Arrow 4 Missile to Defeat Hypersonic Weapons," *National Interest*, September 7, 2021. https://nationalinterest.org/blog/buzz /israel-and-us-develop-new-arrow-4-missile-defeat-hypersonic-weapons-192669.

Ronen, Gil. "Israel's New Hero: The Father of Iron Dome," *Israel National News*, July 12, 2014. https://www.israelnationalnews.com/news/182816.

Said, Summer, Kalin, Stephen. "Israel-Iran Confrontation Forces Gulf Powers to Choose Sides," *Wall Street Journal*, April 16, 2024. https://www.wsj.com/world/middle-east /israel-iran-confrontation-forces-gulf-powers-to-choose-sides-62649a7a.

Samaan, Jean-Loup. "In Golan, a Battle Looms Between Iran and Israel," *The National*, October 26, 2015. https://www.thenationalnews.com/opinion/in-golan-a-battle -looms-between-iran-and-israel-1.32104.

Seitz, Isaac. "Iran's Hypersonic Missiles Summed Up in 4 Words," *National Security Journal*, June 4, 2025. https://nationalsecurityjournal.org/irans-hypersonic-missiles -summed-up-in-4-words/.

Shaham, Udi. "Drones and Navigation Systems: 'Ghost' Is Moving the IDF to the Next Level," *Jerusalem Post*, March 18, 2021. https://www.jpost.com/israel-news/drones -and-navigation-systems-ghost-is-moving-the-idf-to-the-next-level-662450.

Sharon, Jeremy. "Report: Six Iranians Killed in Israeli Strike in Syria, Including Revolutionary Guards General," *Jerusalem Post*, January 19, 2015. https://www.jpost .com/Arab-Israeli-Conflict/Report-Six-Iranians-killed-in-Israeli-strike-in-Syria -including-Revolutionary-Guards-general-388210.

Smith, Frank. "Why Is South Korea Developing an Israeli-Style Iron Dome?," *Al Jazeera*, July 16, 2021. https://www.aljazeera.com/news/2021/7/16/why-is-south-korea -developing-an-israeli-style-iron-dome.

Sprenger, Sebastian. "Israel's IAI plugging Away at German Arrow-3 Order Amid Gaza War," *Defense News*, July 24, 2024. https://www.defensenews.com/global/europe /2024/07/24/israels-iai-plugging-away-at-german-arrow-3-order-amid-gaza-war/.

Stamp, Jimmy. "The History of Rocket Science," *Smithsonian Magazine*, February 2013. https://www.smithsonianmag.com/innovation/the-history-of-rocket-science -4078981/.

Swaine, Jon. "Chuck Hagel to Face Questions over Israel Views Ahead of Defence Secretary Nomination," *The Telegraph*, January 6, 2013. https://www.telegraph.co.uk /news/worldnews/northamerica/usa/9784034/Chuck-Hagel-to-face-questions-over -Israel-views-ahead-of-defence-secretary-nomination.html.

Swaine, Jon, Sohyun Lee, Joyce, Cahlan, Sarah, Piper, Imogen, Monroe, Brian, Hill, Evan, Kelly, Meg. "How Hamas Exploited Israel's Reliance on Tech to Breach Barrier on Oct. 7," *Washington Post*, November 17, 2023. https://www.washingtonpost.com/investigations/2023/11/17/how-hamas-breached-israel-iron-wall/.

Tiron, Roxana. "Israel's Iron Dome Defense in Line for Tripled U.S. Aid," *Bloomberg*, July 23, 2014. https://www.bloomberg.com/news/articles/2014-07-23/israel-s-iron-dome-defense-in-line-for-tripled-u-s-aid.

Tollast, Robert. "Israel's Iron Dome System Overwhelmed on October 7, Inquiry Reveals," *The National*, February 4, 2025. https://www.thenationalnews.com/news/mena/2025/02/04/israels-iron-dome-system-overwhelmed-on-october-7-inquiry-reveals/.

Trevithick, Joseph. "Largest Rocket Barrage from Gaza Ever Hits Central Israel Amid Fears of An Imminent War," *The Drive*, May 11, 2021. https://www.thedrive.com/the-war-zone/40561/largest-rocket-barrage-from-gaza-ever-hits-central-israel-amid-fears-of-an-imminent-war.

Urquart, Conal, Black, Ian, Tran, Mark. "Hamas Takes Control of Gaza," *The Guardian*, June 15, 2007. https://www.theguardian.com/world/2007/jun/15/israel4.

Verter, Yossi. "Netanyahu Quits Government over Disengagement," *Haaretz*, August 7, 2005.

Wilson, Scott. "Obama and Netanyahu Show Unusual Solidarity," *Washington Post*, March 20, 2013. https://www.washingtonpost.com/world/obama-arrives-in-israel-for-three-day-visit/2013/03/20/a01774aa-914f-11e2-9abd-e4c5c9dc5e90_story.html.

Witte, Griff. "Revisiting a War That's Seldom Discussed," *Washington Post*, April 20, 2008. https://www.washingtonpost.com/wp-dyn/content/article/2008/04/19/AR2008041901864.html?hpid=topnews.

Zilber, Neri. "Israel and Gaza Keep Up Their Precarious Dance," *New Lines Magazine*, August 9, 2022. https://newlinesmag.com/reportage/israel-and-gaza-keep-up-their-precarious-dance/.

Ziton, Yoav. "Ehud Barak Isher: Price Bitachon Israel Le-Kipat Barzel" (in Hebrew: Ehud Barak Confirmed: Israel Security Price to Iron Dome), *Yedioth Ahronoth*, June 24, 2012. https://www.ynet.co.il/articles/0,7340,L-4246584,00.html.

Official Documents, Reports

Ben-Israel, Isaac. *Melkhamat Hatilim Harishona: Israel-Khizballah* ("The First Missile War: Israel Hezbollah") (Tel Aviv University, 2007). https://web.archive.org/web/20110722021710/http://spirit.tau.ac.il/government/Downloads/YitzakBIMissiles.pdf.

Brockmann, Kolja, Bromley, Mark, Héau, Lauriane. "Adapting the Missile Technology Control Regime for Current and Future Challenges," SIPRI Policy Brief, December 2022. https://www.sipri.org/publications/2022/sipri-policy-briefs/adapting-missile-technology-control-regime-current-and-future-challenges.

Brom, Shlomo (ed.). *In the Aftermath of Operation Pillar of Defense: The Gaza Strip* (Tel Aviv: Institute for National Security Studies, November 2012).

Central Intelligence Agency. "Egypt: Aspirations for Missile Production," Intelligence Assessment, April 1, 1988 (Declassified on February 11, 2021). https://www.cia.gov/readingroom/document/05857834.

Cohen, Yoram, White, Jeffrey. *Hamas in Combat: The Military Performance of the Palestinian Islamic Resistance Movement* (Washington, DC: Washington Institute for Near East Policy, October 2009).

Commission to Assess the Ballistic Missile Threat to the United States. "Executive Summary of the Report," 104th Congress, July 15, 1998. https://irp.fas.org/threat/bm-threat.htm.

Eisenstadt, Michael. "The Iraqi Artillery Threat," Washington Institute for Near East Policy, February 11, 1991. https://www.washingtoninstitute.org/policy-analysis/iraqi-artillery-threat.

Feickert, Andrew. "The Terminal High Altitude Area Defense (THAAD) System," Congressional Research Service, July 18, 2024.

Fogarty, Francesca. "A Goliath and David Partnership: U.S.-Israel Missile Defense Collaboration from 1983 to 2016," MA Thesis, Creighton University, 2017.

Hadad, Sasson, Fadlon, Tomer, Even, Shmuel (eds.). *Israel's Defense Industry and US Security Aid* (Tel Aviv: Institute for National Security Studies, 2018).

Hinz, Fabian. "Removing the Hype from Iran's 'Hypersonic' Conqueror," International Institute for Strategic Studies, July 14, 2023. https://www.iiss.org/online-analysis/military-balance/2023/07/removing-the-hype-from-irans-hypersonic-conqueror/.

Human Rights Watch. "Israel/Lebanon: Operation Grapes of Wrath," September 1997. https://www.hrw.org/legacy/summaries/s.israel-lebanon979.html.

International Crisis Group. "Hizbollah: Rebel Without a Cause?," Briefing, July 30, 2003. https://www.crisisgroup.org/sites/default/files/hizbollah-rebel-without-a-cause.pdf.

International Institute for Strategic Studies. "Iran's Networks of Influence in the Middle East," IISS Strategic Dossier, 2019.

International Institute for Strategic Studies. "Missile-Defence Cooperation in the Gulf," IISS Strategic Dossier, 2016.

Jaffee Center for Strategic Studies. *War in the Gulf: Implications for Israel* (Boulder, CO: Westview Press, 1992).

Jawhar, Souhayb. "Lebanon: New Strategic Base for Hamas," Carnegie Endowment for International Peace, October 17, 2022. https://carnegieendowment.org/sada/2022/10/lebanon-new-strategic-base-for-hamas?lang=en.

Krasna, Joshua. "A Guide for the Perplexed: The Israeli National Security Constellation and Its Effect on Policymaking," Foreign Policy Research Institute, February 2018. https://www.fpri.org/article/2018/02/guide-perplexed-israeli-national-security-constellation-effect-policymaking/.

Meridor, Dan, Eldadi, Ron. "Israel's National Security Doctrine: The Report of the Committee on the Formulation of the National Security Doctrine (Meridor Committee), Ten Years Later," Institute for National Security Studies, Memorandum no. 187, February 2019.

Nasrallah, Hassan. *Khitaab al radaa', (Speech of Deterrence)*, DVD Video, Dar Al Manar, Beirut, 2010.

Rajagopalan, Rajeswari Pillai, Patil, Sameer. "Future Warfare and Critical Technologies: Evolving Tactics and Strategies," Observer Research Foundation, 2024.

Rostker, Bernard. "Information Paper Iraq's Scud Ballistic Missiles," US Department of Defense, July 25, 2000. https://www.gulflink.osd.mil/scud_info/.

Rubin, Uzi. "Iron Dome: A Dress Rehearsal for War?," Begin Sadat Center for Strategic Studies, Perspective Paper no. 173, July 2012. https://besacenter.org/iron-dome-vs-grad-rocketsa-dress-rehearsal-for-an-all-out-war/.

Rubin, Uzi. "Israel's Air and Missile Defense During the 2014 Gaza War," Mideast Security and Policy Studies Paper no. 111, Begin-Sadat Center for Strategic Studies, Ramat Gan, Israel, 2015. https://besacenter.org/wp-content/uploads/2015/02/111eng_web.pdf.

Rubin, Uzi. *The Missile Threat from Gaza: From Nuisance to Strategic Threat* (Tel Aviv: Begin-Sadat Center for Strategic Studies, 2011).

Samaan, Jean-Loup. "Iron Beam: A New Chapter in Israel's Missile Defence Saga," S. Rajaratnam School of International Studies, Commentary no. 91, June 26, 2023. https://rsis.edu.sg/wp-content/uploads/2023/06/CO23091.pdf.

Shaaban, Omar. "Hamas and Morsi: Not So Easy Between Brothers," Carnegie Endowment for International Peace, October 1, 2012. https://carnegieendowment.org/research/2012/10/hamas-and-morsi-not-so-easy-between-brothers?lang=en¢er=middle-east.

Shabtai, Shay. "Hahatztaidot beKipat Barzel Kvitui Lechshel beKablat Hahachaltot Haleumit" (The acquisition of Iron Dome as an expression of a failure in national decision-making), Begin-Sadat Center, February 2021. https://besacenter.org/wp-content/uploads/2021/02/הצטיידות-בכיפת-ברזל-כביטוי-לכשל-בקבלת-החלטות-הלאומית-1924-Shabtai-Hebrew-final.pdf.

Sharp, Jeremy. "U.S. Foreign Aid to Israel," Congressional Research Service, March 1, 2023. https://www.congress.gov/crs-product/RL33222.

Siboni, Gabi, Bazak, Yuval. "The IDF 'Victory Doctrine': The Need for an Updated Doctrine," Jerusalem Institute for Strategy and Security, June 14, 2021. https://jiss.org.il/en/siboni-idf-victory-doctrine-the-need-for-an-updated-doctrine/.

Sylvia, Noah. "The Israel Defense Forces' Use of AI in Gaza: A Case of Misplaced Purpose," Royal United Services Institute, July 4, 2024. https://www.rusi.org/explore-our-research/publications/commentary/israel-defense-forces-use-ai-gaza-case-misplaced-purpose.

US Congressional Research Service. "US Foreign Aid to Israel," December 22, 2016. https://www.everycrsreport.com/files/20161222_RL33222_38d8a59f2caabdc9af8a6cdabfabb963ae8b63ae.pdf.

Williams, Dylan. "Any New US Aid to Israel Should Prioritize Peacebuilding, Not More Weapons," Responsible Statecraft, Quincy Institute, June 17, 2021. https://responsiblestatecraft.org/2021/06/17/any-new-us-aid-to-israel-should-prioritize-peacebuilding-not-more-weapons/.

Index

Abbas, Mahmoud 35–7, 62, 97, 105
Abraham Accords 96, 155, 171, 188
Accountability (Operation) 31
Adamsky, Dima 69, 139
American Israel Public Affairs (AIPAC)
    113–14, 128, 129
American Jewish Committee 113, 122
Amidror, Jacob 68, 89, 90, 149,152, 161,
    198
Arafat, Yasser 24, 34, 35
Arens, Moshe 25, 30
Army (US) 55, 56, 109, 123–5
Arrow (military system) 4, 9, 12, 22–3, 54,
    60, 71, 74, 87, 107–9, 131, 165–8,
    181–2, 188, 190–1, 198
artificial intelligence 157, 166, 176–9
Ashdod 7, 59, 67, 79, 87, 147
Ashkelon 7, 8, 15, 59, 67, 68, 75, 77, 84,
    147
Ashkenazy, Gabi 47, 151
Assad, Bashar 68, 90, 91, 99, 161
Assad, Hafez 18, 32
Azerbaijan 173, 190

Bahrain 96, 155, 171, 188
Barak, Ehud 25, 30, 33, 34, 48, 52–5, 60,
    64–7, 77–8, 80, 83, 89–92, 103, 114,
    116, 153
Bar-Lev Line 138–9
Be'er-Sheva 15, 67, 68, 74, 77, 79,
    135, 147
Ben Gurion, David 75, 138, 153, 197
Ben-Israel, Isaac 11, 41, 42, 69, 70
Bennett, Naftali 93, 157, 169, 187
Biden, Joe 126, 130–1, 153–4, 168, 172
Blinken, Anthony 130–1
Boehner, John 106
Breaking Dawn (Operation) 99–101
Buchris, Pinhas 48, 50, 53, 60, 65–6
Bush, George W. 6–7, 34, 36, 50, 54,
    104–5, 109–10, 114, 118, 168, 181,
    186

campaign between the wars (concept)
    142, 160
Carter, Ashton 119
Cast Lead (operation) 60–4, 80–1
Central Command 26, 171–2
Cheney, Dick 25–6
Clinton, Bill 64, 93, 103, 115
Cohen, Eliot 138, 140, 195
conceptzia 75, 136
Congress 7, 67, 106–8, 110, 112–14,
    116–18, 120–3, 125–32, 134,
    154, 167, 195. See also House of
    Representatives; Senate
Cult of the offensive (concept) 11, 139

Dado Center 9, 82, 94, 143, 149, 151, 156
Dahya (military concept) 39, 141–2, 144–5
David's Sling 4, 9, 12, 107, 131, 165–8,
    188, 198
Dayan, Moshe 14–15, 139
Decisive Victory (concept) 137, 155–8
deterrence
    and Israel's strategic culture 26, 29, 47,
        94, 142, 145, 156, 158–61
    and missile defense 21, 175, 184, 186,
        199
drones 98, 109, 147–8, 164–6, 172–6,
    179, 182, 189, 191–2, 196, 198.
    See also UAV

Egypt 16–17, 19, 39–40, 80–1, 83–4, 139,
    194
Eilam, Uzi 22
Eisenkot, Gadi 66, 140–2, 144, 149, 154–5,
    157
Elbit Systems 60, 175
Erdogan, Recep 63
Eshkol, Levi 153
Exum, Andrew 117–21, 132

Fatah 6, 36–7, 60, 62, 101
Finkel, Meir 12, 149, 151, 156

Flournoy, Michelle 114–15
Four Mothers (Movement) 33

Gallant, Yoav 160
Gantz, Benny , 78, 93, 168, 172
Gates, Robert 54, 67, 114–15, 117
Gavish, Doron 48, 57–9, 67, 70–1, 137, 148, 170
Gaza
   and status quo 6, 83–4, 92–9, 134, 142, 150–1, 161–2, 184, 196, 198
Gideon (IDF Plan) 140, 149, 157
Gold, Danny 5, 48, 50–1, 56, 65, 69, 78, 168, 195, 197
Golden Dome (US missile defense project) 133, 187
Goldstone (report) 63
Goodman, Micah 6, 93
Gordon, Phil 118
Grapes of Wrath (Operation) 32
Guardian of the Walls (Operation) 96, 99, 126, 146
Gulf War (1990–1991) 9, 16, 23–9, 49, 58, 81, 109, 137

Haaretz 87, 158, 188
Hagel, Chuck 117, 118
Hague Code of Conduct Against Ballistic Missile Proliferation 185–6
Haifa 15, 24, 41, 61, 66, 74, 85, 147, 148
Halutz, Dan 46
Hanegbi, Tzachi 159
Haniyeh, Ismail 36, 99, 165
Hecht, Eado 150, 158
Hezbollah 7–8, 10–12, 16, 29–34, 38–45, 50, 53, 58, 61–2, 90–4, 98–100, 131, 136–7, 139, 141–9, 154–61, 165, 167, 171–5, 183, 186, 188, 192, 196, 198
Home Front Command 28, 29, 38, 73
House Armed Services Committee 122–3
House of Representatives 7, 106, 112, 127, 196
Houthis 146–8, 167, 171, 174, 179, 183, 185–9
Human Rights Watch 32
Hussein, Saddam 18–20, 23–4, 26, 31, 42, 104, 109, 163, 171, 184
hypersonic weapons 133, 166, 173, 179–83

India 181, 187, 189–90
Iran 11, 16, 18–23, 25, 29–32, 42, 51, 84, 90–3, 96, 98–9, 106, 109, 119–21, 126, 131, 134, 148, 154, 163–7, 171–5, 178–9, 182–8, 191
Iran-Iraq War (1980–1988) 18–21
Iraq 11, 16–21, 23–9, 32, 41, 104, 114, 115, 164, 184–6
Iron Beam 9, 12, 168–70, 175, 178, 189, 198
Iron Wall 93, 139–40, 160, 196–7
Islamic Revolutionary Guards Corps 29, 32, 91, 98, 163, 165, 178–9
Israel Aerospace Industries 4, 21–2, 45, 57, 139, 175, 188, 195
Israel Air Force 17–18, 40, 67–8, 71, 108, 162
Israel Defense Forces
   and air defense 2, 10, 17, 27, 42, 48, 57–60, 67–8, 70–4, 77–9, 85–6, 109, 124, 136–7, 146, 148, 150, 153, 159, 163, 166, 170, 172, 176, 178–9, 191
   and civil-military relations 2, 5, 11, 55, 180
   and military culture 5, 25, 138, 158, 177
   and reservists 32, 70–1, 73, 75, 80, 138, 178, 195
Ivry, David 17–18, 20–1, 25, 28–9, 42, 71, 108, 151, 162, 170–1, 194

Jabari, Ahmed 80–1, 100, 144, 146
Jabotinsky, Ze'ev 140, 196, 197
Joint Comprehensive Plan of Action 119, 126
Jordan 16, 24, 164, 172, 185
J-Street 114, 128

Kadima (Party) 64
Kahl, Colin 114–15
Katyusha (rocket) 29–34, 40, 41, 46, 49, 60
Khomeini, Ruhollah 20
Knesset 28, 35, 45, 64, 92, 160, 187
Kochavi, Avi 155–8, 168, 177
Krasna, Joshua 20, 26–7, 46
Kuwait (invasion of) 23–5

Labor (Party) 34, 45–6, 52, 64, 92
Lapid, Yair 100, 157, 168
laser technology (and missile defense) 48, 49, 59, 71, 109, 169, 170

Lavi (fighter jet) 22, 108
Lebanon 9, 17–18, 29–34, 39, 40–2, 46–8,
        50–3, 61–4, 91–3, 100, 144–8, 151,
        153, 155, 159–61, 171, 173, 183,
        195, 198, 199
Lempert, Yael 118
Levin, Chanoch 48, 56–7, 59–60
Levite, Ariel 23, 28–9, 47, 138–9
Likud Party 34, 35, 47, 64, 83
Lipkin-Shahak, Amnon 21
Livni, Tzipi 64, 103
Long, Mary Beth 54–5, 114
Luttwak, Edward 75

McCain, John 103–4, 122
Macron, Emmanuel 164, 191
MAFAT 48–50, 53–7, 60, 65, 68–70, 74,
        77–8, 87, 147, 149, 168
Maginot Line 12, 136, 149–50, 156, 158,
        196, 198
Marine Corps (US) 124–5
Meridor, Dan 46–8
Meshaal, Khaled 62, 84, 99
Missile Technology Control Regime 185–6
Mole Cricket 19 (Operation) 17–18, 42
Morocco 13, 46, 97
Morsi, Mohamed 80, 83
Mossad 95, 138, 161
M-Systems 70
Mughniyeh, Imad 30
Mussawi, Abbas 30

Nagel, Jacob 48–54, 68, 87–8, 118
Nasrallah, Hassan 30–1, 33, 39–40,
        99–100, 144–5, 161, 165
NATO 68, 108, 110, 164, 190, 191
Nautilus 49, 169. *See also* Skyguard
Netanyahu, Benjamin 6, 35, 45, 64–5, 68,
        79–81, 85, 92–7, 104–6, 112, 114,
        118–21, 125–6, 129–30, 132, 134,
        140, 149, 153, 155, 157, 161, 175,
        178, 197
North Korea 181, 182, 190
Northrop Grumman 49–50

Obama, Barack 3, 7, 2, 67, 77, 92, 93,
        103–6, 110–12, 114–21, 125–8,
        132–3, 154, 168, 193, 195
Ocasio-Cortez, Alessandra 127

October, 7 (Hamas' attack on Israel) 1, 6,
        12, 15–16, 37, 73, 75, 130, 135–7,
        144, 146, 150, 153, 158, 160–1,
        193–4, 198–9
Olmert, Ehud 6, 16, 39–40, 42, 45–6, 51,
        61–2, 64, 80, 151
Oren, Michael 78, 105, 114, 116, 126, 136,
        152
Ortal, Eran 82, 143, 148, 150, 156
Oslo Peace Process 6, 33–4, 64, 92, 97

Palestinian Authority 34, 62, 79, 105
Palestinian Islamic Jihad 6, 11, 37, 79, 81,
        84–5, 97, 99–101, 146, 159, 184, 192
Panetta, Leon 115–17
Patriot (missiles) 25–8, 49, 56–8, 74, 86,
        109, 124, 147, 174
Peace for the Galilee (Operation) 30
Pelosi, Nancy 129
People's Army 75, 138. *See also* Israel
        Defense Force & reservists
Peres, Shimon 63–4, 92
Peretz, Amir 4–5, 11, 37, 39–40, 43, 45–6,
        48–53, 55–6, 87, 89, 112, 118, 139,
        150, 168–70, 193–5
Petraeus, David 104
Pillar of Defense (Operation) 78, 79–87,
        94–5, 142, 146
Postol, Theodore 27, 86–8
Proliferation Security Initiative 186
Protective Edge (Operation) 78, 83–6, 89,
        94–6, 142, 147

Qassam Brigades 80, 99
Qassam rocket 8, 34, 46, 103, 148
Qatar 95, 171–2

Rabin, Yitzhak 20–2, 55, 64, 92, 107
Rafael 4, 9, 48, 51, 56–7, 59–60, 65, 68, 70,
        74, 77–8, 88, 123, 149, 167–8, 175,
        188, 188–9, 195
Raytheon 56, 122–3, 167
Reagan, Ronald, xi 12, 21, 106, 108, 110,
        133, 138, 185
Republican Party 4, 28, 103, 105–6, 108,
        110, 113, 117–20, 126, 132–3
Revolution in Military Affairs 137–8, 141,
        166, 172–3
Rice, Condoleezza 37

Romania 190
Rouhani, Hassan 119
Rubin, Uzi 34, 79, 82, 87, 147
Rumsfeld, Donald 45, 110
Russia
    and Middle East policy 182, 188, 191
    Russia-Ukraine War 173–4, 176, 187
    and US rivalry 181

Sanders, Bernie 105, 129–30
Sarkozy, Nicolas 105
Saudi Arabia 23–4, 36, 147, 164, 171–2,
    174, 188
Schumer, Chuck 130
Scowcroft, Brent 25
Scud (missile) 16, 19–20, 23–9, 41–2, 58,
    90, 109, 163, 171, 184
Sderot 8, 11, 13–15, 37–8, 46, 58–9, 73–4,
    103–4, 111, 135, 146, 148, 193–4
Senate (US) 106, 112, 113, 117–18, 120,
    129–30, 196
Shabtai, Shay 47, 52, 66, 151
Shalit, Gilad 38, 80
Shamir, Eitan 82, 94
Shamir, Yitzhak 22, 25, 28, 30–1
Shapiro, Daniel 4, 111, 116–21, 152
Sharon, Ariel 6, 17–18, 21, 25, 34–7, 62,
    64, 69, 84, 139, 153, 162
Shoham, Ophir 50, 65, 70, 77
Siboni, Gabi 52, 156–8, 170
Singapore 187, 190
Sinwar, Yahya 98–9, 144
Sisi, Abdel Fattah 83–4
Six-Day War 6, 16, 93, 105
Skyguard 49–50, 54, 56, 64, 71, 88, 109,
    169–70. *See also* Nautilus
Sky Shield (military program) 191
Soleimani, Qassem 98
South Korea 190
Start-up Nation (concept) 5, 69–71
strategic culture 2, 22, 153, 195
Strategic Defense Initiative 21–3, 106, 138,
    166
Stroul, Dana 113, 155

Suez Canal 17, 69, 139
Summer Rains (Operation) 38
Syria 9, 11, 16–18, 29, 32, 39–40, 42, 68,
    84, 90–2, 99, 125, 151, 161, 163–4,
    167, 188, 194

Tamir (interceptor) 8, 57–9, 74, 122–3,
    160, 190
Tehran 19–20, 32, 99, 106, 119, 165, 174,
    179, 183–4
Terminal High Altitude Area Defense
    (THAAD) 56, 154
Tlaib, Rashida 7, 127–9
Trump, Donald 4, 119, 125–7, 133, 153,
    155, 187
Turkey 63, 173–4
Tzeva Adom 38, 73, 135

United Arab Emirates (UAE) 96–7, 155,
    164, 171, 174, 187–9
United Nations Interim Force in Lebanon
    (UNIFIL) 62
unmanned aerial vehicle (UAV) 12, 99,
    137, 157, 165–6, 172–4, 177, 179,
    183, 186, 192, 194
US-Israel relations
    US military aid to Israel 7, 112, 114,
    116, 130–2, 196

Vulcan Phalanx (military system) 55, 88

Weinberger, Caspar 21
West Bank 16, 33, 35, 43, 84, 97, 99,
    104–5, 127, 155, 161
White House 25–6, 36, 105–7, 108,
    110–12, 115, 118–20, 133
Williams, Dylan 128–9
Winograd (Commission) 40–2, 45

Ya'alon, Moshe 83, 91

Zakheim, Dov 22, 54, 105, 108
Zelensky, Volodymyr 187
Zionism 98, 140, 144, 153, 196–7